WRITING ESSAYS ABOUT LITERATURE

A Guide and Style Sheet

SIXTH EDITION

HEINLE & HEINLE

THOMSON LEARNING

Writing Essays About Literature/ Sixth Edition

A Guide and Style Sheet

Kelley Griffith

Publisher: Earl Mcpeek

Acquisitions Editor: Bill Hoffman

Market Strategist: John Meyers

Developmental Editor: Michell Phifer

Project Editor: Joyce Fink

Art Director: Susan Journey

Production Manager: Suzie Wurzer

Printed in the United States of America

2 3 4 5 6 7 8 9 10   06   05   04   03   02   01

For permission to use material from this text or product contact us:

Tel:	1-800-730-2214
Fax:	1-800-730-2215
Web:	www.thomsonrights.com

ISBN: 0-15-506617-X

For more information contact Heinle & Heinle, 25 Thomson Place, Boston, MA 02210 USA, or you can visit our Internet site at http://www.heinle.com

Library of Congress Catalog Card Number:
00-109639

Cover: Image provided by Photodisc © 2002

WRITING ESSAYS ABOUT LITERATURE

A Guide and Style Sheet

SIXTH EDITION

Kelley Griffith

University of North Carolina at Greensboro

HEINLE & HEINLE

™

THOMSON LEARNING

United States • Australia • Canada • Mexico • Singapore • Spain • United Kingdom *for Gareth and Bronwen*

Preface

Nearly twenty years ago, I wrote the first edition of this book in response to questions students asked when I assigned essays in my literature courses: "What should I look for?" "What's an essay?" "How long should it be?" "Do we have to use outside sources?" "How should I document sources?" Many students had little or no experience writing arguments, not just about literature but about anything. They struggled to get started. This book was my answer to their questions. The initial edition gave a brief introduction to the study of literature, defined key critical terms, explained details of usage (the "style sheet" part of the book), and included sample essays that would illustrate good student writing.

Writing Essays about Literature: A Guide and Style Sheet has evolved over its six editions, and this, the sixth edition, still strives to answer key questions students raise about studying literature and writing about it. First, in Part 1 (Chapters 1 through 6), it provides extensive guidance about reading literature. Chapter 1, "Strategies for Interpreting Literature," undergirds the entire book. Chapters 2 through 5 are discussions of the nature of literature and of the three major literary genres: fiction, drama, and poetry. These chapters define the elements of literature and provide heuristics—questions and "thinking-on-paper" exercises—that lead readers toward their own interpretations. Chapter 6, with its discussions of critical approaches, invites readers to consider all aspects of the study of literature.

Second, the book offers guidance for writing about literature. Chapter 7, "Writing about Literature," serves as an introduction to Part 2. The primary focus of Part 2 is the interpretive essay, but Chapter 7 and subsequent chapters also give attention to more "personal" kinds of writing, such as freewriting, notes, and journals. Chapters 8 through 10 are arranged according to the four stages of the writing process: inventing, drafting, revising, and editing. Chapter 8, "Choosing

Topics," suggests strategies for generating topics. Chapter 9, "Drafting the Essay," emphasizes the argumentative nature of essays about literature. It covers strategies for reasoning, organizing, and moving from early to final drafts. Chapter 10, "Revising and Editing," provides advice about revising, rules for quotations and other matters of usage, and guidelines for the essay's appearance and format.

Third, the book serves as a style guide. Both Chapter 10, with its treatment of usage, and Chapter 11, "Research and Documentation," carry out this purpose. Chapter 11 explains what research papers are, how to find information and opinion, how to incorporate them into essays, and how to document sources using the MLA style. The book concludes with a chapter on taking essay tests and a chapter containing four student essays: one on a poem, one on a short story, one on a play, and one on a novel.

This edition, extensively revised, contains much that is new.

1. The author→work→reader dynamic, introduced in Chapter 1, unifies the book. It calls attention to the rhetorical nature of reading literature and writing about it. An author has ideas and purposes, embodies them in a work of literature, and "sends" the work to us. We "receive" the work, and, after due consideration, we write our own interpretation in an essay and "send" it to other readers. This paradigm emphasizes the hermeneutic thrust of the entire book. Interpretation is why we read on a serious level and why we write.

2. Chapter 2, "What is Literature?" has been rewritten in light of recent theoretical discussions about the nature of literature. It introduces the concept of sites of meaning, "places" we can look to interpret literature.

3. Chapter 6, "Specialized Approaches to Interpreting Literature," has been rearranged to reflect the author→work→reader dynamic. This new arrangement, by pointing beyond the largely formalist approach to literature covered in Chapters 2–4, encourages readers to consider all the "places" where one can find meaning in literature.

4. Chapter 9 includes a discussion of "subjectivity" (use of "I") in essays about literature.

5. There are four new student essays. The research essay on Mary Shelley's *Frankenstein* in Chapter 11 demonstrates how students can use information about an author's life to interpret works of literature. The other new essays are in Chapter 13: one on Edgar Allan

Poe's "The Cask of Amontillado," one on Susan Glaspell's *Trifles,* and one on George Eliot's *Adam Bede.*

6. Accompanying the student essays about short works are full-text versions of the works: Robert Frost's "The Death of the Hired Man" (Chapter 10), Edwin Arlington Robinson's "Richard Cory," Poe's "The Cask of the Amontillado," and Susan Glaspell's *Trifles* (Chapter 13).

7. Rules of usage (Chapter 10) and documentary procedures (Chapter 11) have been updated to reflect the most recent MLA guidelines.

8. The discussion of online resources (in Chapter 11) has been expanded and updated. Along with a new list of helpful Internet addresses, this section now offers a discussion of how to evaluate the quality of Web sites.

I have written this book out of a long-standing love for literature. My hope is that the book's information and suggestions will help readers get as much pleasure from literature as it has given me over the years. The book can serve several related purposes. Teachers can use it as a textbook in introductory courses and as a supplement in advanced ones. Students can use it on their own as an introduction to the study of literature, as a guide to writing essays about literature, and as a reference manual.

I welcome comments and suggestions from users of this book. My e-mail address is <kelley_griffith@uncg.edu>. Regular mail is English Department, University of North Carolina at Greensboro, Greensboro, NC 27402.

Acknowledgments

I owe many people gratitude for their help. I am indebted to the writers whose works I have consulted. For past editions, very helpful were the insightful comments of Laurence Perrine, Frank Garratt (Tacoma Community College), George Gleason (Southwest Missouri State University), John Hanes (Duquesne University), Jacqueline Hartwich (Bellevue Community College), Irving Howe (Hunter College), Edward Pixley (State University of New York at Oneonta), Dexter Westrum (Ottawa University), Jeff Bagato (Virginia Polytechnic Institute), Helen O'Grady (University of Wyoming), Karen Meyers (University of North Carolina at Greensboro), William Tucker (University of North Carolina at Greensboro), Walter Beale (University of North Carolina at Greensboro), Thomas C. Bonner (Midlands Technical College), Nancy Hume (Essex Community College), Gretchen Lutz (San Jacinto College), Robbie Clifton Pinter (Belmont University), Wallace Watson (Duquesne University), Judy Brown (University of British Columbia), Gaye Elder (Abraham Baldwin Agricultural College), Albert J. Griffith (Our Lady of the Lake University), James M. Hutchisson (The Citadel), Ellen N. Moody (George Mason University), John David Moore (Eastern Illinois University), and Tyler Smith (Midlands Technical College).

For this edition I wish to acknowledge the valuable suggestions of Judith Corbin, Eastern Illinois; P. R. Dansby, San Jacinto College; Jim Dervin, Winston-Salem State University; Isabella DiBari, Diablo Valley College; Bruce Gans, Wright College; Becky Roberts, Mt. San Antonio College.

At Harcourt College Publishers I thank Michell Phifer, who oversaw the editing of the book and kept me on schedule. I would also like to thank Joyce Fink, Suzie Wurzer, and Susan Journey, who helped produce this book.

Finally, I am deeply grateful to my family for the encouragement they always give me.

Contents

WRITING ESSAYS ABOUT LITERATURE

A Guide and Style Sheet

SIXTH EDITION

$\mathcal{I}$NTRODUCTION

Introduction

Like all art, literature gives pleasure. It has a certain magic that transports us from the "real" world to seemingly remote and enjoyable places. We can experience this quality without thinking about it. But literature also poses intellectual challenges that do demand thought. For most readers, grappling with these challenges enhances the pleasure of literature. By studying literature, we "see" more of it to appreciate. We learn that, far from being remote from life, literature reflects the real world and helps us locate our places in it.

This book addresses two related questions: (1) How can we read literature? and (2) How can we write about it? The questions are related because we have to read literature well in order to write about it cogently. In turn, writing about literature helps us to understand it.

There are many ways to read and write about literature. This book focuses on one way—interpretation. *Interpretation* is the act of making sense of something, of establishing its meaning. When we interpret literature, we try to discover its meaning. We can all interpret literature at some level, but in order to interpret so that we satisfy our craving for meaning and interest people in our ideas, we have to employ strategies of discovery, analysis, and reasoning. Exploring those strategies—for reading and writing—is the subject of this book.

Part One of this book takes up the first question, how to read. Chapter 1 discusses the process of interpretation and follows up with some basic strategies for interpreting literature. The rest of Part One concentrates on "places" in literature to look for meaning: the properties of literature itself (Chapter 2) and of fiction (Chapter 3), drama (Chapter 4), and poetry (Chapter 5). The concluding chapter of Part

One examines specialized strategies of interpretation, each of which illuminates potential sources of meaning in literature.

Part Two considers the question of how to write. It is organized according to a process that many writers follow: inventing (deciding what to write about), drafting (writing first drafts), revising (writing more drafts), and editing (producing a final draft for "publication"). Throughout Part Two, and most notably in the final chapter, samples of student writing illustrate interpretative writing.

Although each part of the book follows an orderly path—a step-by-step process for reading and writing—you can also use the book as a handbook. Part One covers such things as the elements of literature and of genres (fiction, drama, and poetry), as well as theoretical approaches such as Historicism, New Criticism, Structuralism, Post-Structuralism, New Historicism, Feminist and Gender Criticism. Part Two gives information about, among other things, generating topics, organizing essays, using logic, doing research, documenting sources, handling quotations, and taking tests. The location of all of this material is easy to find, especially when you use the Index of Concepts and Terms located at the back of the book. If you do not remember where a definition or explanation is, just look it up in that index.

We begin, then, with reading.

PART ONE

Interpreting Literature

Strategies for
Interpreting Literature

Why Do People Read Literature?

People read literature for many reasons, but the two most likely reasons are for pleasure and for meaning. We read literature because it is fun and because it speaks to us about important things.

When we read purely for pleasure, we do not usually care what the work means. We just want to escape from the concerns of the day and let the work perform its magic on us. You may remember your first great reading experience, when you were so caught up in a work that you were oblivious to everything else. Reading just for pleasure is like that. We sit down with a book and say to ourselves, "I don't want to think. I just want to enjoy."

But on a more thoughtful level, reading for pleasure and reading for meaning are related. Part of the pleasure of reading comes from the meaning it gives us. On first reading a Raymond Chandler detective novel, for example, we may be gripped by the suspenseful plot. We eagerly turn pages just to find out what will happen next. But upon rereading the novel, and possibly reading other works by him, we discover a thematic and artistic richness we may not have noticed before: how he uses conventions of the detective story—wise guy dialogue, intrigue, suspense, urban settings, stereotypical characters, melancholy hero—to render a moral dimension to his fictional world. We notice his poetic language, his mastery of tone, his insights about American cities, about American obsessions, about high life and low life, wealth and poverty, innocence and crime. As we continue to read Chandler, we move from one level of enjoyment—reading for "escape"—to another—reading for meaning. Or, put another way, we find ourselves reading not just for pleasure and meaning but for pleasure *because* of meaning.

In this book we will explore how to uncover the meanings of works of literature. These include the themes of a work (its comments about the human condition) as well as the workings and effectiveness of such devices as characterization, setting, plot, and language. Although one can study the aesthetic qualities of literature—the devices authors use to give us pleasure—for themselves, here we will consider them as integral to meaning. They are the means by which authors deliver ideas, they influence our response to these ideas, and their appeal often arises from the ideas they embody. On the one hand, we like the ideas in a work because of its artistic devices; on the other, we admire the devices because we like the ideas. Form and content, beauty and truth—they can hardly be separated.

How do we discover meaning in works of literature? We do so through interpretation.

What Is Interpretation?

Interpretation is a process. It is the process of examining the details of works of literature in order to make sense of them. John Ellis, the literary theorist, describes the goals and process of interpretation in this way: interpretation "is a hypothesis about the most general organization and coherence of all the elements that form a literary text." This "organization and coherence" emerges from a "synthesis" between a work's themes and its details. "The most satisfying interpretation," he says, "will be that which is the most inclusive. The procedure of investigation will be that of any inquiry: a continual move between general notions of the coherence of the text, and consideration of the function within the whole of particular parts of it. General conceptions will change in the light of particular observations, and new particular observations will then become necessary in the light of the changed conceptions" (202). Ellis is saying here that as we read, we encounter details of a work and begin to draw conclusions about how they relate to one another, what they mean. As we continue to read, we encounter more details. These may confirm our hypotheses or cause us to replace them with new ones. Once we have finished reading the work, we can decide which hypotheses account for the most details; those hypotheses, Ellis says, constitute the best interpretations.

Many critics today would disagree with Ellis that the best interpretation "covers" or accounts for the most details in a work or that it establishes a "coherence" that unifies the whole work. For one thing, it is hard to say which interpretation covers the most details. For another, the most comprehensive interpretation may not be the most satisfying to a particular reader. We might, for example, want to focus on just one aspect of a work, such as the motivation of a character or the influence of setting. Many works, furthermore, stubbornly resist complete "coherence." But Ellis is correct about how the process of interpretation works. Interpretation is a quest for ideas manifested by a work's details. To be believable and convincing, therefore, interpretations must emerge from the details of the work. If we encounter details that contradict our interpretations, we must adjust the interpretations to accommodate those details.

Interpretation is something we do with more than just literature. It is an unavoidable process in any thinking person's life: Why is Miriam angry with me? Why did Jonathan go to pieces when he took the test? Would this job be better for me than that one? How will my blowup with Lucy affect our relationship? Is the defendant guilty? Should we legalize late-term abortions? What were the causes of World War II? Do human beings have free will? Answering questions like these, from the trivial to the profound, requires interpretation.

A crime scene, for example, demands a similar interpretive process as a work of literature. You, the detective, have just arrived at the scene of the crime. As you examine the details of the scene, you formulate hypotheses about what happened and who is responsible. With the discovery of new evidence, you adjust your hypotheses until, having sifted through all the evidence, you decide who committed the crime. A key difference between crime scenes and works of literature, however, is that literature has authors. Criminals may be "authors" of a sort; they create the crime scene, but they do not want us to know what they have done. Authors, in contrast, want to reach us. The following diagram represents this process of communication:

$$\boxed{\text{Author}} \rightarrow \boxed{\text{Work}} \rightarrow \boxed{\text{Reader}}$$

Authors have ideas, express them in works of literature, and "send" the works to us, their readers. We read ("receive") the works. As receivers, our challenge is to understand authors' ideas. But this challenge is complicated by the nature of literature. Instead of just telling us what their ideas are, authors use "literary" devices—metaphor, symbol, plot, connotation, rhyme, meter, and so forth—to convey ideas. Such devices communicate meaning indirectly. They force us to figure out authors' ideas. It is as if an author says to us, "I want to state my ideas about something, but instead of saying them straight out, I will tell a story and let you figure out what I'm trying to say." Or the author says, "The woman I'm in love with is wonderful, but instead of telling you directly how this is so, I'm going to say, 'My love is like a red, red rose.'" Most authors impose the task of "figuring out" on us, the readers. Such a task requires interpretation. The craft of interpreting literature is called *literary criticism.* Anyone who interprets literature is a literary critic.

How Do We Interpret?

Interpretation of works of literature is the process of thinking about their details in order to see how the details interconnect and what ideas they convey. Interpretation requires us to be active rather than passive readers. When we read purely for pleasure, we are generally "passive," letting the work wash over us, not trying to figure it out. But when we interpret, we need to pay close attention to the potential meaning of details. Keeping in mind the model of author→work→reader, we can think of the author as using literary devices to manipulate our emotions and our beliefs. As interpreters, we should be alert to authors' wiles. Do we agree with the ideas authors try to foist on us? The following are suggestions about how to be active, interpreting readers.

· 1. **Get the facts straight.** The first, most fundamental step in interpreting anything is to see clearly what is in the work, its "facts." For some works, this is easy to do; the details in them are accessible and understandable. But for other works, getting the facts straight may not be so easy. The poetry of seventeenth-century poets like John Donne and George Herbert is notoriously dense and requires close study to understand. Modernist and Post-Modernist authors such as T. S. Eliot, Virginia Woolf, James Joyce, Thomas Pynchon, and Toni Morrison employ innovative techniques that obscure the details of their works. The language of Chaucer and Shakespeare is not quite our language. To understand it we have to rely on glosses (definitions) that editors often place at the bottom of the page. In short, we sometimes have to work hard just to recognize the facts of literary works. When we read, then, we should look up words we do not know. We should track down allusions (to myths, the Bible, historical and biographical events). We should read works slowly and more than once.

2. **Connect the work with yourself.** For each of us, the most important meanings of works of literature will arise from our own experience and beliefs. This does not mean that the reasons people value great authors like Sophocles, Sappho, Virgil, Dante, Shakespeare, Goethe, Emily Dickinson, and George Eliot are unimportant. Such reasons are part of our cultural heritage. Not to be interested in them is to deny ourselves the wisdom of that heritage. Even worse, to care only about our own "meanings" is to cut ourselves off from the rest of humankind. But, that said, unless we can connect a work of literature to our own experiences and interests, it will not live for us.

The "connection" strategy is to actively project ourselves into works of literature, especially ones that seem disconnected from us. We ask, "How would I live under these circumstances?" Take, for example, the writings of the New England Puritans, which may seem remote and forbidding. If you use your imagination to place yourself in the Puritan world, you can capture its connection to your life. How would you think and feel had you lived then—about your family, the wilderness around you, the difficulty of scraping out a living, the harsh winters, the imperatives of your religious beliefs? What would your psychological state—emotional conflicts and tensions—have been? Authors like Nathaniel Hawthorne (in his novel *The Scarlet Letter*, 1850); Arthur Miller (in his play *The Crucible*, 1954); and Maryse Condé (in her novel *I, Tituba, Black Witch of Salem*, 1986) have done just this—projected themselves into Puritan culture and produced highly imaginative rethinkings of it. As readers, we can do the same. By asking questions like the following, we can recover the appeal of works of literature that may at first seem distant from our own lives:

- How are things in the work (characters, incidents, places) similar to things in our lives?
- How does this work challenge our beliefs?
- What new things does the work bring up for us?
- How does this work give us pleasure?
- What is upsetting or unpleasant about it?

3. **Develop hypotheses as you read.** As John Ellis says in the passage on page 8, when we read works of literature, even for the first time, we generate ideas about them. The "hypothesis" strategy makes this action intentional and constant. As you read, raise questions about what the details mean: Why does a particular character act the way she does? What ideas does a character espouse? Why does the author keep using a particular image? rhyme scheme? metrical pattern? As you read, do not feel that you have to give final answers to these questions. Plan to come back to them later. Such questions and tentative answers get us thinking, help us pick up important details that pop up later, and make reviewing the work easier.

4. **Write as you read.** Writing generates ideas and helps us think creatively. By putting concepts in our own words, we make them our own and embed them in our memory. If you own copies of works of literature, write in them: underline passages, circle words, draw arrows from one passage to another. In the margins, write questions, summaries, definitions, topics the author addresses, and tentative interpretations. If something is repeated in a work, note where it first appears ("see page xxx") and make comparisons later. Such notations help us generate ideas about what we are reading. When we review, our markings highlight important places in the work and lead us to synthesize details.

5. **Learn from the interpretations of others.** Although we read alone, interpretation is most fruitful as a shared activity, something we do with others. Knowing what others think helps us decide what we think. One critic wrote that even blurbs on book jackets helped him get his bearings in a work. By learning from the insights and knowledge of others, we place ourselves in a dialogue with them. We listen, agree, disagree, share, and thereby clarify what we believe. Interpretations by professional critics are readily available in books and articles. But equally stimulating are the ideas of people we know— friends, classmates, teachers, colleagues. These people are often nearby, ready to share what they think.

6. **Analyze works of literature.** To *analyze* is to examine the "parts" of something and discover the relationships among them. Analysis is a powerful, necessary strategy for generating and communicating interpretations of anything, not just literature. If, for example, you sell computers, you will do it better if you can analyze them—know how they work and what they can do, thus what they "mean" (how, for example, they can help your customers). The same is true for inter-

preting literature. Being able to analyze literature helps us see how each "part" contributes to the meaning of a work.

In the next chapter, we will consider the "parts" of literature itself and how they contribute to the meaning of works of literature.

Works Cited

Ellis, John. *The Theory of Literary Criticism: A Logical Analysis.* Berkeley: U of California P, 1974.

What Is Literature?

I s a Batman comic book "literature"? What about a physics textbook? a restaurant menu? a university catalog? a television sitcom?
a political speech? the letters we write home? Back about the middle
of the twentieth century, critics thought they knew what literature was
and thus the answer to such questions. The so-called New Critics, who
flourished in the United States from the 1920s until the 1960s, believed
that literature had certain properties that people trained in the writing
and studying of literature could identify. Some of these properties were
to them mysterious, even spiritual, and thus to be intuited rather than
rationally identified. Other properties, however, were objective and
identifiable—such things as imagery, metaphor, meter, rhyme, irony,
and plot. The New Critics confidently identified and evaluated works of
literature, elevating the "great" works of literature to high status. Literature for them consisted, with but few exceptions, of poetry, drama, and
fiction and would definitely *not* have included the kinds of writing listed
at the beginning of this paragraph.

Beginning in the 1960s, however, critics questioned the concept of
literature expounded by the New Critics. The New Critics, they noted,
seemed narrow in policing the literary "canon," that unofficial collection
of works that critics deem worthy of admiration and study. The New Critics were mostly male and Eurocentric, and the works they admired were
usually by males who wrote within the European literary tradition.
Largely excluded from the canon were works by females, persons of color,
and persons who lived outside Europe. Excluded, also, were the genres
(kinds) of "literature" that such outsiders preferred. Because women, for
example, often lacked access to the means of publishing literature, many

wrote in genres that would not normally be published: letters, diaries, journals, memoirs, autobiographies. Why, critics asked, were these genres not "literature"? Because people of color were often politically active, they wrote in genres that furthered political ends: speeches, autobiographies, essays. Why were these not thought of as "literature"? And because some people belonged to "traditional" cultures, their works were often meant to be spoken, not written. Were these works not "literature"?

As a result of such questions and because of the emergence of new theories about language, critics wrestled anew with the question, "What is literature?" At stake were a number of related issues: Which works would get published? Which works were available—in textbooks and paperbacks—to be taught? What groups of people would be valued (because their works were read and appreciated)? If we compare textbook anthologies of English and American literature published circa 1960 with those published today, we can see that the canon now embraces a much broader variety of authors, works, and genres.

Such a comparison reveals how much the concept of "literature" has changed in the past forty years. Some theorists have challenged even the concept of literature. John Ellis argues that literature is not definable by properties, such as rhyme, meter, plot, setting, and characterization. "Nonliterary" works often have such properties—advertisements, popular songs, jokes, graffiti. Rather, the definition of literature is like that of weeds. Just as weeds are "plants we do not wish to cultivate" (38), so literature is identifiable by how people use it. People use works of literature not for their utilitarian purposes—to get something done—but as objects of enjoyment in themselves. Or, as Ellis puts it, a work becomes literature when it is no longer "specifically relevant to the immediate context of its origin" (44). If, for example, a physics textbook stops being read for its information about physics and is read instead for some other reason—say, the elegance of its prose style—then it transcends the "immediate context of its origin" and becomes literature.

Terry Eagleton, another contemporary critic, is even more radical than Ellis: "Literature, in the sense of a set of works of assured and unalterable value, distinguished by certain shared inherent properties, does not exist" (11). Literature—and the literary "canon"—are constructs, established by society: "Anything can be literature, and anything which is regarded as unalterably and unquestionably literature—Shakespeare, for example—can cease to be literature" (10).

Ellis and Eagleton represent a skeptical reaction to the categorical pronouncements of the New Critics, whose definitions excluded many works we value today. Nonetheless, as interpreters of literature, it is helpful for us to know about properties traditionally identified with literature. Not every work may contain all of these, but most will have one or more of them. We can think of these characteristics as "places" to look for meaning in literature.

Literature Is Language

The word *literature* has traditionally meant written—as opposed to spoken—works. But today, given the broadened meaning of the word, it includes oral as well as written works. The works of Homer emerged from an oral tradition, and it is even possible that the author "Homer," whether a single individual or a group of people, was illiterate and spoke his works to a scribe, who wrote them down. What Homer and other oral story tellers have in common with writers is language: The medium of literature, whether oral or written, is language. This raises questions about the "literariness" of media that rely heavily on other means of communication: film, or dance, or certain forms of theater (mime, slapstick, farce), or comic books. Most critics believe that language is a key aspect of literature and that there has to be enough language in a work for it to be considered literature.

Some theorists claim that authors of literature use language in special ways. One of those ways, according to René Wellek, is an emphasis on connotative rather than denotative meanings of words. Scientists, for example, use language for its *denotative* value, its ability to provide signs (words) that mean one thing only. For scientists, the thing the sign represents—the referent—is more important than the sign itself. Any sign will do, as long as it represents the referent clearly and exactly (11). Because emotions render meanings imprecise, scientists try to use signs that eliminate the emotional, the irrational, the subjective. Writers of literature, in contrast, use language *connotatively*—to bring into play all the emotional associations words may have. *Connotation* is the meaning that words have in addition to their explicit referents. An example of connotation is the word *mother*, whose denotation is simply "female parent" but whose connotations include such qualities as protection, warmth, unqualified love, tenderness, devotion, mercy, intercession, home, childhood, the happy past. Even scientific language becomes connotative once it enters everyday speech. When we see Albert Einstein's equation $E = mc^2$, we no longer think just of "Energy equals mass times the speed of light squared" but of mushroom clouds and ruined cities. Or the term *DNA*, which denotes the genetic code of life, connotes the alteration of species or the freeing of innocent people from death row. Some kinds of literature (poetry, for example) rely more heavily on connotation than others. Realistic novels, in contrast to much poetry, may contain precise denotative descriptions of physical objects. But most authors of literature are sensitive to the emotional nuances of words.

The Russian Formalists, a group of theorists who flourished in the Soviet Union in the 1920s, claimed another use of language as a defining quality of literature. The key to literature, they said, is "literary" language, language that calls attention to itself as different from ordinary, everyday language. The term for this quality, invented by Viktor Shklovsky, is "defamiliarisation" (literally, "making strange"). "The technique of art," he said, "is to make objects 'unfamiliar,' to make forms difficult, to increase the difficulty and length of perception, because the process of perception is an aesthetic end in itself and must be prolonged" (quoted in Selden 31). Shklovsky's idea of defamiliarization can apply not just to language but other aspects of literary form—plot, for example, or techniques of drama. The principle of defamiliarization is to "foreground"—give prominence to—something in the work of literature that departs from everyday use or familiar artistic conventions. When authors foreground language, they in effect say, "Hey! Look at my language! See how different it is from ordinary language!" They focus on language for itself. They are fascinated by its sounds, its rhythms, even its appearance on the page. Sometimes they become so interested in these qualities that they subordinate meaning to them. Some nursery rhymes, for example, exhibit a delight in language that virtually deemphasizes meaning, like this one, "Swan":

> Swan, swan, over the sea:
> Swim, swan, swim!
> Swan, swan, back again;
> Well swum, swan!

Here, the anonymous author revels in the repetition of sounds that key off the word *swan*. People who use language in everyday, nonliterary speech and writing also show sensitivity to its sounds and subjective qualities, but writers of literature exploit these qualities more fully, more consciously, and more systematically.

Language is one of the "places" we can look for meaning in literature. We can be alert to how writers convey ideas in their subtle and complex use language. Questions such as these help us focus on such usage: How does an author use language to signal ideas? What seems significant about such things as the author's choice of words (*diction*), ways of constructing sentences (*syntax*), word sounds, repetitions of key words and phrases, archaisms of diction or syntax (as in language that echoes the King James Bible or Shakespeare)?

Literature Is Fictional

We commonly use the term *fiction* to describe prose works that tell a story (for example, fairy tales, short stories, and novels). In fact, however, most works of literature are "fictional" in the sense that something in them signals that readers may set them apart from the context of real life.

A work can be fictional in two ways. First, authors make up—imagine—some or all of the material. This property explains why literature is often referred to as "imaginative literature"; it features invented material that does not exist in the real world. In fantasy fiction, for example, human beings fly, perform magic, remain young, travel through time, metamorphose, and live happily ever after. But even historical fiction, which relies on actual events, is fictional. It includes characters, dialogue, events, and settings that never existed. The three main characters of Hilary Mantel's 1992 novel *A Place of Greater Safety*—Camille Desmoulins, Maximilien Robespierre, and Georges-Jacques Danton—were real people. But the author, while following the outline of their participation in the French Revolution, makes up much of what they do and say.

Second, the fictionality of literature lies also in the artistic control the writer exercises over the work. This artistic control has the effect of stylizing the materials of the work and thus setting it apart from the real. This effect occurs even when the material does accurately mirror the facts of real life or when it states ideas that can be verified in actual experience. Such works would include autobiographies like those by Benjamin Franklin and Frederick Douglass and "true crime" narratives like Truman Capote's *In Cold Blood* (1966) and Norman Mailer's *The Executioner's Song* (1979). Compare, for example, how a newspaper reporter and a poet would describe the same event. Assume that both would describe the event accurately. The reporter would make his or her account correspond as exactly as possible to the event. Just like the poet, the reporter "controls" his or her account by arranging events in order, by choosing apt words, by leaving out details. There is an art to what the reporter does. But the reporter wants us to experience the details of the event, not the report of it. The poet, in contrast, makes his or her *poem* the object of experience. Through the play of language, selection of details, inclusion of metaphor, irony, and imagery, the poet makes the work an artifact, an object of enjoyment and contemplation in itself. Consider Walt Whitman's "Cavalry Crossing a Ford" (1867), a poetic account of an event he no doubt witnessed during the American Civil War:

> A line in long array where they wind betwixt green islands,
> They take a serpentine course, their arms flash in the sun—hark
>   to the musical clank,
> Behold the silvery river, in it the splashing horses loitering stop
>   to drink,
> Behold the brown-faced men, each group, each person a pic-
>   ture, the negligent rest on the saddles,
> Some emerge on the opposite bank, others are just entering the
>   ford—while,
> Scarlet and blue and snowy white,
> The guidon flags flutter gayly in the wind.

Although there are no end rhymes or regular metrical patterns in this poem, readers sense, even if they are not sure why, that this is a work of literature. The way it looks—lines separated, not run together, as they would be in prose. Also, such devices as unusual word choice ("array," "betwixt," "behold," "guidon"), alliteration ("flags flutter"), repeated vowel sounds ("silvery river," "horses loitering"), repeated phrases ("Behold the silvery river," "Behold the brown-faced men"), and colorful imagery ("Scarlet and blue and snowy white") call attention to *how* Whitman describes the event, to the poem itself. In this way, the work becomes "fictional." It transcends the event described. Long after people have forgotten the event, they will take pleasure in the poem.

Even works that are not supposedly fictional, that purport to be about real people and events, become "fictional" by means of literary devices. Two well-known autobiographical examples are Henry David Thoreau's *Walden* (1854) and Richard Wright's *Black Boy* (1945). Thoreau really did live in a cabin at Walden Pond, and we can be fairly sure the events he records in Walden did happen. But Thoreau does so many "literary" things with those events that he causes us to conceive of them in aesthetic and thematic terms. His prose style is highly stylized and "poetic." He emphasizes his own feelings. He collapses the two years he actually spent at Walden into one year, and organizes that year around the four seasons of the year, thus giving the book a kind of "plot." He retells events to illustrate philosophical themes. The text is heavily metaphoric and symbolic. As with Thoreau, Richard Wright records events that actually happened. But here, too, the author employs "literary" devices to make these events vivid. He conveys his intense feelings by means of a first person point of view similar to that a fiction writer would use. His language is charged with emotional intensity. Perhaps most striking, he constructs "novelistic" scenes. These scenes, which have extensive dialogue and minute descriptions of physical actions and details, are almost certainly "fictional" in that it is improbable the author could have remembered the exact words these people said and the physical details he records. We can believe they happened, but Wright fills in details to give them aesthetic impact.

The fictional quality of literature is a second "place" to look for meaning in literature. The fantasy element in literature is fun in itself, but fiction grants authors the option to fill in gaps that always exist in historical events, to make connections that historians cannot. Also, the stylized quality of literature often underscores ideas. Whitman's "Cavalry Crossing a Ford," for example, conveys the impression of light-heartedness, vigor, and gaiety, largely through his selection of details of color, sound, and light. What, then, seems fictional about the work, whether imagined or stylized? What ideas do those qualities suggest?

Literature Is True

Even though works of literature are "fictional," they have the capacity for being "true." This paradox creates one of the most pleasurable tensions in literature: its imaginative and stylized properties (fictionality) against its commentary on the human condition (truth). There are at least three ways that literature can be true. First, literature can be true to the facts of reality, as in descriptions of real people, places, and events—Napoleon's defeat at Waterloo, the operations of a coal mine, the building of the Brooklyn Bridge, the details of human anatomy, the biology of a forest.

More important, literature can be true by communicating ideas about life. Again, the model we presented in Chapter 1 is relevant here:

$$\boxed{Author} \rightarrow \boxed{Work} \rightarrow \boxed{Reader}$$

Authors have certain ideas they want to communicate to readers. They embed them in works of literature and "send" the works to readers. We can most readily spot this purpose when authors directly state their ideas, as in this poem, "My Friend, the Things That Do Attain," by Henry Howard, Earl of Surrey, written in 1547:

> My friend, the things that do attain
> The happy life be these, I find:
> The riches left, not got with pain;
> The fruitful ground; the quiet mind;
>
> The equal friend; no grudge, no strife;
> No charge of rule, nor governance;
> Without disease, the healthy life;
> The household of continuance;
>
> The mean diet, no dainty fare;
> Wisdom joined with simpleness;
> The night discharged of all care,
> Where wine the wit may not oppress:
>
> The faithful wife, without debate;
> Such sleeps as may beguile the night;
> Content thyself with thine estate,
> Neither wish death, nor fear his might.

Here the poet tells us straight out his ideas about how to live the "happy life." Even when authors employ obvious elements of fantasy, they can state their ideas directly. Aesop's animal characters are like no animals in real life: They reason, talk, and act like human beings. But the author uses these fantastic characters to state "morals," shrewd commentaries on the human experience.

More typically, however, authors refrain from stating their ideas directly. Instead, they present them indirectly by means of literary conventions such as plot, metaphor, symbol, irony, musical language, and suspense. All the details of a work make up an imaginary "world" that is based on the author's ideas about the real world. The world of George Orwell's *Nineteen Eighty-Four* (1948), for example, is filled with crumbling buildings, frightened people, children who spitefully turn their parents over to the police, procedures whereby truth is systematically altered, masses of people trapped by their ignorance and selfishness, and officials who justify any deed to achieve power. It is a world without love, compassion, justice, joy, tradition, altruism, idealism, or hope. The facts of this world are patently imaginary—Orwell placed them in the future—but we infer from them that Orwell had an extremely pessimistic view of human nature and human institutions. We sense that he is warning us: the terrible society in *Nineteen Eighty-Four* has already existed in places like Nazi Germany and Stalinist Russia and could spread to other places as well.

Since most works of literature tell stories, two prominent conventions for communicating ideas are *typical characters* and *probable actions*. You may have heard the phrase "stranger than fiction," as if the characters and events in works of fiction are abnormal and bizarre. But, ironically, it is real life that gives us freakish events and inexplicable people. In contrast, authors impose order on the chaos of real life. To do this, they present characters who typify real people, and they recount actions that would probably happen in real life. J. R. R. Tolkien, for example, offers an array of fantasy creatures and kingdoms in *The Hobbit* and its sequel, *The Lord of the Rings*. Yet his characters, whatever they may look like, represent recognizable types of people. The protagonists, Bilbo and Frodo Baggins, for example, typify those gentle, kindly people who would prefer to live in domestic obscurity but who instead play heroic roles in cataclysmic dramas. And the way they behave is probable because it fits the types of people they are. They do not suddenly become supermen with supernatural powers. Like average people, they are vulnerable to superior strength and to their own fears. They succeed because they exhibit the strengths of average people: perseverance, shrewdness, unselfishness, courage, and honesty.

So prominent in literature are typical characters and probable actions that most works of literature are to some extent allegorical. *Allegory* is a kind of literature in which concrete things—characters, events, and objects—represent ideas. Here is a very short allegory:

> Fear knocked at the door.
> Faith answered.
> There was no one there.

In this story, the character "Fear" stands for the idea of fear and the character "Faith" is equivalent to the idea of faith. The setting of the story is a house, which symbolizes our psychological selves. Fear's knocking at the door shows an emotion that everyone experiences. Faith's opening the door shows a possible response to fear. The "moral" of the story, implied in the conclusion, is that we should all have faith because faith makes fear disappear. In longer allegories, such as John Bunyan's *Pilgrim's Progress* (1678), Edmund Spenser's *The Faerie Queen* (1590–1596), and the anonymous medieval play *Everyman* (c.1485), the characters, places, and events are much more complexly developed but nonetheless, as in this allegory, have names that directly indicate the ideas they represent. But even in nonallegorical works, the characters, locations, and events are so typical and probable, that they could almost be given names to represent ideas: Hamlet could be named "Melancholy," Othello could be called "Jealous," Ophelia "Innocent," Romeo "Love Sick," Iago "Sinister," and so forth. We can infer authors' worldviews from the "allegorical" qualities of their works—typical characters, suggestive places, and probable actions.

The near-allegorical quality of literature underscores its expressiveness. Literature is always an expression of the individuals who compose it. Their personalities, emotions, styles, tastes, and beliefs are bound up in their works. As interpreters, our task is to determine objectively what the ideas of a given work may be. We do not, however, have to agree with them. Orwell's worldview is very different from Tolkien's. Orwell shows an average man rebelling against social corruption and failing miserably to do anything about it. He is weak, ineffectual, and controlled by forces outside himself. In Orwell's world, good loses because people are too stupid or greedy or weak to overcome evil. Like Orwell, Tolkien also shows the weakness of average people, but in his worldview, the average person is innately good and potentially strong; such individuals can band together with others and overthrow evil. Orwell is pessimistic about human nature and the future of humanity; Tolkien is optimistic.

Still another kind of "truth" conveyed by literature is the *experience* of reality. Whatever the experience might be—white water rafting, losing a loved one, falling in love, going hungry, overcoming a handicap—authors put us in the midst of it, make us feel it. Such feelings can teach us about experiences we have never gone through. Scientists do not often write novels about their research, but one who did was Björn Kurtén, the Swedish paleontologist. His novel *Dance of the Tiger: A Novel of the Ice Age* features the interaction of *Homo sapiens* and Neanderthal peoples during the Ice Age. Kurtén has published many scholarly books on Ice Age peoples. "Why," he asks in his preface, "write a novel about prehistoric man?" He answers,

> In the last three decades, it has been my privilege to be immersed in the life of the Ice Age. More and more, I have felt there is much to be told that simply cannot be formulated in scientific reports. How did it

feel to live then? How did the world look to you? What were your beliefs? Above all, what was it like to meet humans not of your own species? That is an experience denied to us, for we are all Homo sapiens (xxiii).

In his novel, Kurtén brilliantly succeeds in bringing Ice Age people alive for us. Through the thoughts, conflicts, and daily activities of his characters, we *feel* what it was like to live 35,000 years ago.

Another example is Jessamyn West's novel *The Massacre at Fall Creek* (1975). In the afterword she says she was intrigued by an event that occurred in Indiana in 1824. A white judge and jury convicted four white men of killing Indians, and the men were hanged. Although this event marked the first time in United States history that white men convicted other white men for killing Indians, West could find little information about it. She wondered: What was it like to be convicted for something previously condoned? How did the Indians and whites feel about the event? West's novel is her answer to these questions. Drawing upon her understanding of what most people would go through under those circumstances, she shows us what they *probably* experienced. Furthermore, she causes us to *feel* what they experienced. We live through the gruesome killings. We share the fear of Indian reprisal. We see the callousness of hardened Indian killers. We experience the dawning consciousness of some whites that Indians are human and have rights. We suffer the alienation caused by taking unpopular moral stands. We inhale the circus-like atmosphere of the hangings. With the judge, we puzzle over ambiguous ethical dilemmas. We stand on the scaffold with the condemned.

The truth of literature is the most important "place" to look for meaning in literature. The following questions encapsulate the points we have made here about truth in literature.

1. What ideas does the author seem to state directly?
2. How are the characters typical of human behavior? What ideas do they espouse or seem to represent? Which characters—and thus the ideas associated with them—predominate at the end of the work?
3. What ideas are associated with places and other physical properties?
4. Authors sometimes signal ideas through such devices as titles, names, and epigraphs. (An *epigraph* is a pertinent quotation put at the beginning of a work or chapter.) Examples of suggestive titles are *The Grapes of Wrath* (taken from a line in "The Battle Hymn of the Republic"), *All the King's Men* (from the nursery rhyme "Humpty-Dumpty"),

Pride and Prejudice, Great Expectations, and *Measure for Measure.* What ideas seem embedded in titles, chapter heads, epigraphs, names, and other direct indications of authors' ideas?

5. What do other works by the author suggest about the meaning of this work?

6. As with Björn Kurtén and Jessamyn West on pages 24–25, authors sometimes comment on their own work. What light does such comment shed on the ideas in the work?

7. What feelings does the work elicit in each of us? What do we experience in the work that we have never gone through? What have we experienced that the work brings powerfully to life?

Literature Is Aesthetic

Literature is "aesthetic"; that is, it gives pleasure. The aesthetic quality of literature—its "beauty"—is hard to define and describe. In a sense, it just *is.* Like various other art forms—music, patterns of color in paintings, photographs of sunsets, dance—literature is an end in itself. The pleasure of literature rests in the way authors use literary conventions, such as metaphor, plot, symbolism, irony, suspense, themes, and poetic language. Taken together, they constitute the *form* of the work, the order authors impose on their material. Such order is not typical of real life. In real life, events can be random, disconnected, and inconsequential. Problems can remain unresolved. The murderer may not be caught, the cruel parent may continue to be cruel, the economic crisis may continue, the poor but honest youth may not be rewarded. So many things happen to us that we can hardly recognize, much less remember them all. Nor do we always know which events are important, which trivial. But literature can give order to events in the form of a *plot.* Unimportant events are excluded, cause-and-effect relationships established, conflicts resolved. Events are arranged in logical order so that they form a sequence with a beginning, a middle, and an end. Plot is but one of a multitude of ways artists give order to material. They may also arrange language into patterns, reduce characters to recognizable types, connect details to ideas, elegantly describe settings. In works of literature, all of the elements combine to form an *overall* order, an *overall* coherence.

The aesthetic quality of literature is another "place" to look for meaning in literature. Experiencing the beauty of literature may itself be a kind of meaning. But the aesthetic qualities of literature are bound up with the other kind of meaning, the ideas conveyed by a work. Authors use pleasurable conventions to enhance and communicate ideas. When we study the aesthetics of literature, we ask questions like these: What conventions (of language, plot, characterization, etc.) does the author use to give us pleasure? Why does the author's manipulation of these conventions affect us so strongly? And, especially, how does the author use pleasurable conventions to communicate ideas and make them appealing?

Literature Is Intertextual

Literature is intertextual: It relates to other works of literature, it incorporates established literary conventions, and it belongs to at least one genre of literature. *Genre* is a French word that means "type" or "kind." Literary genres are identifiable by their literary conventions. *Conventions* are features of literature, whether of language, subject matter, themes, or form, that readers can easily recognize. As an example of intertextuality, consider these two poems. The second, by Sir Walter Raleigh, is a response to the first, by Christopher Marlowe.

THE PASSIONATE SHEPHERD TO HIS LOVE

Come live with me and be my love,
And we will all the pleasures prove
That valleys, groves, hills, and fields,
Woods, or steepy mountain yields.

And we will sit upon the rocks,
Seeing the shepherds feed their flocks,
By shallow rivers to whose falls
Melodious birds sing madrigals.

And I will make thee beds of roses
And a thousand fragrant posies,
A cap of flowers, and a kirtle
Embroidered all with leaves of myrtle;

A gown made of the finest wool
Which from our pretty lambs we pull;
Fair lined slippers for the cold,
With buckles of the purest gold;

THE NYMPH'S REPLY TO THE SHEPHERD

If all the world and love were young,
And truth in every shepherd's tongue,
These pretty pleasures might me move
To live with thee and be thy love.

Time drives the flocks from field to fold
When rivers rage and rocks grow cold,
And Philomel becometh dumb;
The rest complains of cares to come.

The flowers do fade, and wanton fields
To wayward winter reckoning yields;
A honey tongue, a heart of gall,
Is fancy's spring, but sorrow's fall.

Thy gowns, thy shoes, thy beds of roses,
Thy cap, thy kirtle, and thy posies
Soon break, soon wither, soon forgotten—
In folly ripe, in reason rotten.

A belt of straw and ivy buds,
With coral clasps and amber studs:
And if these pleasures may thee move,
Come live with me, and be my love.

The shepherds' swains shall dance and sing
For thy delight each May morning:
If these delights thy mind may move,
Then live with me and be my love.

Christopher Marlowe (1600)

Thy belt of straw and ivy buds,
Thy coral clasps and amber studs,
All these in me no means can move
To come to thee and be thy love.

But could youth last and love still breed,
Had joys no date nor age no need,
Then these delights my mind might move
To live with thee and be thy love.

Sir Walter Raleigh (c. 1600)

These poems are intertextual in the three ways mentioned above. First, Raleigh's poem is an almost line-for-line response to Marlowe's. We can understand Marlowe's poem without knowing Raleigh's, but we would miss a lot in Raleigh's poem if we did not know Marlowe's. Second, Marlowe's poem belongs to a genre called pastoral poetry. Third, in composing his poem, Marlowe incorporated the conventions of the pastoral genre: a peaceful, simple rural setting; carefree shepherds (the word *pastor* means "shepherd"); a season of eternal spring; an absence of the difficulties of life—hard work, disease, harsh weather, betrayal; lovers who talk genially about love; and a playful, witty, charming poetic style.

The intertextuality of literature is a rich source of meaning for the interpretation of individual works. We can pose several questions that help us mine this meaning.

1. **What can we learn about a work by considering works related to it?** Authors often have specific works of literature in mind when they compose their own. Sometimes they signal this by means of *allusions:* explicit references to other works. Such allusions are always invitations to compare the author's work with the other works. Dante, for example, by featuring the Latin poet Virgil as a prominent character in *The Divine Comedy*, signals to us that Virgil's writings and especially *The Aeneid* were significant for his work.

Sometimes authors make no overt references to other works, but we infer from the work itself or learn from outside sources, that the author drew from other works. We know, for example, that Dostoevsky was influenced by the works of Charles Dickens, but he does not necessarily say so in his novels. Whether or not authors tell us what other works serve as their reference points, we can ask what ideas and artistic devices from these other works are applicable to the work under study. Raleigh, in "The Nymph's Reply to the Shepherd," openly invites us to compare his poem to Marlowe's. When we do, we see the stark difference between his ideas and Marlowe's.

2. **Can we understand the genre in which the work is written?** Genres are indispensable for both writers and readers of literature. Alastair Fowler, in his comprehensive treatment of genre, *Kinds of Literature: An Introduction to the Theory of Genres and Modes*, says that genres are similar to language. The conventions of each genre constitute a "grammar" that allows us to "read" the genre and works written in it (20). Just as we must learn the structure of a language in order to read it, so must we learn the conventions of genres in order to read literature. People learn popular genres as they grow up—by being read to, watching television, going to movies. But some genres require special training to understand. One reason is that genres are products of particular cultures and times. We can read narrative fiction, for example, because we know its conventions. But a culture could conceivably have no tradition of fiction. If so, its members would find fiction baffling, just as people brought up in the Western tradition usually find Japanese No plays and Kabuki theater puzzling. Another reason is that genres change over time or cease to exist. We may encounter genres even in our own language that puzzle us because we do not know them. To read some works of literature, we have to *recover* their genres. Pastoral poetry, a genre that was enormously popular in Christopher Marlowe's day, is virtually dead as a genre today. To recover it, we can read other poems in the pastoral tradition. And we can refer to historical works, such as M. H. Abrams's excellent *A Glossary of Literary Terms*, for information about pastoral poetry and other unfamiliar genres.

3. **What values does the genre convey?** Genres are cultural phenomena. In contrast to works by an individual author, they emerge from many authors and reflect the interests, ways of life, and values of particular cultures. Detective fiction, for example, became a recognizable genre in the nineteenth century. Critics contend that its conventions mirror the values, troubles, and circumstances of Western culture in the nineteenth century. The detective hero—Edgar Allan Poe's Dupin, Arthur Conan Doyle's Sherlock Holmes—represents Western culture's enormous respect for science. These detectives are dispassionate, analytical, and brilliant. Holmes, in fact, publishes treatises on forensic science. The setting of detective fiction is typically the great industrial cities, which were by-products of nineteenth-century capitalism. These cities, with their mazelike streets and heterogeneous populations, were perfect environments

for intrigue and crime. Dupin works in Paris, Holmes in London. The crime is almost always murder or threat of murder. The pursuit and punishment of the murderer upholds the nineteenth century's respect for the individual. The murderer destroys the individual's most valuable possession, life itself. But the murderer destroys more than just lives. At stake also are the institutions held dear in the nineteenth century—the family, boards of trade, governmental agencies, universities. The detective, by capturing the murderer, purges these institutions of those who would corrupt and destroy them.

Other genres reflect their own cultural contexts. The epic, for example, trumpets heroic deeds and national solidarity. The medieval romance inculcates a code of chivalry. Why, then, did the author choose to compose in this genre? What ideas associated with the genre carry over to this work?

4. **Why is or was the genre appealing?** It is a cold, rainy night. You are home for vacation. Everyone else in the house has gone to bed. You have been saving Stephen King's latest gothic thriller for just such a time. Perfect. You settle in for two hours of uninterrupted escape. The book, of course, need not be horror. It could be science fiction, romance, western, detective, adventure, spy. Maybe you do not care who the author is. You just picked the book off the shelf because it belongs to a genre you like.

   When we do this—read something because it is a kind of literature—we have succumbed to the pleasures of genre. The reasons we like certain genres are part of the "meaning" of what we read—the pleasures the genres give as well as the ideas they convey. We can pinpoint that meaning by investigating the appeal of genres. Why do we and other people like them?

   The same question applies to genres from the past. We can discern what meanings authors may have intended by asking why people liked the genres in which the authors wrote. Authors and readers of pastoral poetry during Christopher Marlowe's time, for example, lived in the city. They liked pastoral poetry because the fantasy of an idealized rural life, with pretty scenes, images, and language, allowed them to escape the grimy, dangerous, and changing cities where they lived.

5. **How does the author challenge or change the genre?** Before authors can compose a work of literature, they have to know its genre well. But when they compose, they almost always rebel against generic formulas. Alistair Fowler describes the process in this way: The "writer who cares most about originality has the keenest interest in

genre. Only by knowing the beaten track, after all, can he be sure of leaving it" (32). Because authors and readers hunger for innovation, every literary work, Fowler says, "changes the genre it relates to." Consequently, "all genres are continuously undergoing metamorphosis. This, indeed, is the principal way in which literature itself changes" (23). An example of a recent "new" genre is "magic realism," a form of fiction that has been popularized by Latin American authors such as Gabriel García Márquez, Isabel Allende, and Laura Esquivel. Combining the characteristics of two genres—realistic fiction and fairy tale—these authors couch trenchant political and social criticism within the delights of erotic romance and supernatural happenings.

We can assume, then, that when authors alter the formulas of genres, they do so purposefully. What shifts in values and aesthetic effects do these changes contribute to the works we want to interpret? Raleigh, by having his female character respond to Marlowe's shepherd in terms of the harsh realities of life, cleverly changes the pastoral genre into a new genre, one we might call the antipastoral. He criticizes not only the ideas that undergird pastoral poetry but the pastoral genre itself.

6. **How do individual conventions of a genre add meaning to a work?**
   Alistair Fowler says that the nucleus of all literary genres is three huge, amorphous categories: fiction, drama, and poetry (5). Within these genres are numerous subgenres. Subgenres, Fowler says, "have the common features of a kind—external forms and all—and, over and above these, add special substantive features" (112). Pastoral poetry, for example, has the overall characteristics of "poetry" but, as we have noted above, has other characteristics that make it a distinctive subgenre of poetry. Our assumption in the next three chapters is that authors choose the genres in which they write. They use the conventions of these genres consciously to communicate ideas. We will, therefore, examine how these conventions work and how they communicate ideas. Like the properties of literature discussed in this chapter—language, fictionality, truth, aesthetics, and intertextuality—each literary convention is a "place" to look for meaning in works of literature.

Works Cited

Abrams, M. H. *A Glossary of Literary Terms*. Fort Worth: Harcourt, 1999.

Eagleton, Terry. *Literary Theory: An Introduction*. Minneapolis: U of Minnesota P, 1983.

Ellis, John. *The Theory of Literary Criticism: A Logical Analysis.* Berkeley: U of California P, 1974.

Fowler, Alastair. *An Introduction to the Theory of Genres and Modes.* Cambridge: Harvard UP, 1982.

Kurtén, Björn. *Dance of the Tiger: A Novel of the Ice Age.* New York: Pantheon, 1980.

Selden, Raman, and Peter Widdowson. *A Reader's Guide to Contemporary Literary Theory.* 3rd ed. Lexington: U of Kentucky P, 1993.

Wellek, René, and Austin Warren. *Theory of Literature.* New York: Harcourt, 1942.

West, Jessamyn. *The Massacre at Fall Creek.* New York: Harcourt, 1975.

Interpreting Fiction

This chapter begins an analysis of the three major genres of literature: fiction, drama, and poetry. The word *genre* comes from French and means "type" or "kind." To identify literary genres is to classify literature into its kinds. Literary critics sometimes disagree about how to classify literature into genres. Some say the genres of literature are tragedy, comedy, lyric poetry, satire, the elegy, and so forth. But for our purpose, we will classify literature into three broad "kinds": fiction, drama, and poetry. This chapter begins with the most popular genre, fiction.

Although literary genres are interesting subjects in themselves, our purpose in this and the next two chapters is to identify things to think about that can help us interpret works of literature. To that end, we will look at many of the best known elements that characterize fiction, drama, and poetry. Our goal when we interpret elements of literature should not be to consider and comment on *every* element of a work. Although all the elements of a work contribute to its meanings, probably only several will stand out to you as the most important ones. Focusing on one or more of these is a fruitful strategy for discovering meaning in texts. The questions and "Thinking on Paper" exercises that follow the discussions of each element should help you do this.

The Nature of Fiction

As a descriptive term, *fiction* is misleading, for although fiction does often include made-up or imaginary elements, it has the potential for being "true": true to the nature of reality, true to human experience.

33

The intellectual activity that most resembles fiction is history. Both writers of history and fiction attempt to create a world that resembles the multiplicity and complexity of the real world. Both history and fiction writers attempt to speculate about the nature of the real world. But fiction differs from history in important ways, and these differences help reveal fiction's nature and uniqueness.

The most obvious difference is that writers of fiction can make up facts but historians must take facts as they find them. In works of history, historians cannot manufacture facts to fill in the gaps of their knowledge. Consequently, the fictional world is potentially more complete and coherent than the historical world. Not only can writers of fiction produce facts at will, they can produce them to fit a coherent plan. If they have an optimistic view of reality, for example, fiction writers can include only positive and affirming facts. Further, they can know more about their worlds than historians (or anyone else) can know about the real world. They can enter their characters' minds, create chains of cause and effect, and foresee the future. A second difference is that writers of fiction must establish some principle of order or coherence that underlies their work. They must establish at least an aesthetic order, and they may also impose a philosophical order upon their materials. Although historians often do both, they need do neither. Like newspaper reporters, historians need only record events as they occur, no matter how unrelated or senseless they may seem. A third difference is that writers of fiction must build conflict into their worlds, whereas historians need not. The events of history are not inevitably characterized by conflict, but the events of fiction almost always are.

All three of these differences point to qualities that make fiction enjoyable: its imaginative, orderly, and dramatic qualities. Two more differences reveal an equally important aspect of fiction—the kinds of reality it deals with and thus the kinds of truth it attempts to expose. The fourth difference, then, is that writers of fiction celebrate the separateness, distinctness, and importance of all individuals and all individual experiences. They assume that human experiences, whatever they are and wherever they occur, are intrinsically important and interesting. In contrast, historians record and celebrate human experiences that affect or represent large numbers of people—wars, rises and falls of civilizations, technological innovations, economic developments, political changes, social tastes, and mores. If historians discuss individuals at all, it is because they affect or illustrate these wider experiences. Henry Fleming, the protagonist of Stephen Crane's novel *The Red Badge of Courage*, has no historical importance. As far as history is concerned, he is an anonymous participant in the Civil War battle of Chancellorsville, one soldier among thousands. Even his deeds, thoughts, and feelings do not necessarily represent those of a typical soldier at Chancellorsville. Yet, in the fictional world, they are important because they are *his* deeds, thoughts, and feelings. We are interested in him not for his connection with an important historical event but simply because he is a human being.

Finally, a fifth difference is that writers of fiction see reality as welded to psychological perception, as refracted through the minds of individuals. In contrast, historians present reality as external to individuals and thus as unaffected by human perception. Both historians and writers of fiction, for example, deal with time. But time for the historian is divisible into exact measurable units: centuries, decades, years, months, weeks, days, hours, minutes, seconds. Time, for historians, is a river in which individuals float like so many pieces of driftwood. In contrast, writers of fiction present time as an experienced, emotional phenomenon, as a river flowing *inside* the mind. Its duration is not scientifically measurable but rather is determined by states of mind, the familiar when-I-am-happy-time-goes-fast, when-I-am-sad-time-goes-slowly phenomenon. Other aspects of reality take on a similar psychological dimension within works of fiction. A house may not be haunted, but a character is so nervous and disoriented that it seems to be. A mountain may not be steep, but a character may be so fatigued from climbing that it seems that way.

The Elements of Fiction

The preceding explanation of the nature of fiction should help you know generally what to expect from it. But fiction, poetry, and drama all have more specific characteristics, and knowing what these are will help you identify and think about them as you read. The rest of this chapter includes definitions of the elements of fiction. Following each discussion are questions and "Thinking on Paper" exercises. Use these definitions, questions, and exercises to develop your own ideas about works of fiction.

Plot

Put simply, *plot* is what happens in a narrative. But this definition is too simple. A mere listing of events, even in the order in which they occur, is not plot. Rather, writers of fiction arrange fictional events

into patterns. They select these events carefully, establish causal relationships among events, and enliven these events with conflict. A
more complete and accurate definition, then, is that plot is a pattern
of carefully selected, causally related events that contains conflict.

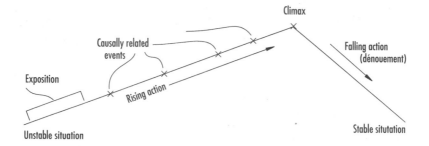

Although writers of fiction arrange events into many patterns, the
most common is that represented by the *Freytag pyramid*, shown above,
which was developed by the German critic Gustav Freytag in 1863
(114–115). Although Freytag meant this diagram to describe a typical
five-act tragedy, it applies to most works of fiction. At the beginning of
this pattern is an *unstable situation*, a conflict that sets the plot in motion.
The author's *exposition* here explains the nature of the conflict. He or
she introduces the characters, describes the setting, and provides historical background. The author next introduces a series of *events*, all related by cause. One event may cause another event, which in turn causes
another event, which causes the next event (husband gets angry with
wife, who gets angry with kids, who get angry with dog, who sulks in
the basement). Or several events may be linked to the same cause (a series of deaths at the beach, all caused by a monster killer shark). Whatever the causal relationship among events, each event intensifies the
conflict so that the plot "rises" toward a *climax*.

The climax is the most intense event in the narrative. The rest of
the story—the *falling action*—is usually brief. It contains events that are
much less intense than the climax and that lead toward the resolution of
the conflict and toward a *stable situation* at the end. Another term for
falling action is *dénouement*, a French word meaning "unraveling."

An example of the Freytag pyramid is the stereotypical fairy tale
in which the youngest son must seek his fortune (unstable situation: He
has no source of income, no home). He goes into a far country whose
king is offering a prize, the hand of his daughter, to anyone who can accomplish three tasks. The hero completes all three (rising action and

climax: Each task is increasingly difficult, but the third is a humdinger and is therefore the climax). The remaining part of the story may contain obstacles, but they are easily overcome. The king praises the hero but does not want his daughter to marry a commoner. The hero reveals that he is not, as he seems, a mere peasant but the son of a nobleman (falling action/dénouement: The conflicts now are minor and easily resolved). The hero marries the princess and lives happily ever after (stable situation: The hero has eliminated the initial conflict; he now has a wife, a source of income, and a home).

There are two general categories of conflict: external and internal. *Internal conflicts* take place within the minds of characters. An example is the good person who wrestles inwardly with temptation. *External conflicts* take place between individuals or between individuals and the world external to individuals (the forces of nature, human-created objects, and environments). The climactic shootout in an American western is an example of a physical, external conflict, but not all external conflicts are physical or violent. A verbal disagreement between two people is also an external conflict.

The forces in a conflict are usually embodied by characters, the most relevant being the protagonist and the antagonist. The term *protagonist* usually means "main character," but it might be helpful sometimes to think of the protagonist as someone who is fighting for something. The *antagonist* is the opponent of the protagonist; the antagonist is usually a person, but can also be a nonhuman force or even an aspect of the protagonist—his or her tendency toward evil and self-destruction, for example. Although a protagonist sometimes fights for evil—Macbeth, for example—we usually empathize with the protagonist and find the antagonist unsympathetic.

Questions about plot Probably the most revealing question you can ask about a work of literature is: What conflicts does it dramatize? For fiction, this is a crucial question. You can break it down into subquestions, each of which might produce interesting ideas: What is the main conflict? What are the minor conflicts? How are all the conflicts related? What causes the conflicts? Which conflicts are external, which internal? Who is the protagonist? What qualities or values does the author associate with each side of the conflict? Where does the climax occur? Why? How is the main conflict resolved? Which conflicts go unresolved? Why?

An example of how you can use these questions to interpret fiction is Ernest Hemingway's story "Hills Like White Elephants." The story consists almost entirely of a dialogue between a young woman and man who are waiting for a train at a tiny station in the Spanish country-side. We learn that they have traveled widely and are lovers—but they are in conflict. About what? The conflict they bring out into the open and discuss aloud concerns an abortion. The woman is pregnant, and the man urges her to have an abortion. He keeps telling her that the abortion will be "simple," "perfectly natural," and will make them "all right" and "happy." But she resists. She asks if after the abortion "things will be like they were and you'll love me" (275). She says that they "could get along" without the abortion (277).

Gradually we realize that although the immediate conflict is about the abortion, there is a deeper, unspoken conflict. This more important conflict—the main conflict—is over the nature of their relationship. The man wants the abortion because it will allow him to continue the rootless and uncommitted relationship he has enjoyed with the woman up to now. The woman, however, wants a more stable relationship, one that having the child would affirm, one that she has apparently believed the man wanted too. Hemingway resolves the conflict by having the woman realize, in the face of the man's continued insistence on the abortion, that the relationship she wants with the man is impossible.

Examining the story's main conflict in this way helps to reveal several important things about the story. At first glance, it seems to have little "action," but examining the conflict reveals what its action is. Studying the conflict also helps to illuminate the characters: The man is selfish and obstinate; the woman is idealistic and somewhat innocent. Analyzing the conflict points to the meaning or theme of the story. Hemingway seems to support the woman's view of the way a loving relationship should be. He makes her the protagonist, the more sympathetic character of the two. Because examining conflict in works of literature is crucial to understanding them, such a study is a rich source of interpretations, perhaps the richest. This discussion of "Hills Like White Elephants" is but one of many examples of what an essay might do with conflict.

■ Thinking on Paper about Plot

1. On one side of a piece of paper, list the external conflicts of the work. On the other side, list the internal conflicts. Draw a line between the external and internal conflicts that seem related.

2. List the key conflicts. For each conflict, list the ways in which the conflict has been resolved, if it has.

3. Describe the turning point or climax. Explain what conflicts are resolved. List the conflicts that are left unresolved.
4. List the major structural units of the work (chapters, scenes, parts). Summarize what happens in each unit.
5. List the qualities of the protagonist and antagonist.
6. Describe the qualities that make the situation at the beginning unstable. Describe the qualities that make the conclusion stable.
7. List the causes of the unstable situations at the beginning and throughout the work.

Characterization

Characters are the people in narratives, and *characterization* is the author's presentation and development of characters. Sometimes, as in fantasy fiction, the characters are not people. They may be animals, robots, or creatures from outer space, but the author endows them with human abilities and human psychological traits. They really are people in all but outward form.

There are two broad categories of character development: simple and complex. The critic and fiction writer E. M. Forster coined alternate terms for these same categories: *flat* (simple) and *round* (complex) characters (67–78). Flat characters have only one or two personality traits and are easily recognizable as stereotypes—the shrewish wife, the lazy husband, the egomaniac, the stupid athlete, the shyster, the miser, the redneck, the bum, the dishonest used-car salesman, the prim aristocrat, the absent-minded professor. Round characters have multiple personality traits and therefore resemble real people. They are much harder to understand and describe than flat characters. No single description or interpretation can fully contain them. An example of a flat character is Washington Irving's Ichabod Crane, the vain and superstitious schoolmaster of "The Legend of Sleepy Hollow." An example of a round character is Shakespeare's Hamlet. To an extent, all literary characters are stereotypes. Even Hamlet is a type, the "melancholy man." But round characters have many more traits than just those associated with their general type. Because it takes time to develop round characters convincingly, they are more often found in longer works than in shorter ones.

Authors reveal what characters are like in two general ways: directly or indirectly. In the *direct* method, the author simply tells the reader what the character is like. Here, for example, is Jane Austen telling us very early in her novel *Pride and Prejudice* what Mrs. Bennet is like:

> She was a woman of mean understanding, little information, and uncertain temper. When she was discontented she fancied herself nervous. The business of her life was to get her daughters married; its solace was visiting and news (3).

When the method of revealing characters is *indirect*, however, the author shows us, rather than tells us, what the characters are like through what they say about one another, through external details (dress, bearing, looks), and through their thoughts, speech, and deeds.

Characters who remain the same throughout a work are called *static* characters. Those who change during the course of the work are called *dynamic* characters. Usually, round characters change and flat characters remain the same, but not always. Shakespeare's Sir John Falstaff (in *Henry IV, Part I* and *Part II*), a round character, is nonetheless static. Dynamic characters, especially main characters, typically grow in understanding. The climax of this growth is an *epiphany*, a term that James Joyce used to describe a sudden revelation of truth experienced by a character. The term comes from the Bible and describes the Wise Men's first perception of Christ's divinity. Joyce applied it to fictional characters. His own characters, like Gabriel Conroy in "The Dead," perfectly illustrate the concept. Often, as in "The Dead," the epiphany coincides with the climax of the plot.

Questions about characters   You can ask many revealing questions about characters and the way they are portrayed: Are they flat, round, dynamic, or static? If they change, how and why? What steps do they go through to change? What events or moments of self-revelation produce these changes? Does what they learn help or hinder them? What problems do they have? How do they attempt to solve them? What types do they represent? If they are complex, what makes them complex? Do they have traits that contradict one another and therefore cause internal conflicts? Do they experience epiphanies? When, why, and what do their epiphanies reveal—to themselves and to us? How do they relate to one another? Do the characters have speech mannerisms, gestures, or modes of dress that reveal their inner selves? Is the character sad, happy, or in between?

The overriding questions that any character analysis attempts to answer are simply: What is the character like? What are the character's traits? Consider the example of the woman in Hemingway's "Hills Like White Elephants," discussed previously. Hemingway drops hints that indicate something about her personality. She compares the Spanish hills to white elephants, a comparison that at first seems capricious but later suggests an imaginative, even artistic, quality that the man cannot comprehend. After she senses the man's true motivation for wanting the abortion, she looks out over the fields of ripe grain, the trees, the river, and the mountains beyond, and tells the man that "we could have all this" but that "every day we make it more impossible." She seems to connect the appreciation of nature—the sympathy they could feel for it—with the moral quality of their relationship. But because their relationship must remain superficial, she says that the landscape "isn't ours any more" (276). Once again, the man lacks the imagination to make the connection, and he fails to grasp her moral point. Hemingway seems to admire the woman's ability to make these comparisons. It underscores her more obvious and admirable desire for a profound and lasting relationship. Another thing we learn about the woman is that she is a dynamic character. At the beginning of the story, she does not fully recognize the falseness of her relationship with the man. She seems genuinely to hope for something better. By the end of the story, however, she knows the truth and, from all appearances, has changed as a result. At the beginning she is innocent and dependent upon the man for her happiness; by the end she has lost her innocence and has become independent.

■ Thinking on Paper about Characterization

1. List the traits of the main characters in the story.

2. Describe the ways the author reveals the traits of a character.

3. Write a description of a complex character in which you try to account for every trait of the character.

4. Describe the emotional reaction a character has to an important event or events.

5. Write a paragraph explaining how and why a character changes.

6. Describe the scene in which a character has an epiphany. Explain what happens and what the character comes to see.

7. Mark the places in which the author or other characters make revealing statements about a character.

Theme

Theme is perhaps the most obvious statement of the "truth" of a work. This discussion of theme, then, is a continuation of the discussion in Chapter 2 (on pages 21–26) of how literature is true. *Theme* is a central idea in the work—whether fiction, poetry, or drama. For many readers, theme is an attractive element because it gives works meaning; it makes them relevant. In identifying a work's themes, consider the following characteristics of theme. First, although the terms *subject* and *theme* are often used interchangeably, it is helpful to distinguish between them. The *subject* is what the work is about. You can state the subject in a word or phrase. The subject of Shakespeare's Sonnet 116 (page 107) is love. In contrast, theme is what the work *says* about the subject. The statement of a work's theme requires a complete sentence, sometimes several sentences. A theme of Sonnet 116 is "Love remains constant whether assaulted by tempestuous events or by time."

Second, a work's theme must apply to people outside the work. For example, it is incorrect to say that the theme of "Rip Van Winkle" is "Rapid change in his environment threatens Rip's identity." This statement is true, but it is not the theme, because it applies only to Rip. You must state the theme in such a way as to include people in general, not just the characters in the story. A correctly stated theme for "Rip Van Winkle," then, would be "Rapid change in environment causes *many people* to feel their identity is threatened." Stating the theme in a work of literature means that you move from concrete situations within the work to generalizations about people outside the work. In this way, literature becomes a form of "philosophy"—universal wisdom about the nature of reality.

A third characteristic of theme is that there may be several, possibly even contradictory, themes in a work. This is especially true of complex works. A subject of Tolstoy's *Anna Karenina* is sacred love versus profane love. But another, equally important subject is social entrapment. One theme of *Anna Karenina*, then, seems to be that people should not abandon "sacred" commitments, such as marriage and parenthood, for extramarital "loves," no matter how passionate and deeply felt they may be. This theme emerges from Anna's desertion of her husband and child for Count Vronsky. An alternate theme is that people, through little fault of their own, can become trapped in painful, long-lasting, and destructive relationships that they want desperately to escape. This theme emerges from Anna's marriage. When she was very young, Anna married an older man whom she now realizes is too petty, prim, and self-absorbed to satisfy her generous and passionate nature. So discordant is her relationship with her husband that it seems no less "immoral" than her affair with Vronsky. Tolstoy, in other words, draws complex, even contradictory lessons from Anna's adultery. She is not simply the sinful person; she is also the driven person. This combination of traits characterizes the condition of many people.

Fourth, we may be hard pressed to find clear themes in some works. There may be so many contradictory or incompletely developed ideas in a work that it seems impossible to say for sure what the work means. Some critics, for example, have cited Edgar Allan Poe's "The Raven" and "The Fall of the House of Usher" as examples of works that lack themes.

Fifth, the subjects and themes of complex works can rarely be accounted for completely. Even when the author says what the work means, we cannot exclude other possibilities. We find evidence of a work's themes in the concrete world the author creates. But we can rarely see all the evidence at once or see all the possible patterns inherent in the work. The best we can do is support our interpretations as logically and with as much evidence as we can. We may disagree with the author's conclusions about a given subject—with his or her theme. Our job is first to identify and understand the work's theme and then, if we are writing about it, to represent it fairly. To do this, however, is not necessarily to agree with the work. We are always free to disagree with an author's worldview.

Sixth, theme may present an intellectual dilemma rather than a "message" that neatly solves the dilemma. Robert Penn Warren's novel *All the King's Men*, for example, raises the problem of morality in politics. A question the novel seems to ask is: How can political leaders in a democratic society do good when citizens are apathetic and easily misled? The character who embodies this question is a well-meaning and gifted politician who uses corrupt and violent means to attain good ends. By telling his story, Warren dramatizes the question. But he never really answers it. You cannot pull a neat moral out of the story of this character's rise and fall. Rather, to state the "theme" of this novel—or one theme—you need to summarize as accurately as you can the problem Warren presents in the way he presents it. You could explain how the problem is worked out in this one character's life, but you could not necessarily generalize from that to all people's lives. Or the generalization might be that politics is morally contradictory, never simply right or wrong.

Questions about theme   The key questions for eliciting a work's theme are: What is the subject (that is, what is the work about)? Then, What is the theme (that is, what does the work say about the subject)? And, finally, In what direct and indirect ways does the work communicate its theme? In "Hills Like White Elephants," Hemingway does not state his subject and theme directly, but given his development of conflict and characterization, it seems fair to say that his subject is love (or loving relationships) and that one possible theme might be something like this:"Loving relationships are impossible without unselfish commitment from both partners."

One strategy for discovering a work's theme is to apply frequently asked questions about areas of human experience, such as the following:

Human nature. What image of humankind emerges from the work? Are people, for example, generally good? deeply flawed?

The nature of society. Does the author portray a particular society or social scheme as life-enhancing or life-destroying? Are characters we care about in conflict with their society? Do they want to escape from it? What causes and perpetuates this society? If the society is flawed, how is it flawed?

Human freedom. What control over their lives do the characters have? Do they make choices in complete freedom? Are they driven by forces beyond their control? Does Providence or some grand scheme govern history, or is history simply random and arbitrary?

Ethics. What are the moral conflicts in the work? Are they clear cut or ambiguous? That is, is it clear to us exactly what is right and exactly what is wrong? When moral conflicts are ambiguous in a work, right often opposes *right*, not wrong. What rights are in opposition to one another? If right opposes wrong, does right win in the end? To what extent are characters to blame for their actions?

Another strategy for discovering a work's theme is to answer this question: Who serves as the *moral center* of the work? The *moral center* is the one person whom the author vests with right action and right thought (that is, what the *author* seems to think is right action and right thought), the one character who seems clearly "good" and who often serves to judge other characters. Not every work has a moral center; but in the works that do, its center can lead you to some of the work's themes. In Dickens's *Great Expectations*, for example, the moral center is Biddy, the girl who comes to Pip's sister's household as a servant. She is a touchstone of goodness for Pip, and when he strays from the good, Biddy and his remembrance of her helps bring him back to it. *Great Expectations* is largely about morality (subject), and by studying Biddy we can uncover some of Dickens's ideas about morality (theme).

When identifying a work's moral center, answer questions such as these: How can we tell that this person is the moral center? What values does the moral center embody? Is the moral center flawed in any way that might diminish his or her authority? What effect does the moral center have on the other characters and on us?

■ Thinking on Paper about Theme

1. List the subject or subjects of the work. For each subject, see if you can state a theme. Put a check next to the ones that seem most important.

2. Explain how the title, subtitle, epigraph, chapter titles, and names of characters may be related to theme.

3. Describe the work's depiction of human behavior.

4. Describe the work's depiction of society. Explain the representation of social ills and how they might be corrected or addressed.

5. List the moral issues raised by the work.

6. Name the character who is the moral center of the work. List his or her traits.

7. Mark statements by the author or characters that seem to state themes.

Setting

Setting includes several closely related aspects of a work of fiction. First, setting is the physical, sensuous world of the work. Second, it is the time in which the action of the work takes place. And third, it is the social environment of the characters: the manners, customs, and moral values that govern the characters' society. A fourth aspect—"atmosphere"—is largely, but not entirely, an effect of setting.

Questions about place   You should first get the details of the physical setting clear in your mind. Where does the action take place?

On what planet, in what country or locale? What sensuous qualities does the author give to the setting? That is, what does it look like, sound like, feel like? Do you receive a dominant impression about the setting? What impression, and what caused it?

Once you have answered these questions, you can move on to questions about place that lead to interpretations: What relationship does place have to characterization and to theme? In some fiction, geographical location seems to have no effect on characters. Indoors or out, in one locale or another, they behave the same. In other works, such as those by Thomas Hardy or Joseph Conrad, place affects the characters profoundly. In the story, "Among the Corn Rows," Hamlin Garland shows how environment brings about a character's decision.

> A cornfield in July is a hot place. The soil is hot and dry; the wind comes across the lazily murmuring leaves laden with a warm sickening smell drawn from the rapidly growing, broad-flung banners of the corn. The sun, nearly vertical, drops a flood of dazzling light and heat upon the field over which the cool shadows run, only to make the heat seem the more intense.
>
> Julia Peterson, faint with fatigue, was toiling back and forth between the corn rows, holding the handles of the double-shovel corn plow while her little brother Otto rode the steaming horse. Her heart was full of bitterness, and her face flushed with heat, and her muscles aching with fatigue. The heat grew terrible. The corn came to her shoulders, and not a breath seemed to reach her, while the sun, nearing the noon mark, lay pitilessly upon her shoulders, protected only by a calico dress. The dust rose under her feet, and as she was wet with perspiration it soiled her till, with a woman's instinctive cleanliness, she shuddered. Her head throbbed dangerously. What matter to her that the king bird pitched jovially from the maples to catch a wandering bluebottle fly, that the robin was feeding its young, that the bobolink was singing? All these things, if she saw them, only threw her bondage to labor into greater relief. (107–108)

Garland shows geographical environment pressuring Julia Peterson into a decision that will affect the rest of her life. Garland has already told us that Julia's parents treat her harshly and force her to work too hard. By emphasizing one sensuous quality, the heat, Garland makes us feel the hardship of her life. She has dreamed of a handsome suitor who will take her away from the farm and give her a life of ease, but the heat makes her feel that anything would be better than this misery. So when a young farmer happens along just after the incident described here and offers her a life of respect and only normal difficulty, she marries him. Garland shows that Julia's environment leads her to settle for less than she really wants. She is not free to choose exactly as she would choose.

Questions about time   Three kinds of time occur in fiction, thus three types of questions about time are important. First, at what period in history does the action take place? Many stories occur during historical events that affect the characters and themes in important ways. Margaret Mitchell's *Gone with the Wind* and Tolstoy's *War and Peace* are examples. To answer this question, you may have to do background reading about the historical period. Tolstoy and Mitchell give you a great deal of historical information in their fiction, but many authors do not. In either case, you may need to supplement facts in the work with what you can find out elsewhere.

Second, how long does it take for the action to occur? That is, how many hours, days, weeks, years are involved? Authors often use the passage of time as a thematic and structuring device: The mere fact that some specific amount of time has passed may be important for understanding characters. Years go by in Alice Walker's *The Color Purple*, for example, allowing her characters to grow and change. But because of her method of telling the stories—through letters—we are not immediately aware of how much time passes until near the end of the book. Because we read the letters one after the other, we get the illusion of time passing quickly. In fact, the letters are written over long intervals, which means that we must consciously slow down the time of the novel to understand its effect on the characters. What clues, then, does the author give to indicate how much time is passing? Is the passage of time in the work relevant to characterization and theme? Is it important to the plausibility of the plot? If an author seems to obscure how much time is passing, why? Does the author use time as a structuring device?

Third, how is the passage of time perceived? Time may seem to move very slowly or very quickly, depending on a character's state of mind. Thus our recognition of how a character perceives time helps us understand the character's internal conflicts and attitudes.

In *Jane Eyre*, for example, Charlotte Brontë intertwines length of time and perception of time. Jane, the narrator, describes her stays at various "houses." She spends about the same amount of time at each house, but the length of her description of each stay is proportional to the value she places on it. She devotes about one fourth of the novel to her stays with the Reeds and at Lowood and one fourth to her stay with the Rivers family. But she devotes over half of the novel to her stay at Thornfield, where she falls in love with Mr. Rochester. The effect of these unequal proportions is to slow down the time spent at Thornfield and thus to emphasize Jane's emotional reaction to the experiences she has there.

Brontë uses this slowing down method with specific events as well. In fact, the novel is a collection of highly charged, intensely felt moments in Jane's life that seem to last far longer than they actually do. The novel opens, for example, with Jane's imprisonment in the hated "red room" of the Reed mansion. As her anger subsides, she becomes aware that the room is "chill," "silent," and "solemn." She recalls that Mr. Reed died there. In a mirror she sees her "glittering eyes of fear moving where all else was still." Daylight "forsakes" the room. She feels "oppressed, suffocated" at thoughts of Mr. Reed's death and the possibility of her own. When she sees a light on the wall, she thinks it is a ghost. She screams. When Mrs. Reed rushes to check on her, she thrusts Jane back into the room and locks the door. Jane faints from hysteria (45–50). The length of this description corresponds to Jane's perception of time, which in turn corresponds to her fear of the room. Each detail is like the tick of a loud clock.

What, then, is the relationship between the length of narrated events and the amount of time in which they occur? Is the author purposely slowing down or speeding up our perception of time? If so, why? What mental states or internal conflicts does a character's perception of time reveal?

Questions about social environment   Often the social environment represented in a work is of little importance. There may even be virtually no social environment. When it is important, however, it affects interpretations of the work. Some questions: What is the social environment portrayed in the work—the manners, mores, customs, rituals, and codes of conduct of a society? What does the author seem to think about them? (Approving? Ambivalent? Disapproving?) How do they affect the characters? Sinclair Lewis spends much of his novel *Babbitt* describing the social environment of his fictional Midwestern city, Zenith. Then he shows that the pressure to conform to this environment is almost irresistible. His characters sometimes want to rebel against this pressure, but they are too weak to do so without extreme guilt or without threat to their economic and social security. Their social environment determines their behavior and entraps them.

Questions about atmosphere   *Atmosphere* refers to the emotional reaction that we and—usually—the characters have to the setting of a work. Sometimes the atmosphere is difficult to define, but it is often found or felt in the sensuous quality of the setting. Our emotional reaction to the Hamlin Garland passage is probably pain, discomfort, weariness, and oppression, mainly because of his emphasis on the thermal sense, the sense of hot and cold. Fruitful questions about atmosphere are: What methods does the author use to create the work's atmosphere? What does the author achieve by creating this atmosphere? Why does the author create this particular atmosphere? Sometimes, the author's purpose may simply be to play upon your emotions. A writer of gothic fiction may just want to scare us. Garland's purpose, however, is more meaningful. He seems to want to convince us of a philosophical point: Physical environment affects human behavior. Joseph Conrad in *Heart of Darkness* creates an atmosphere of mystery, foreboding, and imminent danger to reflect his hatred of colonialism and his belief that "civilized" people are capable of the worst barbarities.

■ Thinking on Paper about Setting

1. Mark the most extensive or important descriptions of physical place. Underline the most telling words and phrases.

2. Characterize physical locales, such as houses, rooms, and outdoor areas.

3. Explain the relationship to the physical place that one or more of the main characters has. Explain the influence that place exerts on the characters.

4. Arrange the main events in chronological order. Indicate when each event occurs.

5. Mark passages where a character's emotional state affects the way the passage of time is presented to us.

6. List the historical circumstances and characters that occur in the work. Explain their importance.

7. List the patterns of behavior that characterize the social environment of the work. For example, people drink heavily, go to church, have tea, gamble, throw parties, get in fights, marry, have children, cheat in business, wander restlessly, and so forth.

8. Mark scenes in which the author or characters express approval or disapproval of these patterns of behavior.
9. Explain the influence one or more of these patterns has on a character or characters.
10. Mark sections that contribute to atmosphere. Underline key words and phrases.
11. List the traits of the atmosphere.

Point of View

Point of view is the author's relationship to his or her fictional world, especially to the minds of the characters. Put another way, point of view is the position from which the story is told. There are four basic points of view, four positions the author can adopt in telling the story.

Omniscient point of view   In the omniscient position, the author—not one of the characters—tells the story, and the author assumes complete knowledge of the characters' actions and thoughts. The author can thus move at will from one place to another, one time to another, one character to another, and can even speak his or her own views directly to the reader as the work goes along. The author will tell us anything he or she chooses about the created world of the work. Many of the great eighteenth- and nineteenth-century novels use an omniscient point of view; examples are Hawthorne's *The Scarlet Letter*, Hardy's *Tess of the D'Urbervilles*, Fielding's *Joseph Andrews*, and Eliot's *Adam Bede*.

Limited omniscient point of view   When the limited omniscient position is used, the author still narrates the story but restricts (limits) his or her revelation—and therefore our knowledge—of the thoughts of all but one character. This character may be either a main or peripheral character. One name for this character is "central consciousness." A device of plot and characterization that often accompanies this point of view is the character's gradual discovery of himself or herself until the story climaxes in an epiphany (see page 40). Examples of the limited omniscient point of view are Hawthorne's "Young Goodman Brown," Stephen Crane's "The Open Boat," and, for the most part, Austen's *Pride and Prejudice*. Sometimes the author restricts the point of view so severely that we see everything solely through the mind of a single character, like sunlight filtered through a stained glass window. The later fiction of Henry James experiments with this severe restriction of the limited omniscient point of view. His story "The Beast in the Jungle" and his novel *The Ambassadors* are examples. Other writers, such as James Joyce, Virginia Woolf, and William Faulkner, carry James's experiments further with a "stream of consciousness" technique, which puts the reader literally in the mind of a character. In the first section of Faulkner's *The Sound and the Fury* we experience the chaotic thoughts of a mentally retarded man, and we view the novel's world solely through his mind. A short story that uses a stream-of-consciousness technique is Katherine Anne Porter's "The Jilting of Granny Weatherall."

First-person point of view   In the first-person position, the author's role as story teller is even more restricted: One of the characters tells the story, eliminating the author as narrator. Whereas in the limited omniscient point of view the author can reveal anything about one character—even things the character may be dimly aware of—here, the narration is restricted to what one character *says* he or she observes. The character–narrator may be a major character who is at the center of events or a minor character who does not participate but simply observes the action. Examples of first-person narratives are Dickens's *Great Expectations,* Twain's *Huckleberry Finn,* Fitzgerald's *The Great Gatsby,* Poe's "The Cask of Amontillado," and Melville's "Bartleby the Scrivener." An unusual use of the first-person point of view is the epistolary narrative, which reveals action through letters. (An *epistle* is a letter, and *epistolary* means "written in letters.") Samuel Richardson's *Pamela,* Henry James's "A Bundle of Letters," and Alice Walker's *The Color Purple* are all epistolary narratives.

Objective (dramatic) point of view   In the objective position, the author is more restricted than in any other. Though the author is the narrator, he or she refuses to enter the minds of any of the characters. The writer sees them (and lets us see them) as we would in real life. This point of view is sometimes called "dramatic" because we see the characters as we would the characters in a play. We learn about them from what they say and do, how they look, and what other characters say about them. But we do not learn what they think unless they tell us. This point of view is the least common of all. Examples are Ernest Hemingway's "Hills Like White Elephants" and "The Killers," Stephen Crane's "The Blue Hotel," and Shirley Jackson's "The Lottery."

Tone   *Tone* is also an aspect of point of view since it has a great deal to do with the narrator. Tone is the narrator's predominant attitude toward the subject, whether that subject is a particular setting, an event, a character, or an idea. The narrator conveys his or her attitude through the way narrative devices are handled, including choice of words. Sometimes the narrator will state point blank how he or she feels about a subject; more often, the narrator's attitude is conveyed indirectly. Jack Burden, the narrator of Robert Penn Warren's *All the King's Men*, maintains a flippant and cynical tone through most of the narration. Jake Barnes, the narrator of Hemingway's *The Sun Also Rises*, maintains a stoical, hard-boiled tone. Dr. Watson, the narrator of the Sherlock Holmes stories, manifests a bemused, surprised tone.

Questions about point of view   Point of view is important to an understanding of a story in two main ways. First, the author may choose a particular point of view to emphasize one character's perception of things. Point of view also influences *our* perception of things. The omniscient narrator can tell us what a character thinks, but the limited omniscient and first-person points of view make us *experience* what the character thinks. An author may even include several points of view in the same work. Dickens in *Bleak House* shuttles back and forth between a first-person narrative and an omniscient narrative. We see that the first-person narrator has a more limited view of things than the omniscient narrator. Point of view here becomes a means of developing character and of making a point about the limits of human perception.

Second, point of view is important when you suspect the trustworthiness of the narrator. A preliminary question is: Who tells the story? But a searching follow-up question is: Can you trust the narrator to tell us the truth about the events, characters, and setting of the story? You can almost always trust omniscient narrators. But you should be suspicious about first-person narrators and the "centers-of-consciousness" characters in limited omniscient stories. Sometimes these characters distort what they observe. Ask, then, if circumstances such as their age, education, social status, prejudices, or emotional states should make you question the accuracy or validity of what they say and think. Ask, also, if the author differentiates between his or her view of things and the characters' views.

Mark Twain makes such a distinction in *Huckleberry Finn*. When Huck sees the Grangerford house, he says, "It was a mighty nice family, and a mighty nice house, too. I hadn't seen no house out in the country before that was so nice and had so much style." He proceeds to describe the interior with awe and reverence. Although Huck is impressed with the furnishings, Twain clearly is not. We recognize Twain's attitude from the details Huck provides: the unread books, the reproductions of sentimental paintings, the damaged imitation fruit, the crockery animals, the broken clock, the painted hearth, the tablecloth "made out of beautiful oilcloth," the piano "that had tin pans in it" (85–88). Huck also shows his admiration for Emmeline Grangerford's poetry by reproducing some of it to share with us (87–88). But we see, as Twain wants us to see, that the poetry is terrible.

Finally, Huck is awestruck by the family's aristocratic bearing: "Col. Grangerford was a gentleman, you see. He was a gentleman all over; and so was his family. He was well born. . . . He didn't have to tell anybody to mind their manners—everybody was always good mannered where he was" (89). Yet he fails to see, as Twain and we see, the ironic contrast between the family's good manners and its irrational and murderous feud with another family. Twain's handling of point of view in this novel helps to develop both character and theme. By presenting Huck's credulous view of things, it develops Huck as an essentially innocent person. By ironically contrasting Twain's view to Huck's, it underscores the author's harsher and more pessimistic perception of "reality."

Once you have determined a work's point of view, ideas should emerge from two general questions. Why has the author chosen this point of view? What effects does it have on other elements of the story—theme, characterization, setting, language? Some follow-up questions are: What effect does the author's point of view have on us and the way we view the world of the work? For example, if the point of view is first person, we have a much more limited view than if it is omniscient. The omniscient point of view makes us feel as though we understand everything about the world of the work, as though everything revealed by the omniscient narrator is true. What perspective of the world, then, does the author want us to have? Also, what do we learn about the nature of human perception from the author's handling of first person and especially limited omniscience? Henry James's limited omniscience often shows people as blind to the needs and desires of other people and of themselves as well. If the point of view is first person, is the narrator telling the story to someone? If so, to whom? How do they react? What do we learn about the narrator from that fact? If the point of view is objective (dramatic), does it seem as though the narrator is emotionally uninvolved and rationally objective about the characters and events? What do we gain by not being able to enter the characters' minds?

■ Thinking on Paper about Point of View

1. Identify the point of view of the story. Describe how the story would change if it were told from each of the other points of view.
2. List the main characters in the story. Write a paragraph on one or more characters, explaining how the story would be different if that character were narrating it.
3. Mark places where the narrator or central consciousness differs from our view of reality or fails to see important truths that we or other characters see.
4. Mark places that are particularly expressive of the narrator's tone. List the characteristics of tone.

Irony

Authors use irony pervasively to convey their ideas. But irony is a diverse and often complex intellectual phenomenon difficult to define in a sentence or two. Generally, *irony* makes visible a contrast between appearance and reality. More fully and specifically, it exposes and underscores a contrast between (1) what is and what seems to be, (2) between what is and what ought to be, (3) between what is and what one wishes to be, and (4) between what is and what one expects to be. Incongruity is the method of irony; opposites come suddenly together so that the disparity is obvious to discriminating readers. There are many kinds of irony, but four types are common in literature.

Verbal irony Verbal irony is perhaps the most common form of irony. Most people use or hear verbal irony daily. In verbal irony, people say the opposite of what they mean. For example, if the day has been terrible, you might say, "Boy, this has been a great day!" The hearer knows that this statement is ironic because of the speaker's tone of voice and facial or bodily expressions or because the hearer is familiar with the situation and immediately sees the discrepancy between statement and actuality. Understatement and overstatement are two forms of verbal irony. In *understatement*, one minimizes the nature of something. "Greg Maddox pitched a pretty good game," one might say after seeing a no-hitter. Mark Twain's famous telegram is another example of understatement: "The reports of my death are greatly exaggerated." In *overstatement* one exaggerates the nature of something. After standing in a long line, you might say, "There were about a million people in that line!"

Why do people use verbal irony? One reason is that verbal irony is more emphatic than a point-blank statement of the truth. It achieves its effect by reminding the hearer or reader of what the opposite reality is and thus providing a scale by which to judge the present reality. Verbal irony often represents a mental agility—wit—that people find striking and, as with the Mark Twain retort, entertaining. Verbal irony in its most bitter and destructive form becomes sarcasm, in which the speaker condemns people by pretending to praise them:

> Oh, you're a real angel. You're the noble and upright man who wouldn't think of dirtying his pure little hands with company business. But all along, behind our backs, you were just as greedy and ruthless as the rest of us.

Situational irony   In situational irony, the situation differs from what common sense indicates it is, will be, or ought to be. It is ironic, for example, that General George Patton should have lived through the thickest of tank battles during World War II and then, after the war, have been killed accidentally by one of his own men. It is ironic that someone we expect to be upright—a minister or judge—should be the most repulsive of scoundrels. Authors often use situational irony to expose hypocrisy and injustice. An example is Hawthorne's *The Scarlet Letter*, in which the townspeople regard the minister Arthur Dimmesdale as sanctified and angelic when in fact he shamefully hides his adultery with Hester Prynne, allowing her to take all the blame.

Attitudinal irony   Situational irony results from what *most* people expect, whereas attitudinal irony results from what one person expects. In attitudinal irony, an individual thinks that reality is one way when, in fact, it is a very different way. A frequent example in literature is naïve characters—Fielding's Parson Adams, Cervantes's Don Quixote, Dickens's Mr. Micawber, Voltaire's Candide—who think that everyone is upright and that everything will turn out for the best, when in fact people they encounter treat them unfairly and events are hurtful.

Dramatic irony   Dramatic irony occurs in plays when a character states or hears something that means more to the audience than to the character. An example is the play *Oedipus Rex*. Like all Greek tragedies, *Oedipus Rex* dramatizes a myth that its audiences know. Thus, when

Oedipus at the beginning boasts that he will personally find and punish the reprobate who killed King Laius, the audience recognizes this boast as ironic. Oedipus does not know—but the audience does—that he himself is the unwitting murderer of Laius. Although dramatic irony gets its name from drama, it can occur in all forms of literature. The key to the existence of dramatic irony is the reader's foreknowledge of coming events. Many works become newly interesting when we reread them because we now know what will happen while the characters do not; this dramatic irony intensifies characterization and makes us aware of tensions that we could not have known about during our initial reading.

Questions about irony   The first question to ask is: What are the most obvious ironies in the work? The second is: How are the ironies important? What, for example, are their implications? Shirley Jackson's "The Lottery" is layered with irony. An essay might deal with one of its ironies, such as the ironic contrast between the placid country-town setting and the horrible deeds done there. The setting seems like everyone's nostalgic image of the ideal American small town, with its central square, post office, country store, cranky old men, gossipy housewives, laconic farmers, mischievous children, settled routine, and friendly atmosphere. Is Jackson implying, then, that "normal" American communities conduct lotteries to decide which of their members is to be destroyed by the others? The answer is probably yes, she is suggesting just this. Americans are guilty of conducting "lotteries," perhaps not exactly in this manner, but with equal arbitrariness and cruelty. Instead of making this point directly, however, she implies it through the use of irony. And she achieves a much greater emphasis than if she were to state her accusation directly. She shocks us by associating something we agree is horrible with a way of life we think of as "normal" and benign. The irony packs an emotional wallop that captures our attention and gets us thinking.

Other, more specific questions about irony are these:
Verbal irony: If characters constantly use verbal irony, why? What do we learn about their attitudes toward the world? Does their verbal irony usually take the form of sarcasm? Are they, then, bitter, and disappointed or simply realistic?

Situational irony: What are the most obvious situational ironies? Are the characters aware of the situational ironies? At what point do they become aware of them? Should we blame the characters for creating situational ironies or not understanding them? Does the author, for example, want us to do something about them—to reform society and ourselves?

Attitudinal irony: What attitudes do the characters have that contradict reality? Are we supposed to admire the characters who misconstrue the world, or are we to blame them for being naïve and deluded? What troubles do they encounter because of their attitudes?

Dramatic irony: What do you know about coming events or past events in the work that the characters do not know? When and what do they say that triggers this disparity? What does the author want us to think of them when they say these things? What effect does dramatic irony have on the plot? Does it, for example, make the plot suspenseful?

■ Thinking on Paper about Irony

1. Mark examples of verbal irony, either by the narrator or other characters. Explain how a character's verbal irony helps characterize him or her.

2. Mark episodes in which a character's beliefs and expectations are contradicted by reality. Explain the importance to characterization of these episodes.

3. List instances of situational irony; identify people, for example, whom we expect to behave in one way but who behave quite differently. Explain the importance to theme of these instances.

Symbolism

In the broadest sense, a symbol is something that represents something else. Words, for example, are symbols. But in literature, a *symbol* is an object that has meaning beyond itself. The object is concrete and the meanings are abstract. Fire, for example, may symbolize general destruction (as in James Baldwin's title *The Fire Next Time*), or passion (the "flames of desire"), or hell (the "fiery furnace"). Symbols, however, are not metaphors; they are not analogies that clarify abstractions, such as the following metaphor from Shakespeare's Sonnet 116:

love is an ever-fixèd mark,
That looks on tempests and is never shaken.

Here, the abstract concept (the referent) is "love" and the clarifying concrete object is the stable mark (buoy, lighthouse, rock) that tempests cannot budge. A symbol, in contrast, is a concrete object with no clear referent and thus no fixed meaning. Instead, it merely suggests the meaning and, in an odd way, partly *is* the meaning. For this reason, the meaning of symbols is difficult to pin down. And the more inexhaustible their potential meaning, the richer they are.

There are two kinds of symbol: public and private. *Public symbols* are conventional, those that most people in a particular culture or community would recognize as meaning something fairly definite. Examples of public symbols are the cross, the star of David, the American eagle, flags of countries, the colors red (for "stop") and green (for "go"), and the skull and crossbones.

Private symbols are unique to an individual or to a single work. Only from clues in the work itself can we learn the symbolic value of the object. There are many examples of private symbols in literature. In F. Scott Fitzgerald's *The Great Gatsby*, there is an area between the posh Long Island suburbs and New York City through which the major characters drive at various times and which Fitzgerald calls a "valley of ashes." It is a desolate, gray, sterile place, and over it all broods a partly obliterated billboard advertisement that features the enormous eyes of Doctor T. J. Eckleburg, an optometrist. Fitzgerald invests this area with symbolic meaning. He associates it with moral decay, urban blight, the oppression of the poor by the wealthy, meaninglessness, hell, and violent death. At one point he connects the eyes with failure of vision, at another with God, who sees all things. But we never know exactly what the valley of ashes represents; instead, it resonates with many possible meanings, and this resonance accounts for its powerful suggestiveness.

Questions about symbolism   Not every work uses symbols, and not every character, incident, or object in a work has symbolic value. You should ask the fundamental question: What symbols does the work seem to have? You should, however, beware of finding "symbols" where none were intended. A second question, then, is necessary to the believability of any interpretation based on symbols: How do you know they are symbols? What does the author do that gives symbolic meaning to the elements you mention? Once you answer this question, you can move on to a third and more interesting question: What does the symbol mean? In Hemingway's *A Farewell to Arms*, for example, the following dialogue between Frederic Henry and Catherine Barkley suggests that Hemingway intended a symbolic meaning for rain; it also suggests what the symbol represents:

> [Frederic says] "It's raining hard."
> "And you'll always love me, won't you?" [Catherine replies]
> "Yes."
> "And the rain won't make any difference?"
> "No."
> "That's good. Because I'm afraid of the rain."
> "Why? . . . Tell me."
> "All right. I'm afraid of the rain because sometimes I see me dead in it."
> "No."
> "And sometimes I see you dead in it. . . . It's all nonsense. It's only nonsense. I'm not afraid of the rain. I'm not afraid of the rain. Oh, oh, God, I wish I wasn't." She was crying. I comforted her and she stopped crying. But outside it kept on raining. (125–126)

Throughout the novel, Hemingway's recurrent association of rain with destruction of all kinds broadens its significance from a mere metaphor for death to other and more general qualities such as war, fate, alienation, foreboding, doom, and "reality." Because of these associations, the last sentence of the novel is more than just a description of the weather: "After a while I went out and left the hospital and walked back to the hotel in the rain" (332). The sentence seems to suggest that Frederic is stoically and bravely facing the harsh realities—including Catherine's death, the war, the arbitrariness and cruelty of fate—represented by the rain.

■ Thinking on Paper about Symbolism

1. List the symbols in the work.
2. State why you think the objects are meant as symbols.
3. Mark the descriptions or episodes that give the symbols meaning.
4. List each symbol's possible meanings.

Other Elements

In this chapter we have treated the elements most obviously identified with fiction. But other elements are also sometimes important in fiction: dialogue, description, metaphor, poetic use of language, diction. We will discuss these other elements in the next two chapters.

Works Cited and Consulted

Abrams, M. H. *A Glossary of Literary Terms.* Fort Worth: Harcourt, 1999.

Austen, Jane. *Pride and Prejudice.* Riverside Editions. Boston: Houghton, Mifflin, 1956.

Brontë, Charlotte. *Jane Eyre.* New York: Penguin, 1966.

Forster, E. M. *Aspects of the Novel.* New York: Harcourt, 1954.

Freytag, Gustav. *Freytag's Technique of the Drama.* 5th ed. Trans. Elias J. MacEwan. Chicago: Scott, Foresman, 1894.

Friedman, Norman. *Form and Meaning in Fiction.* Athens: U of Georgia P, 1975.

Garland, Hamlin. "Among the Corn Rows." *Main-Traveled Roads.* Signet Classics. New York: New American Library, 1962. 98–121.

Hemingway, Ernest. *A Farewell to Arms.* New York: Scribner's, 1957.

———. "Hills Like White Elephants." *The Short Stories of Ernest Hemingway.* New York: Scribner's, 1966. 273–278.

Twain, Mark. *The Adventures of Huckleberry Finn.* Riverside Editions. Boston: Houghton, Mifflin, 1958.

Interpreting Drama

D
rama contains many of the elements of fiction. Like fiction, drama contains plot, characters, theme, and setting. Like fiction, drama uses irony and symbolism. And indeed, you can read a play as you would a short novel, using your imagination to fill in all the "missing" material you typically find in fiction: character description, background information, vivid action scenes. Similarly, drama often contains many of the elements of poetry, and you can read the poetic passages in plays just as you read any poetry. Because of the great similarity of drama to fiction and poetry, the definitions, questions, and exercises stated in the preceding chapter on fiction and in the following chapter on poetry are all equally valid for drama. Use them to generate your own interpretations of the plays.

The Nature of Drama

Drama is different from fiction and most poetry in one essential way: It is meant to be performed. Some theorists of drama argue that a play is incomplete *until* it is performed. According to the critic Bernard Beckerman in *Dynamics of Drama*, "a play is a mere skeleton; performance fleshes out the bones" (3). When you read a play, you miss qualities the playwright intended as a part of the play. For one thing, you miss the audience, whose physical presence and reactions to the performance influence both the performance and your perception of the play. For another, you miss the set designers' vision of the atmosphere and physical world of the play. You miss the interpretive art of the actors and the illusion they can create of real life unfolding before your eyes. You miss the physical and emotional *experience* of drama that a production can give you.

This is not to say that reading a play carefully is not worth doing. Sometimes in a performance we miss aspects of plays that most people can catch only when reading the play. This is especially true of plays written in poetry. When Romeo and Juliet first speak to each other, for example, Shakespeare has them develop a complex metaphor (a pilgrim coming to a shrine) and speak in sonnet form. It is unlikely that a playgoer, upon hearing this exchange, would think, "Aha! That was a sonnet!" Rather, we typically notice such devices by reading carefully. Even if our purpose is to produce the play, we must read carefully because productions are based on interpretations of the plays. "Literary" devices such as a sonnet may not be immediately recognizable by the audience, but they provide clues to how the playwright wanted the play performed. In fact, everything in the play is a clue to its possible performance and thus deserves studious attention.

To read a play with an eye to how the play might be produced, therefore, is to understand the play as the playwright conceived it. Since we examine the elements of fiction and poetry in Chapters 3 and 5, we will concentrate in this chapter on how you can use the possible performance of drama as a means of understanding its elements.

The Elements of Drama

Plot

Because the playwright has only a short time (two or so hours) to develop plot and because the playwright's audience experiences the play in one sitting, with little immediate opportunity to review it, the playwright must keep the plot simple and clear enough for an audience to grasp during the length of the performance. This means that the playwright cannot indulge in numerous subplots or in intricate plot complications; otherwise the playgoer would become confused. Playwrights, therefore, limit the number of characters in the play. (The fewer the characters, the simpler the plot can be.) Playwrights also emphasize conflict to keep the audience involved in the action and establish easily discernible patterns of cause and effect.

Although the playwright can present physical action without having to use words, the action (and the conflict implicit in the action) must be understandable to the audience. The most important and almost inevitable means for doing this is *dialogue*—people talking to people. Playwrights, then, strive to make every word of dialogue help move the plot forward. The near inevitability of dialogue also means that playwrights focus largely on conflicts between people rather than conflicts between people and nonhuman forces. In contrast, fiction need not represent characters' words or thoughts and so is freer to depict conflicts between people and nonhuman forces. Jack London's short story "To Build a Fire" does give the thoughts of the protagonist; but otherwise there is no "dialogue," just the protagonist's conflict with the harsh Yukon landscape. It would be very difficult for a play to duplicate this kind of conflict. Plays sometimes do portray conflicts between people and nonhuman forces, but these conflicts are revealed through dialogue and usually through conflicts between the characters.

Because the time and space for a presentation is limited, certain kinds of action—battles and sports activities, for example—cannot be represented fully or literally on the stage. These activities must be concentrated or symbolized. A duel onstage, for example, might represent an entire battle; a plantation house that in act one is sparkling new but in act four is ramshackled might represent the activities that have brought a once-grand family to the brink of ruin. Sometimes the playwright places activities offstage. A character might describe events that have just taken place, but the audience does not see these events. It learns about them only through the dialogue.

The actions that take place during the presentation of the play—onstage or offstage actions—are usually only a part of a larger series of events. Bernard Beckerman helpfully distinguishes the two sets of actions by the terms *plot* (what occurs during the play) and *story* (what occurs before, during, and after the play) (171–172). The "plot" of *Oedipus Rex*, for example, is Oedipus's attempt to rid Thebes of a blight and his resulting discovery of who he is and the nature of his crimes. The "story" of the play is Oedipus's entire history, starting with his parents' attempt to kill him when he was an infant and ending with his death at Colonus. Some plays feature a plot that is only a small part (but usually a very important and climactic part) of a story. Other plays feature a plot that is almost equivalent to the story. Shakespeare's *Macbeth*, for example, has almost no important past and future events; nearly all the action occurs within the play itself. Thus the plot and story of *Macbeth* are nearly equivalent. The events in *Hamlet*, however, occur after a murder and a marriage and, long before that, a war between Denmark and Norway, all of which profoundly affect the action within the play itself; the conclusion of the play, furthermore, suggests what the future of Denmark will be like under its new ruler, the Norwegian king Fortinbras.

The plotting in drama depends in part on establishing *audience expectations* of what will happen in the immediate future, as the play is unfolding. Both fiction and poetry, in contrast, focus more on what has already happened. The playwright, of course, predetermines the events in a play; but as we watch, we experience the illusion that the action is occurring in the present and that neither we nor the characters know what will happen next. This effect of expectation is heightened in drama because as we watch the play we have little time to reflect on what has happened, whereas when we read a novel we can pause and think about what we have read. Playwrights often predict our expectations about certain kinds of action and certain kinds of characters and fulfill our expectations or surprise us by thwarting them.

The *structural divisions* of plays affect plot. Playwrights usually provide structural divisions to give playgoers physical relief—a few moments to stand up, walk about, stretch, or reflect (however briefly) on what they have seen. Structural divisions also serve to allow set changes. In addition to such performance considerations, structural divisions also mark segments of the plot. *Formal structural divisions* are those specified in the play or the program—acts and scenes. *Informal structural divisions* can be smaller units within an act or scene, units not identified as such by the playwright but that nonetheless have a self-contained quality. In formal structural units, the playwright might call for the curtain to come down, the lights to go off, or the characters to leave the stage to signal the end of a unit. Shakespeare often ends his units with a couplet. In informal units, none of these things may happen; instead, the units may just flow together. Characteristic of all of them, however, is a rising action, a climax, and possibly a brief falling action. The climax of these units is usually a moment of revelation, either to the main characters, to other characters, or to the audience. An example is Hamlet's recognition at the climax of the play-within-a-play scene that King Claudius has murdered his father, the former king. All of the units of a play contribute to the rising action of the entire play and lead finally to its main climax.

Questions about plot

Simplicity: We said that plot in drama needs to be relatively simple and clear. In the play you are studying, is it? If not, why would the playwright want to create confusion about the important conflicts and cause-and-effect relationships? Sometimes the playwright *tries* to create such confusion. Congreve in *The Way of the World*, for example, creates a pattern of relationships so confusing that an audience is hard pressed to figure out who has done what to whom, especially at the breakneck speed the play is usually performed. He probably does this purposefully to indicate the complicated texture of Restoration upper-class society and the difficulty of finding one's way through it safely and honorably. Basic questions are: What are the main conflicts? What has caused the conflicts existing at the beginning of the play? What causes the conflicts that emerge during the course of the play? Who is in conflict with whom? Why? Are any of the characters in conflict with forces larger than just individuals—society, for example, or fate? How are the conflicts resolved?

Location of action: What actions occur offstage? Why does the author elect to place some actions offstage and other actions onstage? In *Macbeth*, for example, Shakespeare has the murder of King Duncan (at the beginning of the play) occur offstage, but later he has the murder of Banquo and, in another scene, the murder of Macduff's family (or part of it) occur onstage. Why, then, does he choose to put one murder offstage and other murders onstage? Questions that should lead to answers to this are: How do the characters react to the offstage events? Shakespeare probably places Duncan's murder offstage because he wants the audience to focus attention on Macbeth and Lady Macbeth's reaction to the murder. Related questions are: What does the playwright use to represent or symbolize action that occurs offstage? When Macbeth returns from killing Duncan, he carries the murder weapons, all covered with blood. His hands are covered with blood. When Lady Macbeth returns from smearing blood all over the sleeping guards, *her* hands are covered with blood. The more we see of this blood and the more they talk about it, the more grisly and physical and sticky the murder seems. Without actually describing the murder, Shakespeare uses a physical image—blood—and the characters' reaction to it to signal what the murder was like.

Plot versus story: What is the "plot" of the play? What is the "story"? If the plot is only part of the story, why does the playwright choose this part? What has happened before the play begins? What will happen afterward? As Beckerman points out, if the plot is only part of a larger or continuing story, the characters are more likely to seem at the mercy of forces beyond their control; whereas, if the plot and story are roughly equivalent, the characters will seem more free to choose and mold their own fate (172). The plot of *Romeo and Juliet*, for example, is only one episode—the final episode, we hope—of a generations-long, murderous, and irrational family feud. Romeo and Juliet are therefore "star-crossed" and "death-marked"; try as they will, they cannot escape the undertow of their families' history. Even Prince Escalus, the only person in the play with both power and good sense, can do nothing to avert the concluding tragedy. Macbeth and Lady Macbeth, in contrast, choose to do evil at the beginning of the play and thus give rise to the forces that destroy them.

Audience expectations: What expectations does the plot call up in the audience? Does the playwright fulfill those expectations? If not, how and why not? Most traditional comedy, for example, offers young lovers as staple characters. We expect the lovers, after suitable complications, to find happiness together, usually signaled at the end by betrothal or marriage. But sometimes the playwright introduces potential lovers, gives us something like a light comic tone, creates comic complications, but thwarts our expectations that they will marry. Examples are Etherege's *The Man of Mode*, Molière's *The Misanthrope*, and Shaw's *Mrs. Warren's Profession*. Another example is Chekhov's *The Cherry Orchard*, which he called a comedy, even though it is not always played as such. In this play, the main character, Lopakhin, and the adopted daughter of the family he is trying to rescue from economic disaster, seem meant for each other. There is much talk throughout the play of their marrying. Such a marriage would seem to be good for both of them. They agree to marry, and since they are sympathetic characters, the audience wants them to marry. Yet they never do. Why does Chekhov create the expectation and even hope of their marriage and then abort it? The answer to this question provides insight into Chekhov's purposes in *The Cherry Orchard*; and since he uses the same device in other plays—*Three Sisters*, for example—the answer throws light on his entire dramatic method.

Formal and informal divisions: What are the formal structural divisions of the plays? How many are there—three acts? four? five? How do the formal divisions reflect the playwright's purposes and materials? Oscar Wilde's *The Importance of Being Earnest*, for example, is divided into three acts. The first act takes place in London, the second and third in the country. This division reflects the double-identity motif in the plot because the main character pretends to have two identities: a city identity and a country identity. The first two acts reflect these opposing identities. The third act, however, synthesizes the first two. Events and revelations allow the main character to blend his city and country identities into one happy whole. The structure of the play, then, neatly reflects a "thesis, antithesis, synthesis" pattern of oppositions and resolution of oppositions.

What are the informal units of the play? For *all* the units, what are the climaxes of each? What is revealed in the climax—to the main character featured in the unit, to other characters, to the audience? How is a particular unit important to the whole play? What is the main climax of the play? What do you learn from it?

■ Thinking on Paper about Plot

1. List the conflicts revealed in each major section of the play (usually acts, but sometimes scenes).

2. Explain how one or more of these conflicts is first made evident. Pay close attention to dialogue.

3. Summarize how a conflict is developed throughout the whole play and how it is resolved.

4. Summarize the events, either in the past or present, that cause conflict. If there is one event that caused or causes all the conflicts, summarize it in detail and explain why and how it is so important.

5. List the external conflicts. How are they represented on stage? Through dialogue? Through physical action? Through symbolic stage props?

6. List the events that precede the action of the play. Explain the effect, if any, of these prior events on the action.

7. Summarize the events in each major structural unit of the play. Explain the relationship of the play's units to the plot's structure. Show how the action in each unit rises to a climax.

8. Mark some informal structural divisions in the play. Note the rising action and climax of these units.

9. Describe one important scene in detail. Explain how the characters' actions and dialogue reveal conflict. Explain the importance of the scene to the whole play.

10. Describe the climax of the play. Explain what conflicts are resolved.

11. List the main plot and the subplots. Explain the relationship of the subplots to the main plot.
12. List the events that occur offstage. Explain why the playwright has one or more of these occur offstage rather than onstage.
13. Summarize the situation at the beginning of the play and state what you expect to happen. Explain how the play does or does not fulfill those expectations.

Characterization

As with plot, the playwright must keep character portrayal simple enough for an audience to understand during the course of a single performance. The playwright must therefore rely heavily on flat characters, especially stereotyped ("stock") characters, whose personalities and moral traits are easily caught and remembered by the audience. The playwright may even use unsubtle stratagems of dress, dialect, physical movements, and names to communicate these traits. In Restoration and eighteenth-century comedy, for example, the names signal the traits of comic flat characters: Mrs. Loveit, Sir Fopling Flutter, Snake, Pert, Mr. Oldcastle, Lady Wishforit, Lady Sneerwell, Smirk, Handy. The playwright must also rely on static characters more heavily than dynamic characters because time-restricted performance limits the opportunity to make character changes plausible.

Edward Pixley has pointed out that when the play is dominated by flat characters, the plot hinges mainly on external conflicts; the focus is on action. When the play includes round characters, the plot deals largely with internal conflicts, the focus is on characterization (12). In Wilde's *The Importance of Being Earnest*, for example, all the characters are flat; the charm of the play lies not in character development but in the witty language, in the mild satire rippling through the dialogue, and in the plot complications resulting from the confusion of identities. In contrast, Ibsen's *Hedda Gabler* presents a complex, round character, Hedda herself; and the interest of the play lies in what she will do next and why she will do it. Hedda does not change during the play, but her character traits intensify and become clearer to the audience. Round characters, therefore, hold the audience's attention by changing or, if they don't change, by becoming more intense. In either case, continual revelations about the characters grip the audience's interest.

Although the playwright may depend to an extent on exterior details to reveal character traits, the playwright's most important device for character development is dialogue—what the characters say and what they say about one another. But performance time is limited; the words of the dialogue cannot describe the character fully. Playwrights, therefore, rely heavily on implication in the dialogue and on "gaps"— information left out—to indicate what characters are like and what physical things they might be doing. Some critics mark this distinction with the terms *text* for the written dialogue and *subtext* for the implications and gaps. All literary genres make use of implication and gaps, but drama and poetry almost *must* rely on them because both genres are such compressed forms of communication.

A simple example of text and subtext is the scene near the beginning of *Hamlet* in which Hamlet, after a long absence, meets his university friends Horatio and Marcellus. The night before this meeting, Horatio and Marcellus have seen the ghost of Hamlet's father. But Hamlet doesn't know about the ghost; instead, he complains about his mother's marrying so soon after his father's death:

HAMLET: Would I had met my dearest foe in heaven
             Or ever I had seen that day [the wedding day], Horatio!
             My father—methinks I see my father.
HORATIO: Where, my lord?
HAMLET: In my mind's eye, Horatio.
HORATIO: I saw him once. 'A was [he was] a goodly king. (1.2.
             182–188)

If you were the actor playing Horatio, how would you say the line "Where, my lord?" The "gap" here is the nature of Horatio's response to Hamlet's statement, "My father—methinks I see my father." To fill the gap, you have to determine from the context how Horatio takes that statement (Shakespeare does not tell you how, as a novelist might), and you have to communicate his reaction to the audience by the way you say the line and by your physical demeanor. You might phrase the line as an incredulous question: "What? You see your father? But how could you, he's dead?" Or you might say it as a reflection of what you take to be Hamlet's witty mood: "I know you're joking, Hamlet. But tell me anyway. Where do you see your father?" But another possibility is that you would say it in astonishment, as if you take it literally. After all, *you* had seen the ghost of Hamlet's father just a few hours before. You probably think Hamlet has now spotted the ghost, and so you say,

"Good Lord, do you see it, too? Where?" And you look fearfully around, trying to see the ghost too. When Hamlet indicates that he is only remembering his father, you calm down. At this point you might pause and make appropriate gestures to indicate your shift from fear and astonishment to calmness. The fact that you *have* made such a shift is indicated by your response to Hamlet: "Yes. Once, when the king was alive, I saw him too. He was an impressive-looking king." This last statement shows that Horatio has moved from thinking about a supernatural phenomenon (the ghost) to thinking about a natural one (Hamlet's father when he was alive).

This brief example illustrates the greatest value of understanding a play's subtext. By "reading" the implications and the gaps in the play, you uncover the inner states of the characters—what is going on in their minds and what their hidden nature is. You also establish a correspondence between the character's inner state and what the character says and does (the character's outer state). Interpretation of subtext is essential for actors, who must figure out how to say the dialogue and what to do onstage. But it is important for readers, too, even though a reader may not work out intonation and physical movements in as much detail as actors do. The reason for this importance is that a character's inner world is the key to the character's makeup and actions. Horatio, in the example above, is a flat character, and the problem of exposing his inner state is relatively uncomplicated. But doing so gives the performance— whether seen by an audience or imagined by a reader—vividness. Horatio springs to life. He is not just an automaton reading lines; he is a real person. As for round characters, the difficulty of uncovering their inner states is much greater, yet their complexity and hiddenness of inner state makes them fascinating. Great characters like Oedipus, Macbeth, Hamlet, and Hedda Gabler grip our imaginations just because their inner states are complex and mysterious. The only way we can expose these inner states is by interpreting the subtext of the play.

Closely related to subtext in drama is *mask wearing*. Nearly every play employs the mask as a device for developing plot and characterization. Juliet wears a "mask"—pretends to be different from the way she really is—in order to fool her parents and run away with Romeo. Hamlet puts on a mask of madness to root out the murderer of his father. Hedda pretends to be the contented housewife in order to secure the wealth and social status she thinks she deserves. Macbeth and Lady Macbeth pretend to be the loyal servants and gracious hosts of King Duncan while plotting his murder. The audience may be fully aware of the mask and thus the disparity between appearance and reality, as, for example, in Juliet's case. Or the audience may at first be as unaware of the mask as are the other characters in the play, as in Hedda's case. And sometimes the mask wearers are themselves unaware or partially unaware of their masks; that is, they deceive themselves. Oedipus, for example, does not know that he is masking his true identity of king murderer. In all cases, both plot and characterization turn on revelation—the tearing away of the mask. At these moments of revelation, the audience and at least some of the characters see the reality behind the mask. Often the final unmasking comes at the climax of the plot. In *Othello*, for example, the climax occurs when Iago's mask is ripped away before Othello's shocked eyes.

Questions about characterization and plot If the characters are flat, what are their dominant traits? their function in the plot? How do they help establish the conflicts in the plot? If the characters are dynamic, how do they change—from what to what? If they are static, do their traits intensify or become clearer as the play moves on? If the characters are round, what can you learn from the subtext of the play about their inner states?

What "masks" are the characters wearing? Who is hiding what from whom? When are the masks removed? What causes their removal, and what are the results? In general, how would you play a particular character if you were the actor? What physical devices would you use? Hedda Gabler, for example, is aristocratic, proud, and forceful; she seems strong but has an inner fragility. Her rival, Thea, is hesitant, unsophisticated, and afraid; she seems weak but has an inner strength. If you were acting these characters, how would you present yourself physically to convey these qualities? How would you show that Hedda seems strong but is in fact weak? You may not actually act Hedda, of course, but determining a physical presence for her helps you analyze her and thus understand her better.

■ Thinking on Paper about Characterization

1. List the character traits of each major character.
2. List the devices, such as dress, names, and gestures, that help establish the traits of a character.
3. Describe in detail the traits of a complex character, especially contradictory and seemingly inexplicable traits.
4. Explain a character's motivations for doing the things he or she does. Focus especially on what the character seems to want. Explain the situations from which the character's motivations seem to emerge.

5. Describe the strategies a character devises for getting what he or she wants. Explain how effective those strategies are.

6. Describe the miscalculations a character makes and the effect they have.

7. Summarize how a character intensifies, changes, or comes into sharper focus for the audience. Trace the intensification, change, or focus through each major unit of the play. Explain what causes it.

8. Summarize a scene in which a major character faces a crisis. Explain what we learn about the character from the character's words and actions.

9. Summarize a scene in which a major character has a startling or affecting revelation. Explain what the revelation is, what causes it, and its effect on the character's future.

10. Explain how you would portray one of the characters in an important scene. Show how your performance would reveal the character's inner state.

11. Explain the relationship a major character has with the other major characters. Describe the alliances and conflicts the character has with the other characters. Describe the attitudes the character has toward the other characters and their attitudes toward him or her.

12. If there is one character who exerts control—intentionally or unintentionally—over other characters, describe that character in detail and explain the source and nature of that control. Describe the other characters' reactions to that control.

13. List the masks characters wear. Explain why a character wears a mask.

14. Trace one or more of these masks throughout the play. Explain how effectively the mask accomplishes the character's purpose.

15. Summarize the scene in which the mask is dropped. List the effects of the mask being dropped.

Setting

Because of the limited time and space of dramatic productions, a play cannot create a "world" in the same detail and breadth a novel can. The worlds of novels like Tolstoy's *War and Peace* and Hugo's *Les Miserables*, with their multitude of characters, scenes, physical places, and battles, are impossible to show in drama. Rather, such worlds can be represented only fragmentarily. The playwright must use a shorthand method of presenting the setting so that the playgoer grasps enough information about it to understand whatever relationship it might have to characterization and theme. Sometimes the relationship is minimal, sometimes very close. *Setting* in drama is the same as in fiction: the social mores, values, and customs of the world in which the characters live; the physical world; and the time of the action, including historical circumstances.

The playwright has three main ways of communicating setting to an audience. First, we learn about setting from the characters' dialogue, dress, and behavior. In Sheridan's *School for Scandal*, we know immediately that the world of this play is leisured upper-class English society. We know this from the elaborately polite and mannered way in which the characters carry themselves and from the names they so freely drop—Sir Harry Bouquet, Lord Spindle, Captain Quinze, Lady Frizzle, the Dowager Lady Dundizzy. In *Hedda Gabler* the conversations between Hedda and Judge Brack let us know that they are aristocrats and that Hedda's husband and his family are middle class. Second, we learn about setting from the sets produced by the set designer. Sheridan doesn't tell us what the interiors for *School for Scandal* should look like. He says simply that throughout the play the setting is "London" and that in act one it is "Lady Sneerwell's house." A set designer, however, would do research on the interior design of fashionable homes in late-eighteenth-century England and produce that image on stage. The set, in short, should "say" that these people are aristocrats.

Third, we learn about setting from the knowledge we *bring* to the performance. The playwright alludes to the nature of the setting and assumes we will fill in the details. As Americans, for example, we have relatively little trouble understanding the setting of Arthur Miller's *The Crucible*, even though it is set in seventeenth-century New England. Miller expects us to know something about the Salem witch trials and about the McCarthy "witch-hunts" of the 1950s, and most Americans who see that play do know about them.

A problem surfaces, however, when the audience does not have the supplemental information to complete the setting of the play—audiences from other cultures or other time periods. Chekhov's plays are a case in point. *The Cherry Orchard*, for example, plays against a background of Russian history that Chekhov assumes we know: the reform acts of Czar Alexander II (1855–1881), including the freeing of the serfs in 1861 and the establishing of the *zemstvo* system of local self-government; Alexander's assassination by anarchists in 1881; the rigid autocracy of the next czar, Alexander III (1881–1894); and the ineffectual and repressive reign of his successor, Nicholas II (1894–1917), which revived revolutionary movements in the late 1890s. *The Cherry Orchard* focuses on the passing of a decrepit aristocratic order and the rising of a vigorous middle class and financial order. For us even to recognize this concern, it helps to know a little Russian history. Otherwise, we may be confused about why the aristocrats are so nostalgic, whimsical, and impractical in the face of imminent financial disaster. Chekhov wants us to see that their attitude is both a result and a cause of this historical change.

Playwrights and set designers can choose to give their sets symbolic value. Sets need not be symbolic. The sets in *School for Scandal* will usually be a literal suggestion of aristocratic drawing rooms and mean nothing more than that. To create the illusion of real rooms, the set designer can use physical detail lavishly—furniture, wallpaper, decorative doodads, architectural features, paintings, and clothes. But aspects of sets can take on symbolic or representational meaning. The simplest representational set is a bare stage, which can represent anything the playwright wants—a battlefield, a heath, a forest, or a gothic cathedral. The playwright can be blatantly symbolic, assigning obvious meanings to physical objects. Thornton Wilder does this in *Our Town* when he uses stepladders to represent houses. The playwright can also combine a realistic with a symbolic method. In *Hedda Gabler*, for example, Ibsen calls for solidly "real" things to be put in the two rooms we see of the Tesman house—an armchair, footstools, sofa, tables, French windows, and flowers in vases. But certain objects—Hedda's pistols, the portrait of General Gabler (Hedda's father), and the piano—become closely associated with her and her psychological disorders. Equally suggestive are the two rooms: one a large, elegant drawing room located in the front part of the stage and the other a smaller sitting room located in back. In act one Hedda's piano is in the drawing room, but in act two it is out of sight in the back room. In fact, as the play proceeds, the back room becomes more and more "Hedda's room" and the drawing room "Tesman's room." Even the portrait of General Gabler is in the back room. At the end of the play, Hedda retreats to the back room, pulls the curtains, frantically plays the piano, and shoots herself. It is as if the back room represents an increasingly restricted physical and emotional space for Hedda, until at last it becomes her prison and coffin.

Questions about setting   What do you learn about the setting from characters' behavior and dialogue? What kind of sets does the play seem to call for? What costumes would you have the actors wear? What costumes would best fit particular characters? Does the play seem to require background knowledge on your part to understand its setting? What are the symbolic possibilities in particular objects or in larger portions of the set? What relationships does the setting have to characterization? What emotional feel—atmosphere—does the setting have? What relationships does the setting have to theme?

■ Thinking on Paper about Setting

1. For each major unit of the play, describe the place where the action occurs. If the playwright gives a description of the place, summarize the description. If the playwright does not give a description, use information from the dialogue to construct a description. Explain the relationship of place to action, characterization, and theme.

2. Identify the time of day of each unit of the play. Explain how the time of day is represented on stage and its effect on the characters and the action.

3. Identify the time of year of each unit of the play. Explain the relationship of time of year to action, characterization, and theme.

4. Identify the historical period of the play. Give any background information that would be useful for understanding the play. Explain the relationship of the historical period to action, characterization, and theme.

5. Describe the atmosphere of each major unit of the play.

6. Describe the costumes the characters wear. Explain the relationship between costumes, characterization, and theme.

7. Describe your design for the physical world—sets, costumes, sounds, lighting, the works—of one major unit of the play. Explain the reasons for your choices.

8. List the details of setting that have symbolic value. Explain what each symbolizes. Explain the relationship of symbolism to characterization and theme.

9. Explain each major character's attitude toward the setting.

Theme

Playwrights build themes into their plays through the development and interrelationship of all the elements of drama, most of which are the same as for fiction. Three methods of developing theme, however, are particularly noteworthy: repetitions, symbols, and contrasts. All three lend themselves well to drama. Audiences can pick up on them easily during performances.

Repetitions can take many forms—a character's performing the same gesture over and over again, repeating the same phrase, stating the same idea, or appearing at regular intervals. But for repetitions to relate to theme, they must develop ideas. Shakespeare does just that in *Hamlet* by repeating and intertwining three concepts: Denmark as "rotten," human beings as sinful, and the king's role as crucial to the health of the state. He characterizes Denmark by repeatedly comparing it to a garden overrun with weeds and to a diseased body, analogies borne out by Hamlet's partial madness and Ophelia's complete madness and suicide. He has key characters dwell on the sinful nature of humankind. The queen says that her own soul is "sick," "as sin's true nature is" (4.5.16).The king says that his "offense is rank, it smells to heaven" because it has "the primal eldest curse" upon it (Cain's murder of Abel, 3.3.36-37). And Hamlet says that even the best people seem to have "some vicious mole of nature in them" that leads them from purity to corruption (1.4.24). (All three of these statements connect sin to sickness.) The corrupt state of Denmark, Shakespeare implies, is the result of the king's sin. For, as one character says, the king is like the hub of a wheel whose spokes connect to "ten thousand lesser things" (3.3.11-23). Whatever the king does affects everyone in the state.

As we noted, *symbolism* can enrich setting; but, in fact, symbolism bears on both characterization and theme as well. It is often hard to separate the effect of symbolism on all three elements. In *Hedda Gabler*, for example, Ibsen contrasts Hedda's and Thea's hair to symbolize their different character traits. Hedda's hair is thin and dull; Thea's is thick and luxuriant. Hedda dates her long-standing rivalry with Thea from their school days, when Hedda threatened to "burn off" Thea's hair. Hedda seems at times to want to inspire people to create, but her efforts end up as destructive; whereas Thea has an innate and unconscious gift for inspiring creativity. This wellspring of inspiration and fertility is symbolized by Thea's hair, which helps explain Hedda's animosity toward it. It's hard to say just what Ibsen's themes in *Hedda Gabler* are; he may simply be trying to present, not explain, Hedda's mysterious perversities. But one implication of the hair symbolism may be that creativity is a mysterious quality existing even in someone as innocent and nonintellectual as Thea and that it may not have anything to do with the intellectual sharpness and forcefulness of people like Hedda. Whatever Ibsen's themes are, they are inextricably bound up with his characterization of Hedda and Thea.

A simpler—that is, easier to interpret—example of thematic symbolism occurs in Lorraine Hansberry's *A Raisin in the Sun*. Mrs. Younger, the main character, is the mother of a large extended family, but her environment—a stultifying, roach-infested, inner-city tenement—has kept her from giving the best of life to her children. The house she wants to buy in the suburbs becomes equivalent to new "earth" in which her children and grandchild can "grow," because, as she says, they are her "harvest." To emphasize the analogy between the house and a garden, Hansberry shows Mrs. Younger constantly dreaming of working in the garden at the new house, and, as a moving present, her children give her garden tools. The most visible symbol of Mrs. Younger's frustrations and aspirations, however, is a sickly houseplant she has been trying for years to nurture. The audience sees the plant sitting in the window. Mrs. Younger fusses over it. Her children chide her for messing with it, but she persists. The last thing we see her do is say goodbye to the oppressive apartment and carry the plant out the door. At the new house, it will revive in the sunshine and clean air of a better world. The message seems clear: People are like plants; they become healthy—mentally, morally, and physically—only in hospitable environments.

Like symbolism, *contrast* helps develop not just theme but characterization and plot. We have already seen many examples of contrast in the plays we have discussed so far: romantic love (Romeo and Juliet) versus social requirements (the Montagues and the Capulets), Thea versus Hedda, Macbeth versus Duncan, old Russia versus new Russia, Hamlet's father versus the new king. Often, playwrights repeat situations but vary them in such ways that the differences have thematic implications. In *Macbeth*, for example, Shakespeare places nearly identical events at the beginning and end. At the beginning, Scotland has just defeated Norway. The traitorous Thane of Cawdor is executed, and Macbeth triumphantly displays the head of another rebel by putting it on a stake. As a reward for valor, the king designates Macbeth the new Thane of Cawdor. At the end of the play, another battle is fought; Macbeth is killed as a "usurper," and his head is cut off and held aloft as a sign of revenge and victory. Ironically, Macbeth has changed places with the first Thane of Cawdor in both name and nature, and the circumstances of their deaths are almost identical.

A more far-reaching example of contrast is the Surface brothers in Sheridan's *School for Scandal*. Joseph Surface pretends to be good, but he is in fact selfish and destructive. Charles Surface leads a carefree and careless life; he seems to be a wastrel, but he is in fact generous and honest. Their uncle and benefactor, Sir Oliver Surface, a brusque but warmhearted man, has just returned to England after a long absence and wants to ferret out the true nature of his two potential heirs. To do this he visits each brother separately, disguised as someone else. Both scenes are so similar that an audience cannot fail to notice the similarity; Sheridan uses the similarity to contrast the brothers. The first scene, with Charles, does indeed expose his good qualities. The audience now knows how the scene will go and gleefully awaits the second scene, in which the despicable Joseph will unwittingly reveal his selfishness and pride. This contrast not only develops plot and character, it also points a moral—that the appearance of goodness is worthless without the practice of goodness.

Questions about theme   What repetitions occur in the play? What meaning can you draw from these repetitions? What symbols does the author deliberately establish? How do you know they are symbols? What do the symbols seem to mean?

What contrasts does the playwright establish? Which are the obvious contrasts and which are the not-so-obvious contrasts? In *Romeo and Juliet*, for example, we easily spot the contrast between the lovers and the parents, but other contrasts are suggestive: Romeo is different from Juliet and is perhaps partly to blame for their deaths; Prince Escalus is different from the parents; the nurse's attitude toward love contrasts starkly with Juliet's; the friar's attitude toward love is different from Romeo's. Any one or a combination of these contrasts would make a good focus for interpretation. How is contrast related to the conflicts in the plot? Hedda and Thea are not only different from each other, they are in conflict. What values, then, do the contrasting sides of a conflict manifest?

■ Thinking on Paper about Theme

1. List the subjects of the play (the issues or problems the play seems to be about). State themes for each of these subjects (what the play seems to be saying about these issues and problems).

2. Mark speeches and sections of dialogue that help develop a particular theme. Look especially for "the big speech," which will typically be longer than most and will forcefully state a theme. Hamlet's "To

be or not to be" speech is an example. There may be more than one "big speech." Summarize them and explain how the actions of the play develop their ideas.

3. Explain in detail how an important scene helps develop themes.

4. Trace the development of one theme throughout the play. Mark all the passages that help develop this theme. Summarize the plot as it relates to this theme.

5. List the images (sensuous images, metaphors) that recur in the play. Explain the ideas they seem to develop.

6. List other repetitions (characters' actions and words, characters' obsessions, scenes, details of setting). Explain their relationship to characterization and theme.

7. List the symbols in the play. For each symbol, list its meanings.

8. Describe the important contrasts in the play (of characters, scenes, values, actions, physical objects). Explain how these contrasts help expose character traits and develop theme.

Irony

The presence of an audience at performances of plays affects profoundly the way plays are written and the way productions are conceived. The actors, of course, pretend to be real people involved in real human relationships. But unlike real life, these fictional activities are witnessed by an audience of total strangers. It is as if the front wall of your neighbor's house were taken away and the whole neighborhood were standing outside watching everything your neighbors are doing, hearing everything they are saying. The playwright or producer must decide whether to exclude or include the audience as participants in the play. If the choice is to exclude the audience, the production assumes that no one is watching. The production establishes a physical and psychological distance between the performance and the audience (the performance lighted, the auditorium dark; the performance up on stage, the audience down and away from the stage), and the actors pretend the audience is not there. If the choice is to include the audience, then measures are taken to bring the audience "into" the play. The physical distance between performance and audience may be reduced (by building the stage out into the auditorium or by having the actors circulate among the audience). The actors may look at the audience, gesture to it, or talk to it as if the audience were another person. Shakespeare's drama includes these possibilities with its numerous asides and soliloquies.

One prominent device that relies entirely on the presence of an audience, and on what the audience is thinking, is dramatic irony. *Dramatic irony* in effect does acknowledge the presence of the audience because it gives the audience the privilege of knowing things that one or more characters do not know. Dramatic irony occurs when characters say or do something that has meaning the audience recognizes but the characters do not. The concept of dramatic irony can be extended to all situations in which characters are blind to facts the audience knows. Sometimes only the audience is aware of the ironic contrast between the character's words or actions and the truth; sometimes the audience shares this knowledge with other characters onstage.

In the two parallel scenes in *School for Scandal*, for example, the audience knows that Sir Oliver Surface is wearing a mask to test his nephews—and, of course, Sir Oliver knows—but the nephews do not. So the audience recognizes as ironic everything the nephews do and say that works for or against their self-interest, particularly in the case of Joseph, who would treat Sir Oliver with meticulous courtesy if only he knew who he was. In another scene from this play, Lady Teazle hides behind a screen while her husband, unaware of her presence, talks about her. When he says that he wants to leave her a lot of money upon his death, but that he does not want her to know about it yet, we recognize his statement as ironic because we know—and he does not—that Lady Teazle has heard everything.

A powerful example of dramatic irony occurs in the last scenes of Shakespeare's *Othello*. Before Desdemona goes to bed, she sings a song about a man who accuses his love of being promiscuous. She asks Emilia, her lady-in-waiting, if any woman could so treat her husband. Emilia says that some might for the right "price," but Desdemona says that she could not do so "for the whole world." The audience recognizes her comments as ironic, because Othello, unbeknownst to Desdemona, is nearly insane with the belief that she is a "whore" and plans to kill her for it. Later, when Othello is strangling Desdemona, he boasts that even if he is "cruel" he is at least "merciful" because he will kill her quickly without allowing her to "linger in . . . pain." But his "mercy" contrasts horribly with our knowledge of her innocence and the quality of mercy she justly deserves. When he defends his murder to Emilia, he says,

Cassio did top her. Ask thy husband [Iago] else.
O, I were damned beneath all depth in hell
But that I did proceed upon just grounds
To this extremity. Thy husband knew it all. (5.2. 137–140)

We know, and poor Othello is about to find out, that Iago has betrayed him and that he has in truth had no "just grounds" for the "extremity" of his deed.

Questions about irony   To what extent does the playwright seem to want the audience involved in the action? How would you perform such audience-involving devices as soliloquies and asides? To whom, for example, would you have the actors make asides? What advantages are there in performing the play as if the audience is not there?

Like fiction and poetry, drama uses all kinds of irony. Verbal irony is very prevalent simply because drama relies so heavily on dialogue. Sometimes the director and actors themselves must decide whether particular lines are ironic. When Thea, for example, tells Hedda about inspiring Loevborg to write his book, Hedda interjects comments such as "Poor, pretty little Thea"; "But my dear Thea! How brave of you!"; "Clever little Thea!" (284–289) It is almost certain that Hedda means these statements ironically. The actress would probably say them, then, with enough sarcasm to let the audience know how Hedda really feels about Thea's successes, but not with enough bite to let the slow-witted Thea pick up on the irony.

What are the ironies, then, in the play you are studying? How do they relate to characterization and theme? Most important, what dramatic ironies does the playwright build into the play? Do the dramatic ironies—such as Othello's repeated description of Iago as "honest"—create a pattern of revelation or meaning? Why do the dramatic ironies appear where they do in the play?

■ Thinking on Paper about Irony

1. Explain the extent to which the play seems to invite audience participation.
2. Mark the instances in the play of dramatic irony. Explain what the dramatic irony reveals about characterization and theme.

3. Mark the instances of verbal irony. Explain what the verbal irony reveals about the characters who use it.

4. List the instances of situational irony. Explain the importance of situational irony to characterization and theme. (For a definition of situational irony, see Chapter 3.)

5. List the instances of attitudinal irony. Explain the importance of attitudinal irony to characterization and theme. (For a definition of attitudinal irony, see Chapter 3.)

Subgenres

The best-known subgenres of drama are tragedy and comedy, but there are many others: melodrama, theater of the absurd, allegory, comedy of manners, the spectacle, the masque, modern drama, farce, and tragicomedy. Some, like musicals, opera, and ballet, shade into other art forms.

Definitions of subgenres can lead to fruitful interpretations of individual works. The definition of *tragedy*, for example, began with the first and most famous discussion of it, that in Aristotle's *Poetics*. Aristotle based his definition on an inductive examination of Greek tragedy, and he seems in particular to have had Sophocles's plays in mind. His definition focuses primarily on the effect of the play on the audience and on the nature of the tragic hero. The hero, he says, inspires "pity" and "fear" in the audience: pity because the hero doesn't deserve his fate and fear because the hero's fate could be anyone's. The audience, in other words, identifies deeply with the tragic hero. The hero is noble but flawed. He has one principal flaw—in Sophocles, usually the flaw of pride. This flaw Aristotle called a *hamartia*, literally a "miscalculation." Because of the hero's flaw, he suffers emotionally and experiences a reversal of fortune, moving abruptly from a high place (high social position, wealth, responsibility, purity) to a low place. Before this reversal occurs, the hero understands for the first time his flawed state and his error-filled ways. This moment is the "recognition" and usually occurs at the climax of the play. The hero recognizes that he is responsible for his deeds and that they contradict a moral order inherent in the entire cosmos. The effect of the play on the audience is to induce a *catharsis*, a feeling of emotional release and exuberance.

Aristotle planned to write as comprehensively on *comedy* as on tragedy, but either that part of the *Poetics* was lost, or he never got around to it. It is hard to see, however, how he could have made comedy any less enigmatic than it still appears to us, for the nature of comedy is difficult to pin down, both artistically and psychologically. Numerous essays have been written trying to explain why people laugh, and all are speculative. Laughter is only one of the puzzling aspects of comedy. Most people would agree on some of the aspects of comedy. Comedy is the depiction of the ludicrous; that is, a gross departure from the serious. Therefore, in order to see something as comic, you must first understand what is "serious." Drama communicates to a community of playgoers, so the comic in drama is closely related to what the community *thinks* is serious. If the community thinks that proper attire for men is a business suit, tie, and polished shoes, then a gross distortion of that dress—by a clown in a circus, for example—would be comic. The basic methods of signaling the ludicrous are incongruity and exaggeration. It is incongruous for a haughty, spiffily dressed man, walking nose in the air, to slip and fall face first into a mud hole or to be hit in the face with a cream pie. Further, comedy must cause no pain to the audience. This means that the audience cannot identify as deeply with comic figures as it does with tragic figures and that the method of presentation—language, acting, setting—must communicate an air of "fantasy." Through its methods and style, the production constantly says, "This isn't true. It's only a joke." The fantasy element in comedies helps explain why they almost always end happily, whereas tragedies end unhappily. Finally, the characters in comedy are more "realistic" than in tragedy. They are more like us, whereas in tragedy they are, even in their flawed state (sometimes *because* of their flawed state), far nobler than we are.

Questions about subgenres   Definitions of genres and subgenres are useful only if they help you understand specific works. Aristotle was trying to understand Greek tragedy, so it does non-Greek tragedies an injustice to rigidly apply his definition to them. The same goes, really, for anyone's definition of a subgenre because literature is too varied and complex a phenomenon to fit neatly into categories. You should use definitions like Aristotle's as insights into the probable nature of a work and base your questions on those insights. You can take every part of these definitions of tragedy and comedy and turn each into a probing question aimed at a specific work: What is the character's major flaw? Does he or she have more than one flaw? When does the recognition scene occur? What does the character recognize? What incongruities cause the comedy? What do the incongruities reveal about the playwright's attitude toward the characters and setting? Are there hints of satire in these incongruities? How does the playwright establish the detachment necessary for us to laugh?

You might also apply definitions like these to works that do not quite fit the categories and see what you come up with. Some people regard *Hedda Gabler* as something like a "tragedy" but not exactly an Aristotelian tragedy. Will any parts of Aristotle's definition apply to *Hedda Gabler?* Which fit well? Which do not? Does Hedda have a "tragic flaw"? Is she responsible for her actions? Is she to blame for the harm she causes? Does she have a moment or moments of recognition? Is she nobler than we are? Does she experience a "reversal"? How does the audience feel after seeing or reading the play? Does the audience experience pity and fear for Hedda?

Some of the most interesting questions about subgenres emerge from plays that mix subgenres. Why, for example, are there comic elements in Shakespeare's tragedies? Is *The Cherry Orchard* a comedy? a tragedy? both? Are we supposed to laugh or cry at the fate of Chekhov's ineffectual aristocrats? If Aristotle's definition or someone else's provides no explanation for some feature of a play, can you invent an explanation of your own?

■ Thinking on Paper about Subgenres

1. If you know the subgenre to which the play belongs (tragedy, comedy, farce, and so forth), find a good definition of the subgenre. List the characteristics of the subgenre.

2. Take one item from the list and explain how well it applies to the play. If *Hamlet* is a tragic character, for example, what might be his tragic flaw? What constitutes his reversal? When does he experience a recognition? How does the audience respond to him?

Works Cited and Consulted

Abrams, M. H. *A Glossary of Literary Terms.* Fort Worth: Harcourt, 1999.

Aristotle. *Aristotle's Poetics: A Translation and Commentary for Students of Literature.* Trans. Leon Golden. Commentary O. B. Hardison, Jr. Tallahassee: UP of Florida, 1981.

Beckerman, Bernard. *Dynamics of Drama: Theory and Method of Analysis.* New York: Drama Book Specialists, 1979.

Corrigan, Robert W., ed. *Tragedy: A Study of Drama in Modern Times.* New York: Harcourt, 1967.

———. *Comedy: Meaning and Form.* New York: Harper, 1981.

Hansberry, Lorraine. *A Raisin in the Sun.* New York: New American Library, 1987.

Ibsen, Henrik. *Hedda Gabler and Other Plays.* Trans. Una Ellis-Fermor. New York: Penguin, 1988.

Pixley, Edward, George Kernodle, and Portia Kernodle. *Invitation to the Theatre.* 3rd ed. San Diego: Harcourt, 1985.

Shakespeare, William. *Hamlet.* Ed. Willard Farnham. Pelican Shakespeare. Baltimore: Penguin, 1957.

———. *Othello.* Ed. Gerald Eades Bentley. Pelican Shakespeare. Baltimore: Penguin, 1958.

Sheridan, Richard Brinsley. *The School for Scandal. Four English Comedies.* Ed. J. M. Morrell. Harmondsworth, England: Penguin, 1950.

Interpreting Poetry

Poetry shares many elements with its sister genres, drama and fiction. And indeed, many works of drama and fiction are written in the form of poetry. Plays by Shakespeare, Goethe, Molière, Marlowe, Maxwell Anderson, and T. S. Eliot; narrative works by Homer, Chaucer, Dante, Longfellow, Milton, Spenser, Tennyson, and Browning are examples. But poetry usually differs from prose drama and fiction in several key ways. In general, it is more concentrated—that is, poetry says more in fewer words. Poets achieve this concentration by selecting details more carefully, by relying more heavily on implication (through figurative language, connotation, and sensuous imagery), and by more carefully organizing the form of their poetry (through rhythmic speech patterns and "musical" qualities such as rhyme). Because of the relative shortness of poetry and because of its greater concentration, it demands a more complete unity than prose fiction; nearly every word, sound, and image contributes to a single effect.

Poetry is a complex subject. The following is a *brief* survey of its elements, with questions and exercises that should help you generate interpretations of individual poems.

The Elements of Poetry

Characterization, Point of View, Plot, Setting, and Theme

Some poems—"narrative" poems—are very similar to prose fiction and drama in their handling of characterization, point of view, plot, and

87

setting. Thus many of the same questions one asks about a short story, novel, or play are relevant to these poems. Most poems, however, do not offer a "story" in the conventional sense. They are usually brief and apparently devoid of "action." Even so, a plot of sorts may be implied, a place and time may be important, a specific point of view may be operating, and characters may be dramatizing the key issues of the poem. In any poem there is always one "character" of the utmost importance, even if he or she is the only character. This character is the speaker, the "I" of the poem. Often the speaker is a fictional personage, not at all equivalent to the poet, who may not be speaking to the reader but to another character, as is the case in Marvell's "To His Coy Mistress" and Browning's "My Last Duchess." The poem might even be a dialogue between two or more people, as in ballads such as "Edward" and "Lord Randal" and in Frost's "The Death of the Hired Man." Thus the poem can be a little drama or story, in which one or more fictional characters participate. But more typically, one character, the "I," speaks of something that concerns him or her deeply and personally. Such poems are called "lyric" poems because of their subjective, musical, highly emotional, and imaginative qualities. They are songlike utterances by one person, the "I."

Questions about characterization, point of view, plot, setting, and theme   In analyzing poetry, your first step should be to come to grips with the "I" of the poem, the speaker. You should answer questions such as: Who is speaking? What characterizes the speaker? To whom is he or she speaking? What is the speaker's tone? What is the speaker's emotional state? Why is he or she speaking? What situation is being described? What are the conflicts or tensions in this situation? How is setting—social situation, physical place, and time—important to the speaker? What ideas is the speaker communicating? Matthew Arnold's "Dover Beach" provides an example of how you can use most of these questions to get at the meanings of a poem.

DOVER BEACH

MATTHEW ARNOLD

The sea is calm to-night.
The tide is full, the moon lies fair
Upon the straits; on the French coast the light
Gleams and is gone; the cliffs of England stand,
Glimmering and vast, out in the tranquil bay.

Come to the window, sweet is the night-air!
Only, from the long line of spray
Where the sea meets the moon-blanched land,
Listen! you hear the grating roar
Of pebbles which the waves draw back, and fling,
At their return, up the high strand,
Begin, and cease, and then again begin,
With tremulous cadence slow, and bring
The eternal note of sadness in.

Sophocles long ago
Heard it on the Aegean, and it brought
Into his mind the turbid ebb and flow
Of human misery; we
Find also in the sound a thought,
Hearing it by this distant northern sea.

The Sea of Faith
Was once, too, at the full, and round earth's shore
Lay like the folds of a bright girdle furled.
But now I only hear
Its melancholy, long, withdrawing roar,
Retreating, to the breath
Of the night-wind, down the vast edges drear
And naked shingles* of the world.

Ah, love, let us be true
To one another! for the world, which seems
To lie before us like a land of dreams,
So various, so beautiful, so new,
Hath really neither joy, nor love, nor light,
Nor certitude, nor peace, nor help for pain;
And we are here as on a darkling plain
Swept with confused alarms of struggle and flight,
Where ignorant armies clash by night.

*beaches covered with pebbles

Because Dover is an English port city, one of several points of departure for the European continent, the speaker has apparently stopped for the night on his way to Europe. As he looks out of his hotel window, he speaks to another person in the room, his "love" (last stanza). Arnold traces the speaker's train of thought in four stanzas. In the first stanza, the speaker describes what he sees, and his tone is contented, even joy-ous. He sees the lights on the French coast and the high white cliffs of Dover "glimmering" in the moonlight. He invites his companion to share the glorious view. As he describes the sound of the surf to her, his tone alters slightly; the sound reminds him of "the eternal note of sad-ness." This melancholy tone deepens in the second stanza. There the speaker connects the sea sound with a passage in Sophocles, probably the third chorus of *Antigone*, which compares the misery of living under a family curse to the incessant roar of a stormy sea beating against the land.

In the third stanza, the remembrance of Sophocles's comparison leads the speaker to make a more disturbing comparison of his own. He likens the sea to faith—apparently religious faith, both his own and that of his age. He says that at one time the "Sea of Faith" was full but now has withdrawn, leaving a "vast," "drear," and coarse world. By the fourth stanza, the speaker has fallen into near despair. He says that what merely looks beautiful—the panorama seen from his window—is only a false image of the world, which in reality is absurd and chaotic. He has only one hope, his companion, whom he now urges to be true to him as he is true to her. The speaker, in short, is an erudite, thoughtful, but deeply troubled person. The poem takes him from momentary content-edness to near hopelessness. The stimulus for his train of thought is the place of the poem—Dover Beach—and the companion to whom he ad-dresses his remarks. All these elements—thoughts, place, and compan-ion—are interrelated.

■ Thinking on Paper about Characterization, Point of View, Plot, Setting, and Theme

Many of the exercises one does on poetry consist of marking the poem itself. You might, then, photocopy the poem you want to interpret and write on the photocopy rather than the book. Some photocopy ma-chines will enlarge images. Since poems are often published in small print, taking advantage of this feature would allow you to better see the poem and have more space to write. You might want to make more than one copy of the poem. Use different copies for marking different as-pects of the poem.

1. Find the subject, verb, and object of every sentence in the poem. Sometimes this will be easy; reading poetry will be like reading

clear prose. But sometimes it will not. Because poetry often conforms to structural requirements and because it is a condensed form of communication, sentence structures are sometimes distorted and words are left out. In such cases, you will have to put the sentence in normal order and insert missing words.

2. Paraphrase the poem. This helps you understand every sentence or, at least, the major sections of the poem. The two paragraphs immediately following "Dover Beach" (pp. 89–90), for example, are a paraphrase of the poem.

3. Identify the speaker of the poem. Underline the words and phrases that help characterize the speaker and bring out the speaker's concerns. Describe in detail the traits of the speaker and of any other characters in the poem.

4. Describe the situation of the poem: where the speaker is, what time of day it is, what season of the year, what historical occasion, to whom the speaker is speaking, why. List the external and internal conflicts of the poem.

5. State the issues that concern the speaker (what the poem is about). Explain the speaker's ideas (the themes of the poem). Note any changes in the speaker's mood or ideas as the poem moves from unit to unit. Explain what the speaker is trying to accomplish.

6. Describe the speaker's tone (angry, lyrical, hopeful, bitter, nostalgic, sarcastic, compassionate, admiring, sorrowful, amused, and so forth). Note any changes of tone.

7. If the speaker is not the poet, estimate the poet's attitude toward the speaker and to the issues raised by the poem. Indicate any differences between the poet's attitude and the speaker's.

8. Describe important contrasts made in the poem. Explain their relationships to characterization and theme.

9. Relate the poem's title to its themes.

10. Explain any allusions in the poem. An *allusion* is a reference to historical events and people, to mythological and biblical figures, and to works of literature. Allusions invite comparison between the work at hand and the items referred to. An example of an allusion is Arnold's reference to Sophocles in "Dover Beach." Arnold invites us to bring the weight of Sophocles's tragedies to bear on the subject matter of his poem. An allusion is a compact way of adding meaning to the work. Explain, then, the implications of the allusions.

Diction

Basically, *diction* refers to the poet's choice of words. Poets are sensitive to the subtle shades of meanings of words, to the possible double meanings of words, and to the denotative and connotative meanings of words. As we say in Chapter 2, *denotation* is the object or idea—the referent—that a word represents. The denotation of a word is its core meaning, its dictionary meaning. *Connotation* is the subjective, emotional association that a word has for one person or a group of people. Poets often choose words that contribute to the poem's meaning on both a denotational and a connotational level.

Questions about diction   Examine the words in a poem for all their possible shades and levels of meaning. Then ask how these meanings combine to create an overall effect. Note, for example, the effect that connotation creates in William Wordsworth's "A Slumber Did My Spirit Seal."

A SLUMBER DID MY SPIRIT SEAL

WILLLIAM WORDSWORTH

A slumber did my spirit seal;
I had no human fears—
She seemed a thing that could not feel
The touch of earthly years.

No motion has she now, no force;
She neither hears nor sees;
Rolled round in earth's diurnal course,
With rocks, and stones, and trees.

In order to create the stark contrast between the active, airy girl of the first stanza with the inert, dead girl of the second, Wordsworth relies partly on the connotative effect of the last line. We know the denotative meaning of "rocks, and stones, and trees," but in this context the emotional or connotative meaning is unpleasant and grating. Rocks and stones are inanimate, cold, cutting, impersonal. And although we usually think of trees as beautiful and majestic, here the association of trees with rocks and stones makes us think of tree roots, of dirt, and thus of the girl's burial. The rocks and stones and trees are not only not human, they confine and smother the girl. Another example of connotation is the word *diurnal*, which means "daily." But the Latinate *diurnal* has a slightly more formal connotation than the prosaic *daily*. The effect of the word is to make the processes of nature—death, the revolving of Earth, the existence of rocks and stones and trees—seem remote, remorseless, and inevitable.

Be alert for wordplay—double meanings and puns. The speaker in Andrew Marvell's "To His Coy Mistress," for example, tries to persuade a reluctant woman to make love with him. His argument is that time is running out, and unless we take opportunities when they appear, we will lose them. He concludes his speech with a pun:

> Thus, though we cannot make our sun
> Stand still, yet we will make him run.

That is, we cannot stop time (make the sun stop), but we can bring about new life (a child: "son"), who will "run," and thus defeat decay and death. Some poets, such as e.e. cummings, make imaginative wordplay a dominant trait of their poetry. In "anyone lived in a pretty how town," cummings uses pronouns on two levels of meaning. The words *anyone* and *noone* mean, on the one hand, what we expect them to mean ("anybody" and "nobody"); but on the other hand they refer to two people, male and female, who fall in love, marry, and die.

■ Thinking on Paper about Diction

1. Circle all the words you do not know. Look them up in the dictionary.

2. Underline words that seem especially meaningful or well chosen. For each word, explain denotations and connotations.

3. Underline any wordplay such as double meanings and puns. Explain what the wordplay adds to the sense of the poem.

4. Underline any uses of "unusual" words—slang, profanity, archaisms, foreign language words, made-up words. Explain what qualities and meanings these words add to the poem. Discuss how the poem would be different without them.

5. Identify the level of diction in the poem (formal, informal, colloquial, slangy, dialect). Explain what the poem gains from the use of this level. Explain what it would lose by changing to a different level.

6. Explain how the choice of words contributes to the speaker's tone.

Imagery: Descriptive Language

When applied to poetry, the term *imagery* has two meanings. First, imagery represents the descriptive passages of a poem. Although the word *imagery* calls to mind the visual sense, poetic imagery appeals to all the senses. Sensuous imagery is pleasurable for its own sake, but it also provides concreteness and immediacy. Imagery causes the reader to become personally and experientially involved in the subject matter of the poem. Further, the poet often uses descriptive imagery to underscore other elements in a poem. The selection of detail and the vividness imparted to images help create tone, meaning, and characterization.

An example of descriptive imagery is the first stanza of John Keats's narrative poem "The Eve of St. Agnes":

> St. Agnes' Eve—Ah, bitter chill it was!
> The owl, for all his feathers, was a-cold;
> The hare limped trembling through the frozen grass,
> And silent was the flock in woolly fold;
> Numb were the Beadsman's fingers, while he told
> His rosary, and while his frosted breath,
> Like pious incense from a censer old,
> Seemed taking flight for heaven, without a death,
> Past the sweet Virgin's picture, while his prayer he saith.

This stanza appeals to the thermal sense (the chill of the evening, the frozen grass), the sense of touch (the beadsman's numb fingers), the visual sense (the beadsman saying his rosary before the picture of the Virgin), the sense of motion (the hare trembling and limping through the grass, the beadsman's frosted breath taking flight toward heaven), and the sense of sound (the silent flock, the sound of the beadsman's monotonous prayer). The dominant sensuous appeal, however, is to the thermal sense. Keats uses every sensuous image in the stanza to make us feel how cold the night is.

Imagery: Figurative Language

Critics today use *imagery* in a second sense. They use it to mean figurative language, especially metaphor. *Figurative language* is the conscious departure from normal or conventional ways of saying things. This could mean merely a rearrangement of the normal word order of a sentence, such as the following: "Sir Gawain the dragon slew" or "With this ring I thee wed." Such unusual rearrangements are called "rhetorical" figures of speech. But much more common and important to poetry is a second category of figurative language: tropes. *Tropes* (literally, "turns") extend the meaning of words beyond their literal meaning, and the most common form of trope is metaphor. *Metaphor* has both a general and a specific meaning. Generally, it means any analogy. An *analogy* is a similarity between things that are basically different. Specifically, metaphor means a particular kind of analogy and is contrasted with the simile. A *simile* uses *like* or *as* to claim similarities between things that are essentially different; for example, "Her tears were like falling rain." The following stanza from Shakespeare's "Fair Is My Love" contains several similes (indicated by the added italics):

Fair is my love, but not so fair as fickle;
Mild as a dove, but neither true nor trusty;
Brighter than glass, and yet, *as glass is, brittle;*
Softer than wax, and yet, *as iron, rusty;*
A lily pale, with damask dye to grace her;
None fairer, nor none falser to deface her.

A metaphor also claims similarities between things that are essentially unlike, but it eliminates the comparative words (such as *like*) and thus equates the compared items. For example, "My heart was a tornado of passion" (not "My heart was like a tornado of passion"). The poem "Love Is a Sickness" by Samuel Daniel contains three metaphors—love is a sickness, love is a plant, love is a tempest—indicated here by the italics:

LOVE IS A SICKNESS

SAMUEL DANIEL

Love is a sickness full of woes,
    All remedies refusing.
A *plant* that with most cutting grows,
    Most barren with best using.
            Why so?

More we enjoy it, more it dies,
If not enjoyed it sighing cries,
            Hey ho.

Love is a torment of the mind,
    A *tempest* everlasting,

And Jove hath made it of a kind
Not well, nor full, nor fasting.
                    Why so?

More we enjoy it, more it dies,
If not enjoyed it sighing cries,
                    Hey ho.

Analogies can be directly stated or implied. The similes and metaphors in the above poems by Shakespeare and Daniel are directly stated analogies; but when Daniel in the last lines of each stanza says that love "sighs," he implies a kind of analogy called *personification;* he pretends that love has the attributes of a person. When the poet develops just one analogy throughout the whole poem, the analogy is called an *extended metaphor.* Thomas Campion's "There Is a Garden in Her Face" contains an extended metaphor comparing the features of a woman's face to the features of a garden:

THERE IS A GARDEN IN HER FACE

THOMAS CAMPION

There is a garden in her face,
Where roses and white lilies grow,
A heavenly paradise is that place,
Wherein all pleasant fruits do flow.
There cherries grow, which none may buy
Till "Cherry ripe!"* themselves do cry.

Those cherries fairly do enclose
Of orient pearl a double row;
Which when her lovely laughter shows,
They look like rosebuds filled with snow.
Yet them nor peer nor prince can buy,
Till "Cherry ripe!" themselves do cry.
Her eyes like angels watch them still;
Her brows like bended bows do stand,
Threatening with piercing frowns to kill
All that attempt with eye or hand
Those sacred cherries to come nigh,
Till "Cherry ripe!" themselves do cry.

*A familiar cry of London street vendors

Questions about imagery   Imagery is an important—some would argue the most important—characteristic of poetry. You should try to identify the imagery of a poem. Ask, then, what senses the poet appeals to and what analogies he or she implies or states directly. Ask, *Why* does the poet use these particular images and analogies? In "Dover Beach," for example, Arnold uses both descriptive and metaphorical imagery meaningfully. He emphasizes two senses: the visual and the aural. He begins with the visual—the moon, the lights of France across the water, the cliffs, the tranquil bay—and throughout the poem he associates hope and beauty with what the speaker sees. But the poet soon introduces the aural sense—the grating roar of the sea—which serves as an antithesis to the visual sense. These two senses create a tension that mirrors the conflict in the speaker's mind. The first two stanzas show the speaker merely drifting into a perception of this conflict, connecting sight with hope and sound with sadness. By the third stanza, he has become intellectually alert to the full implications of the conflict. He signals this alertness with a carefully worked out analogy, his comparison of the sea with faith. In the fourth stanza, he sums up his despairing conclusion with a stunning and famous simile:

> And we are here as on a darkling plain
> Swept with confused alarms of struggle and flight,
> Where ignorant armies clash by night.

This final analogy achieves several purposes. First, it brings the implication of the descriptive imagery to a logical conclusion. No longer can the speaker draw hope from visual beauty; in this image, he cannot see at all—it is night, the plain is dark. He can only hear, but the sound now is more chaotic and directly threatening than the mere ebb and flow of the sea. Second, the analogy provides an abrupt change of setting. Whereas before, the speaker visualized an unpeopled plain, now he imagines human beings as agents of destruction. He implies that a world without faith must seem and be arbitrary and violent. Finally, the analogy allows the speaker to identify his own place in this new world order. Only loyalty is pure and good, so he and his companion must cling to each other and maneuver throughout the world's battlefields as best they can.

■ Thinking on Paper about Descriptive Language

1. Mark the descriptive images. For each image, name the sense appealed to. Characterize the dominant impression these images make.

2. Explain the relationship of descriptive images to the speaker's state of mind.

3. Describe how the descriptive images create a sense of the time of day and season of the year.

4. Note any progression in the descriptive images; for example, from day to night, hot to cold, soft to loud, color to color, slow to fast.

5. Explain how the descriptive images help create atmosphere and mood. Slow movements, for example, are conducive to melancholy; speed to exuberance and excitement.

■ Thinking on Paper about Figurative Language

1. Mark the similes in the poem. Underline or circle the words that signal the comparisons (words such as *like, as, similar to, resembles*). Explain the implications of the analogies (that is, what they contribute to the meaning of the poem).

2. Mark the metaphors in the poem. Explain the implications of the analogies.

3. Mark any personification in the poem. Underline the words and phrases that make the personification clear.

4. Poets often use analogies to help make an abstract quality, such as "love" or "my love's beauty" or "my current predicament" or "the destructive effect of time" or "God's grandeur," concrete and knowable. They do so by comparing the abstract quality to something the reader knows well. Almost always this "something" is a physical object or reality. Name the abstract quality the poet wants to clarify and the object the poet is comparing it to. List the qualities of the object. Explain how the comparison has clarified the abstraction.

5. List the senses appealed to in each analogy. Describe the dominant sensuous impression created by the analogies.

Rhythm

All human speech has rhythm, but poetry often regularizes that rhythm into recognizable patterns. These patterns are called *meters*. Metrical patterns vary depending on the sequence in which one arranges the accented (á) and unaccented (ă) syllables of an utterance. The unit that determines that arrangement is the foot. A *foot* is one unit of rhythm in a verse. Probably the most natural foot in English is the iambic, which has an unaccented syllable followed by an accented syllable (ăá). Here are the most common metrical feet:

iamb (iambic) ăá	ăbóve
trochee (trochaic) áă	lóvelў
anapest (anapestic) ăăá	ŏvĕrwhélm
dactyl (dactylic) áăă	róyăltў
spondee (spondaic) áá	bréak, bréak

Poets further determine the arrangement of metrical patterns by the number of feet in each line. The following names apply to the lengths of poetic lines:

monometer (one foot)

dimeter (two feet)

trimeter (three feet)

tetrameter (four feet)

pentameter (five feet)

hexameter (six feet)

heptameter (seven feet)

octameter (eight feet)

A very common line in English poetry is iambic pentameter; it contains five iambic feet. Shakespeare wrote his plays in iambic pentameter, and the sonnet is traditionally composed in iambic pentameter (see pages 107–108 for some examples).

Another feature of line length is that each line may have a fixed number of syllables. When people speak of iambic pentameter, they usually think of a line containing five accented syllables and ten syllables in all. Even if the poet substitutes other feet for iambs, the number of syllables in the line comes out the same—ten for iambic pentameter, eight for iambic tetrameter, six for iambic trimeter, and so forth. When a line of poetry is measured by both accents and syllables, it is called *accentual–syllabic*. Most English poetry is accentual–syllabic, as in these iambic tetrameter lines from "To His Coy Mistress":

Hăd wé bŭt wórld ĕnoúgh, ańd tiḿe,
Thĭs cóynešs, ládў, weré nŏ críme.

Each line has four iambic feet—four accented syllables, eight syllables in all. But not all English poetry is accentual–syllabic. Sometimes it is just accentual. Traditional ballads, for example, often count the number of accents per line but not the number of syllables:

"O whére hae ye beén, Lord Rándal, my són?
O wheŕe hae ye beén, my hańdsome young mán?"
"I hae beén to the wíld woód; móther, máke my bed soón,
For I'm weáry wi huńting, and fáin wald lie dówn."

The third line of this stanza contains six accented syllables but thirteen (not twelve) syllables. The first two lines contain four accents but ten (not eight) syllables. And the last line contains four accents but twelve (not eight) syllables. The important factor in purely accentual lines is where the accent falls; the poet can freely use the accents to emphasize meaning. One of the accents in line three, for example, falls on *wild*, which expresses the treacherous place from which Lord Randal has returned.

Because individuals hear and speak a language in different ways, *scanning* a poem (using symbols to mark accented and unaccented syllables and thus to identify its metrical pattern) is not an exact science. Some poets establish easily recognizable—often strongly rhythmical— metrical patterns, and scanning their poems is easy. Other poets use more subtle rhythms that make the poetic lines less artificial and more like colloquial language. The best poets often deliberately depart from the metrical pattern they establish at the beginning of the poem. When you scan a poem, therefore, you need not force phrases unnaturally into the established metrical pattern. Always put the accents where you and most speakers would normally say them. The poet probably intends them to go there.

When you scan a poem, be alert for caesuras. A *caesura* is a strong pause somewhere in the line. You mark a caesura with two vertical lines: ‖ Consider the caesuras in this jump-rope rhyme:

Cinderella, dressed in yellow,
Went upstairs ‖ to kiss a fellow.
Made a mistake; ‖ kissed a snake.
How many doctors did it take?
One, two, three, four . . .

A likely place for a caesura is in the middle of the line, and if the meter of the poem is tetrameter, then a caesura in the middle neatly divides the line in half. Such is the case in lines 2 and 3 of this poem. A caesura may also occur near the beginning of a line or near the end. Or there may be no caesuras in a line, as is probably the case in lines 4, 5, and possibly 1 of this poem. Caesuras often emphasize meaning. Caesuras in the middle of lines, for example, can emphasize strong contrasts or close relationships between ideas. In line 3, both the caesura and the rhyme of "mistake" with "snake" link the abstraction (the mistake) with the action (kissing the snake).

A profound example of the relationship between meaning and caesura—indeed, between meaning and all the qualities of poetic sound—is Shakespeare's Sonnet 129:

SONNET 129

WILLIAM SHAKESPEARE

Th' expense of spirit ‖ in a waste of shame
Is lust in action; ‖ and, till action, lust
Is perjured, murderous, bloody, full of blame,
Savage, extreme, rude, cruel, not to trust;
Enjoyed no sooner ‖ but despisèd straight;   5
Past reason hunted; ‖ and no sooner had,
Past reason hated, ‖ as a swallowed bait,
On purpose laid ‖ to make the taker mad;
Mad in pursuit, ‖ and in possession so;
Had, having, and in quest to have, extreme;   10
A bliss in proof; ‖ and proved, a very woe;
Before, a joy proposed; ‖ behind, a dream.
All this the world well knows; ‖ yet none knows well
To shun the heaven ‖ that leads men to this hell.

Here Shakespeare establishes a pattern of contrasts and similarities, and uses caesura and other sound devices to establish them. One of these devices is the accentual pattern. Like most sonnets, this one has ten syllables per line and is supposed to be iambic pentameter. But for many of these lines, Shakespeare has only four accents per line, not five. This allows him to make some of his comparisons equal in weight. Line 5, for example, has a strong caesura and four accented syllables:

Enjóyed no soóner || but despiśèd straíght.

The effect is to contrast strongly the two emotional states, pleasure and guilt; and since Shakespeare puts guilt last, he gives it more weight. Lines 11 and 12, however, contain caesuras and five accents each, making the two-part divisions within the lines unequal. Note how this relates to the meaning of the lines:

A bliśs in próof; || and próved, a véry wóe;
Befóre, a jóy propósed; || behińd, a dréam.

The "weaker" sides of the lines contain the pleasure part of the equation and emphasize the brevity and insubstantial quality of pleasure; the "strong" sides emphasize either naïve expectation or guilt.

Questions about rhythm   Metrics has many uses in poetry. It provides a method of ordering material. It creates a hypnotic effect that rivets attention on the poem. Like the rhythmic qualities of music, it is enjoyable for itself. Children, for example, take naturally to the strongly rhythmic qualities of nursery rhymes and jump-rope rhymes; jump-rope rhymes, in fact, are that rare form of literature that children teach each other. But probably the greatest importance of metrics is that it establishes a pattern from which the poet can depart. Good poets rarely adhere to the metrical pattern they establish at the beginning of the poem or that is inherent in a fixed form like the sonnet. Sonnet 129, on page 101, is a striking example. Sometimes poets stray from the established pattern to make the language sound more colloquial. Such is partly the case in "Dover Beach" and Browning's "My Last Duchess," both of which are spoken by fictional characters. Sometimes poets alter the pattern to emphasize specific aspects of the poem's content. This is why you should be sensitive to the natural rhythms of the language when you scan a poem. Take, for example, these lines from Sonnet 129: Lust is like

a swallowed bait,	7
On purpose laid to make the taker mad:	8
Mád iñ pŭrsuít, añd iñ pŏsséssiŏn só;	9
Hád, háving, añd iñ quést tŏ háve, ĕxtréme;	10
A bliss in proof; and proved, a very woe;	11
Before, a joy proposed; behind, a dream.	12

All these lines fit the iambic scheme except lines 9 and 10. Why? A possible reason is that Shakespeare wanted to emphasize certain words in these two lines, particularly the first words in each. The accents in line 10 are especially emphatic, for the accents emphasize the past ("had"), the present ("having"), the future ("quest" and "have"), and the psychological and moral nature of all three ("extreme").

Questions to ask about rhythm in poetry, then, are these: Which metrical pattern does the poem use? What is appealing about the pattern? How closely does the poet stick to the established pattern? If closely, why and what effect is the poet striving for? For example, does the poem have a singsong quality? If so, why does the poet do this? Where does the poem vary from the established pattern? Why? How does the poet use pauses, especially caesuras, within each line? Why?

■ Thinking on Paper about Rhythm

1. Count the number of syllables for each line. Write the number at the end of the line.

2. Read the poem aloud, then mark the accented and unaccented syllables of each line.

3. Draw a vertical line between each foot in the line.

4. Identify the metrical pattern (iambic, trochaic, and so forth) and the length of the lines (pentameter, hexameter, and so forth).

5. Use two vertical lines to mark the caesuras in the poem. Explain how the caesuras relate to the sense of each line.

6. Underline the places where the poet departs from the established metrical pattern of the poem. Explain how these departures relate to the sense of each line. Show which words are emphasized by the departures.

7. Explain the appropriateness of the metrical pattern to the poem's meaning.

8. Describe how easy or difficult it is to read the poem aloud. Does its metrical pattern slow you down? Or does it allow you to read smoothly? Explain how the difficulty or ease of reading the metrical pattern relates to the poem's meaning and purpose.

Sound

Poets delight in the sound of language and consciously present sounds to be enjoyed for themselves. They also use them to emphasize meaning, action, and emotion, and especially to call the reader's attention to the relationship of certain words. Rhyme, for example, has the effect of linking words together. Among the most common sound devices are the following:

onomatopoeia—The use of words that sound like what they mean ("buzz," "boom," "hiss," "fizz," "pop," "glug").

alliteration—the repetition of consonant sounds at the beginning of words or at the beginning of accented syllables ("the *w*oeful *w*oman *w*ent *w*ading *W*ednesday").

assonance—the repetition of vowel sounds followed by different consonant sounds ("*O*, the gr*o*ans that *o*pened to his ears").

consonance (or *half-rhyme*)—the repetition of final consonant sounds that are preceded by different vowel sounds ("the beas*t* climbed fas*t* to the cres*t*"). Consonance is the opposite of alliteration, which features initial consonant sounds.

rhyme—the repetition of accented vowels and the sounds that follow. There are subcategories of rhyme:
  masculine rhyme (the rhymed sounds have only one syllable: "ma*n*–ra*n*," "detec*t*–correc*t*").
  feminine rhyme (the rhymed sounds have two or more syllables: "*subtle*–re*buttal*," "de*ceptively*–per*ceptively*").
  internal rhyme (the rhymed sounds are within the line).
  end rhyme (the rhymed sounds appear at the ends of lines).
  approximate rhyme (the words are close to rhyming: "book–buck," "watch–match," "man–in").

Edgar Allan Poe's "To Helen" illustrates many of these sound devices:

TO HELEN

EDGAR ALLAN POE

Helen, thy beauty is to me
Like those Nicean barks of yore,
That gently, o'er a perfumed sea,
alliteration   The weary, way-worn wanderer bore
To his own native shore.   5

masculine rhyme/ end rhyme

consonance

On desperate (seas) long wont to roam   6
Thy hyacinth hair, thy classic (face)
Thy Naiad (airs) have brought me home   approximate rhyme   8
To the glory that was (Greece)
And the grandeur that was Rome.

assonance

Lo! in yon brilliant window-nich   11
How statue-like I (see)(thee) stand!   internal rhyme
The agate lamp within thy hand,
Ah! Psyche, from the regions which
Are Holy Land!

Questions about sound   It's easy to lose yourself in an analysis of the mechanical intricacies of a poem's sound structure and forget why you are making the analysis in the first place. You start with the question: What sound devices does the poet use? But you move on to ask: Why does the poet use them? How do they help establish the poem's tone, atmosphere, theme, setting, characterization, and emotional qualities? What meanings do they suggest? In Poe's "To Helen," for example, the alliteration in line 4 ("*w*eary, *w*ay-*w*orn *w*anderer") underscores the fatigued state of the wanderer. The consonance of "seas" and "airs" in lines 6 and 8 emphasizes the contrast between them; one is "desperate" but the other assuages despair. And the assonance in line 11 ("*i*n yon br*i*lliant w*i*ndow-n*i*ch"), with its emphasis on high, tight, "i" sounds, helps to characterize the luminosity of the place where Helen, statuelike, stands.

Be especially alert to relationships between ideas established by rhyme, most notably by internal rhyme and end rhyme. Rhyme is, of course, a musical device that makes the sound of the poem attractive to the ear, but it can be used meaningfully as well. Turn back to Sonnet 129 and examine the complex sound associations Shakespeare creates there. The words sound rough, almost painful, with their harsh consonants, all of which illustrate the frustrated and frenetic emotional state Shakespeare ascribes to lust. Note the variation on "s" sounds in the first line:

Th' expense of spirit in a waste of shame

Line 3 begins a list of qualities, and Shakespeare divides and associates them through assonance and alliteration: Lust

Is perjured, murderous, bloody, full of blame.

The words *perjured* and *murderous* are linked by assonance (the "er" sounds) and focus on evil deeds (falsehood, murder), leading to the second half of the line. The words *bloody* and *blame* are linked by alliteration and focus on the results of evil deeds, especially murder: blood and guilt. The linkages signaled by the poem's end rhyme are also meaningful: shame/blame, lust/not to trust, no sooner had/make the taker mad, extreme/dream, yet none knows well/leads men to this hell.

In the poem you are analyzing, what linkages of meaning are there to *all* the sound qualities of the words—especially to the obvious ones, such as alliteration, internal rhyme, and end rhyme? What light do these linkages throw on the themes of the entire poem?

■ Thinking on Paper about Sound

1. Underline instances of alliteration, assonance, and consonance in the poem. Explain the relationship between these devices and the sense of the lines where they occur.

2. Circle rhymed words. Explain what similarities and contrasts the rhymed words call attention to.

3. Circle words that have meaningful or attractive sound qualities, such as onomatopoetic words. Explain how these words add to the poem's sense.

4. When the sounds of a poem are harsh and grating, the effect is called *cacophony*. When they are pleasing and harmonious, the effect is called *euphony*. Underline instances of cacophony or euphony. Explain how they relate to the poem's sense.

5. Describe any sound devices in the poem that catch you by surprise. Explain how and why the poet uses such surprises.

Structure

Poets give structure to their poems in two overlapping ways: by organizing ideas according to a logical plan and by creating a pattern of sounds. Arnold arranges "Dover Beach" in both ways, as do most poets. He divides the poem into four units, each of which has a pattern of end rhyme, and he arranges the whole poem rhetorically—that is, by ideas. Each unit elaborates a single point, and each point follows logically from the preceding one.

Perhaps the most common sound device by which poets create structure is end rhyme, and any pattern of end rhyme is called a *rhyme scheme*. Rhyme scheme helps to establish another structural device, the *stanza*, which is physically separated from other stanzas (by a space inserted between each stanza) and usually represents one idea. The stanzas in a poem typically resemble one another structurally. They have the same number of lines, length of lines, metrical patterns, and rhyme schemes. Poets can, of course, create any rhyme scheme or stanza form they choose, but they often work instead within the confines of already established poetic structures. These are called *fixed forms*. Stanzas that conform to no traditional limits, such as those in "Dover Beach," are called *nonce forms*. The most famous fixed form in English is the *sonnet*. Like other fixed forms, the sonnet provides ready-made structural divisions by which a poet can organize ideas. But it also challenges poets to mold unwieldy material into an unyielding structure. The result is a tension between material and form that is pleasing to both poet and reader.

All sonnets consist of fourteen lines of iambic pentameter. The two best known kinds of sonnets are named for their most famous practitioners. A *Shakespearean sonnet* rhymes abab/cdcd/efef/gg and has a structural division of three quatrains (each containing four lines) and a couplet. A *Petrarchan sonnet* rhymes abbaabba in the octave (the first eight lines) and cdecde in the sestet (the last six lines). Poets often vary the pattern of end rhyme in these kinds of sonnets; this is especially true of the sestet in the Petrarchan sonnet. Note, for example, the sonnet below by Wordsworth. Each kind of sonnet has a *turn*, a point in the poem at which the poet shifts from one meaning or mood to another. The turn in the Shakespearean sonnet occurs between lines 12 and 13 (just before the couplet). The turn in the Petrarchan sonnet occurs between the octave and the sestet. In both forms, the part of the poem before the turn delineates a problem or tension; the part after the turn offers some resolution to or comment on the problem, and it releases the tension.

SONNET 116

WILLIAM SHAKESPEARE

three quatrains	Let me not to the marriage of true minds	a
	Admit impediments. Love is not love	b
	Which alters when it alteration finds,	a
	Or bends with the remover to remove:	b 4

Oh, no! it is an ever-fixèd mark,	c	
That looks on tempests and is never shaken;	d	
It is the star to every wandering bark,	c	
Whose worth's unknown, although his height be taken,	d	8
Love's not Time's fool, though rosey lips and cheeks	e	
Within his bending sickle's compass come;	f	
Love alters not with his brief hours and weeks,	e	
But bears it out even to the edge of doom.	f	12
If this be error and upon me proved,	g	
I never writ, nor no man ever loved.	g	14

three quatrains (cont'd)

turn →
couplet

Shakespeare molds the ideas and images of this poem to fit its form perfectly. He states the theme—that love remains constant no matter what—in the first quatrain. In the second, he says that cataclysmic events cannot destroy love. In the third, he says that time cannot destroy love. Finally, in the couplet, he affirms the truth of his theme.

THE WORLD IS TOO MUCH WITH US

WILLIAM WORDSWORTH

The world is too much with us; late and soon,	a	
Getting and spending, we lay waste our powers;	b	
Little we see in nature that is ours;	b	
We have given our hearts away, a sordid boon!	a	4
This Sea that bares her bosom to the moon,	a	
The winds that will be howling at all hours,	b	
And are up-gathered now like sleeping flowers,	b	
For this, for everything, we are out of tune;	a	8
It moves us not.—Great God! I'd rather be	c	
A Pagan suckled in a creed outworn;	d	
So might I, standing on this pleasant lea,	c	
Have glimpses that would make me less forlorn;	d	
Have sight of Proteus rising from the sea;	c	
Or hear old Triton blow his wreathèd horn.	d	14

octave

turn →

sestet

Wordsworth uses the structure of the Petrarchan sonnet to shape his ideas. In the octave he states his general theme: that materialistic values and activities dull our sensitivity to nature. But he divides the octave into two quatrains. In the first he states his theme; in the second he exemplifies it. He then uses the sestet to suggest an alternate attitude, one that might produce a greater appreciation of nature's mystery and majesty.

Questions about structure You can find definitions of many fixed forms—ballad, ode, heroic couplet, Alexandrine stanza, rhyme royal stanza, Spenserian stanza, and so forth—by looking them up in handbooks of literature (such as those by Abrams and Harmon and Holman). However, since poets do not always use fixed forms, and since there are many ways to give poetry structure, try to answer this question: What devices does the poet use to give the poem structure? Does the poet use rhyme scheme, stanzas, double spaces, indentations, repetition of words and images, line lengths, rhetorical organization? As with rhythm and sound, a follow-up question is of equal consequence: How does the poem's structure emphasize or relate to its meaning? An example of such a relationship is the final stanza of "Dover Beach," in which Arnold uses end rhyme to emphasize opposing worldviews:

Ah, love, let us be true	a
To one another! for the world, which seems	b
To lie before us like a land of dreams,	b
So various, so beautiful, so new,	u
Hath really neither joy, nor love, nor light,	c
Nor certitude, nor peace, nor help for pain;	d
And we are here as on a darkling plain	d
Swept with confused alarms of struggle and flight,	c
Where ignorant armies clash by night.	c

The rhyme scheme of the first four lines is almost the same as the next five lines; the only difference is the addition of the fifth line. This similarity divides the stanza in half, and the difference in rhymes corresponds to the difference of the ideas in the two halves (the new, beautiful world versus the war-torn, chaotic, threatening world).

■ Thinking on Paper about Structure

1. Mark the rhyme scheme of the poem or stanza. (Use the three examples on pages 107, 108, and above as models for doing this.)
2. Draw horizontal lines between each division or unit of the poem. In a sonnet, for example, mark divisions between quatrains, couplets,

octaves, and sestets. (Use the same poems mentioned in the above assignments.)

3. Summarize the meaning of each division of the poem. In a Shakespearean sonnet, for example, summarize the meaning of each quatrain and the couplet. In a Petrarchan sonnet, summarize the meaning of the octave (and the quatrains within the octave) and the sestet. For both kinds of sonnet, indicate how the meaning changes after the turn.

4. Within the poem or stanza, summarize the relationships between ideas suggested by the end rhyme. A couplet, for example, wherever it may appear in the poem or stanza, almost always states one idea or indicates a close connection between the sense of the two lines.

5. If one or more lines are shorter or longer than most of the others, describe the effect of that differing length on the sense and impact of the poem or stanza.

6. Account for variations from the established rhyme scheme. Explain how the variations relate to the sense of the poem or stanza.

7. Describe and explain the significance of subtle differences between sections or stanzas in a poem. Ballads, for example, often rely on *incremental repetition*—the repeating of phrases and lines from stanza to stanza but with slight changes. The changes enhance suspense by altering the meaning of each stanza.

8. Outline the units of meaning in the poem. That is, indicate where the poet moves from one idea to another. Show how the units of meaning relate to visual structural divisions (such as stanzas), if they do.

9. Describe the imagery of each unit. Show what images dominate each unit. Show differences in imagery from unit to unit. Explain how the images help create the sense of the unit.

10. Some poems, for instance ballads, the songs in Shakespeare's plays, and popular songs, were meant to be sung. For one of these poems, explain the effect of this intention on the poem (choice of words, metrical pattern, rhyme, other sound devices, stanzaic form). If you can, listen to a recording of the song.

11. Some poems, such as George Herbert's "Easter Wings" and many of the poems by e. e. cummings, create an effect by the way they look on the page. Choose one such poem and explain the relation-

ship between how it looks and other elements of the poem, including rhyme scheme, metrical pattern, line length, word choice, and meaning.

Free Verse

One sometimes puzzling form of poetry is *free verse*. It is puzzling because it seems to lack obvious structural elements. The first practitioner of free verse in modern times was Walt Whitman (beginning with the 1855 edition of *Leaves of Grass*). Many people, when they saw Whitman's poetry for the first time, wondered if it was really poetry. They asked why any "prose" writings could not be arranged into lines of varying lengths and be called poetry. Since Whitman's time, many poets have written in free verse, and there is one very well-known antecedent to Whitman's free verse: the Bible. Hebrew poetry has its own complicated system of rhythms and sound associations, but when it is translated into English it comes out as free verse. Here is a well-known example (from the 1611 King James translation):

> The Lord is my shepherd; I shall not want.
> He maketh me to lie down in green pastures; he leadeth me beside the still waters.
> He restoreth my soul; he leadeth me in the paths of righteousness for his name's sake.
> Yea, though I walk through the valley of the shadow of death, I will fear no evil, for thou art with me; thy rod and thy staff they comfort me.
> Thou preparest a table before me in the presence of mine enemies; thou anointest my head with oil; my cup runneth over.
> Surely goodness and mercy shall follow me all the days of my life, and I will dwell in the house of the Lord forever.

Free verse is "free" in certain ways. It avoids strict adherence to metrical patterns and to fixed line lengths. But it is not entirely "free," because it creates rhythm and sound patterns in other ways. First, it often relies on the sound qualities of words to establish associations within words—assonance, alliteration, internal rhyme, and so forth. Second, it creates rhythm by repeating phrases that have the same syntactical structure. See the Twenty-third Psalm, for example: "He maketh me," "he leadeth me," "he restoreth my soul," "he leadeth me." A more blatant example appears in the "out of" phrases in the first section of Whitman's "Out of the Cradle Endlessly Rocking":

> Out of the cradle endlessly rocking,
> Out of the mockingbird's throat, the musical shuttle,
> Out of the Ninth-month midnight . . .

Third, free verse can establish rhythms within lines by means of phrases of about equal length. Finally, free verse can vary lines meaningfully. Whitman, for example, will sometimes have a series of long lines and then one very short line that comments pertly on the preceding lines or resolves a tension within them.

Questions about free verse   Questions about free-verse poetry should be similar to questions about any poetry. What structural devices—divisions within the poem, line length, repeated syntactical units—does the poet use, and how do they complement the poet's meaning? What patterns of imagery—descriptive and figurative—does the poet use? What sound devices does the poet weave into the poem? Why does the poet choose the words he or she does? Who is the speaker, and to what situation is the speaker responding?

■ Thinking on Paper about Free Verse

1. Read the poem aloud. Note the phrases that create the rhythm of the poem.
2. Underline repeated phrases in the poem, as with the "out of the cradle" phrase in Whitman's poem.
3. Mark with double vertical lines the caesuras in each line of the poem.
4. Mark the accents in each line of the poem.
5. Explain why the lines end where they do.
6. Note any variation between short phrases and long phrases. Explain how these variations relate to the sense of the poem.
7. Explain the relationship between the rhythms of the poem and its meaning and purpose.

8. Mark and account for all of the sound qualities of the poem: alliteration, assonance, cacophony, euphony, internal rhyme, and so forth.

Symbolism

Symbolism appeals to poets because symbols are highly suggestive yet succinct. As we say in Chapter 4, a symbol is an object—usually a physical object—that represents an abstract idea or ideas. The most powerful symbols are those that do not exactly specify the ideas they represent. An example of a symbol in poetry occurs in the Twenty-third Psalm, quoted on page 111. The poem begins with a metaphor: God is like a shepherd and I (the speaker) am like one of his sheep; just as a shepherd takes care of his sheep, so will God take care of me. But the poem shifts from metaphor to symbol with phrases such as "green pastures," "still waters," and particularly "the valley of the shadow of death." The meanings of "green pastures" (nourishment, security, ease) and "still waters" (peace, sustenance, calm) are fairly easy to ascertain. But the meaning of "the valley of the shadow of death" is more difficult. It does not seem to mean just death, but a life experience—perhaps psychological or spiritual—that is somehow related to death (the "shadow" of death) that we must journey through (through the "valley"). Perhaps the indefiniteness of this phrase, combined with its ominous overtones, explains the grip it has had on people's imaginations.

Another example of a symbol in poetry is William Blake's "The Sick Rose" (1794):

THE SICK ROSE

WILLIAM BLAKE

O Rose, thou art sick.
The invisible worm
That flies in the night
In the howling storm

Has found out thy bed
Of crimson joy,
And his dark secret love
Does thy life destroy.

This poem might be understandable as a literal treatment of horticulture: a real rose beset by an insect that preys on roses. But Blake probably means for us to see the rose, the worm, and the action of the worm as symbolic. For one thing, the poem occurs in Blake's collection of poems *Songs of Experience*, suggesting that it represents the ominous aspects of life, particularly human life. For another, much of the poem makes little sense unless it can be taken symbolically: the "howling storm," the bed of "crimson joy," the worm's "dark secret love," for example. What, then, do these things represent? One interpretive approach would be to consider word meanings that Blake, who read widely in symbolic Christian literature, may have had in mind. The archaic meaning of "worm" is dragon, which in Christian romance represented evil and harks back to the devil's appearance to Eve as a snake. Also in Christian romance, the rose represented female beauty and purity and sometimes represented the Virgin Mary. Blake seems, then, to be symbolizing the destruction of purity by evil. The poem probably also has sexual implications, since, for example, the worm (a phallic image) comes at "night" to the rose's "bed." In general, the poem may represent the destruction of all earthly health, innocence, and beauty by mysterious forces. The point is that although we get the drift of Blake's meaning, we do not know precisely what the symbolic equivalents are. Yet the symbols are presented so sensuously and the action so dramatically that the poem grips us with a mesmerizing power.

When you read poetry, be alert for symbols, but persuade yourself—and your reader—that the objects you claim to be symbols were intended as such by the author. Remember that not *every* object in a poem is a symbol. What, then, are the symbols in the poem you are reading? Why do you think they are symbols? What do they mean? In answer to this last question, offer reasonable and carefully thought out explanations for your interpretations. Stay close to what the author seems to have intended the symbols to represent.

■ Thinking on Paper about Symbolism

1. Circle the symbols in the poem.

2. List the possible meanings of each symbol. Explain what evidence suggests these meanings.

3. Explain what each symbol contributes to the overall meaning of the poem.

Works Consulted

Abrams, M. H. *A Glossary of Literary Terms.* Fort Worth: Harcourt, 1999.

Fussell, Paul, Jr. *Poetic Meter and Poetic Form.* New York: Random House, 1967.

Harmon, William, and C. Hugh Holman. *A Handbook to Literature.* 7th ed. Englewood Cliffs: Prentice-Hall, 1995

Preminger, Alex, and T. V. F. Brogan, eds. *The New Princeton Encyclopedia of Poetry and Poetics.* Princeton U P, 1993.

Specialized Approaches to Interpreting Literature

Literary Criticism and Theory

Before the twentieth century, there was little systematic attempt to interpret works of literature, to probe their meanings. Gerald Graff, in *Professing Literature*, his history of literary studies in higher education, says that before then there was a widespread "assumption that great literature was essentially self-interpreting and needed no elaborate interpretation" (20). Instead, students studied classical works such as the *Aeneid* and the *Odyssey* to learn Latin and Greek grammar. They used bits and pieces of literature in English, such as Mark Antony's funeral speech in *Julius Caesar*, for training in oratory (28, 41). Otherwise, people could not believe that "the literature in one's own language needed to be taught in formal classes instead of being enjoyed as part of the normal experience of the community" (19).

Even so, prior to the twentieth century, the investigation of the nature and value of literature had had a long and distinguished history, beginning with Plato and Aristotle and continuing into modern times with such figures as Sir Philip Sidney, John Dryden, Samuel Johnson, William Wordsworth, Samuel Taylor Coleridge, and Matthew Arnold. But their investigations focused primarily on evaluation, not interpretation. They explored what literature is and praised or condemned works that failed to meet whichever standards they deemed essential. In *The Republic*, to cite one extreme example, Plato condemned *all* literature because it stirs up the passions—lust, desire, pain, anger—rather than nurtures the intellect. At the end of the nineteenth century, however, universities began to include courses in modern literature, and teachers and writers began to give attention to interpreting literature.

Accompanying this shift in attitude was the growth of literary theory. In *Literary Theory: A Very Short Introduction* (1999), Jonathan Culler defines literary theory generally as "the systematic account of the nature of literature and of the methods for analyzing it" (1). Through the first half of the twentieth century, a handful of new theories influenced the interpretation and teaching of literature. The most important of these was New Criticism, whose methodology was practical and accessible. But with the discovery of French structuralism in the 1960s, new literary theories swamped the old ones and elicited an enormous body of writings. To get a sense of the scale of this output, compare the *MLA International Bibliography of Books and Articles on the Modern Languages and Literatures* (*MLAIB*) of 1960 to that of today. "MLA" stands for the Modern Language Association, the now huge organization for scholars of modern languages and literatures. Compared to the one-volume *MLAIB* of 1960, the present version consists of five titanic volumes accompanied by expensive and sophisticated computer software.

This near-obsessive interest in literary interpretation and theory is cause for wonder. Right now there seems to be no end to it. "One of the most dismaying features of theory today," Culler says, "is that it is endless. It is not something that you could learn so as to 'know theory.' It is an unbounded corpus of writings which is always being augmented as the young and the restless, in critiques of the guiding conceptions of their elders, promote the contributions to theory of new thinkers and rediscover the work of older, neglected ones" (15). For those who come new to literary theory, Culler's book is an excellent place to begin. Rather than describe in detail the various theoretical approaches (New Criticism, structuralism, deconstruction, feminism, and so forth), Culler addresses the issues that theory since 1960 has taken up. There are numerous books that survey theories. Very readable is Raman Selden and Peter Widdowson's *A Reader's Guide to Contemporary Literary Theory* (1997). One that examines the usefulness of recent theories to interpretation is K. M. Newton's *Interpreting the Text: A Critical Introduction to the Theory and Practice of Literary Interpretation* (1990).

Places for Interpretation

Taking our cue from Culler, we will not survey all current theoretical approaches in this chapter. Rather, we will use some of them to highlight the "places" interpreters can look to find meaning in works of literature. So far, we have concentrated on the work itself—how we can use properties of literature and genres as avenues to meaning in individual works. An expanded version of the author/work/reader pattern, introduced in Chapter 1, provides a comprehensive diagram of all the places to look for meaning in literature.

All of reality

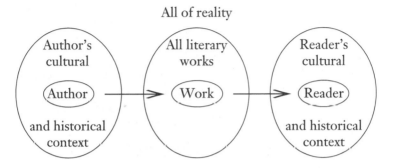

This diagram highlights four general sites of meaning. The first centers on the author, who begins the process of creation and communication. It includes the circumstances of the author's life (biography); the author's values, intentions, and methods of composition (the author as artist); and the events, patterns of life, and beliefs of the author's time (history). The second centers on the work. It encompasses the artistry and elements of the work (its form), the language of the work (its linguistic makeup), and the work's relationship to other works and literary practices (its intertextuality). The third centers on the reader. It includes the individual reader: his or her interests, reading skills, and knowledge. Included also are groups of readers, such as those who first read the work as well as those who read the work now. And, as with authors, it focuses on the influence of environment on readers. The final place is all of reality. This includes the work's connection to the world outside it, its "truth." Just as the work is surrounded by all of reality, so too are authors and readers, all of whom have their own understanding of "reality." Using what they know, authors incorporate aspects of reality in their works. In turn, readers, based on what they know, try to ascertain reality in works of literature.

Interpreters of literature typically deal with more than one of these sites of meaning. When we interpret a work of literature, for example, we may focus largely on the work itself, but we may also draw upon information about an author's life or about philosophical concepts of reality. M. H. Abrams, who in *The Mirror and the Lamp* (1953) originated the concept of sites of meaning, says that theoretical approaches almost always touch on more than one of these places, but most "exhibit a discernible orientation toward one only" (6). We will discuss theoretical approaches here according to which place they mainly illuminate. Since the work of literature is central to all attempts to interpret it, we will start with it.

The Work

Three theoretical approaches—New Criticism, structuralism, and post-structuralism—demand concentrated study of the work of literature itself. Although all three insist that interpreters pay close attention to the details of individual works, structuralism and especially post-structuralism are strong reactions against many of the assumptions of New Criticism. Closely related to the study of individual works is the study of how a work relates to other works, its *intertextuality*. In Chapter 2, we looked at one kind of intertextuality—authors' reliance on conventions and genres to create their own works. In this chapter, we will examine another approach to intertextuality: archetypal criticism.

Basic questions about meaning in individual works include the following:

- What meanings do elements within the work—characterization, plot, irony, setting, and so forth—suggest?

- What works are alluded to within the work? What meanings do those works suggest for this one?

- To what genre(s) does this work belong? What meanings associated with the genre(s) are present in this work?

- What meanings do repeated patterns—archetypes—convey in this work?

New Criticism

A product of the rise of Modernism, New Criticism was one of the twentieth century's first theories about interpreting literature. Although New Criticism began well before World War II, with the criticism of T. S. Eliot and I. A. Richards, it received its fullest expression after the war by such critics as John Crowe Ransom, W. K. Wimsatt,

Allen Tate, Cleanth Brooks, and Robert Penn Warren. These and other New Critics published best-selling textbooks that established practical and easily understood ways of teaching and studying literature. These ways continue to influence the study of literature in higher education.

The term *New Criticism* comes from the title of a book published by John Crowe Ransom in 1941, *The New Criticism*. Ransom surveyed the work of recent ("new") critics and thereby made clear some of his own critical principles. Other critics who agreed with Ransom came to be called the New Critics. The New Critics broke dramatically with the nineteenth-century emphasis on historical and biographical background. They held that understanding and appreciating a work of literature need have little or no connection with the author's intended meanings, with the author's life, or with the social and historical circumstances that may have influenced the author. Everything the reader needs to understand and appreciate a work is contained within the work itself.

The New Critics saw their method as "scientific." The work is a self-contained phenomenon made up of "physical" qualities—language and literary conventions (rhyme, meter, alliteration, plot, point of view, and so forth). These qualities can be studied in the same way a geologist studies a rock formation or a physicist the fragmentation of light particles. But some New Critics, like Cleanth Brooks, claimed that the meaning contained in works of literature cannot be paraphrased, cannot be separated from the work's form. One can state what a work is "about" or summarize a work's themes, but a work's meaning is far more complex than such statements alone. Brooks argued that a work's complexity lies in its "irony" or paradoxes. A *paradox* is a statement that seems contradictory but is nonetheless true. Statements such as "the first shall be last" or "you must lose your life to gain it" are paradoxes. Brooks claimed that good works of literature are filled with paradoxes. In William Wordsworth's poem "It Is a Beauteous Evening," for example, a child seems oblivious to the beauty of nature but is, paradoxically, more aware of it than anyone else. The young lovers in John Donne's poem "The Canonization" discover paradoxically that by rejecting life they capture its intensity.

The New Critics used their theories about literature to judge the quality of works of literature. A "good" work, they believed, should contain a network of paradoxes so complex that no mere summary of the work can do them justice; yet, a good work should also have unity. The author achieves this unity by balancing and harmonizing the conflicting ideas in the work. Everything in the work is meaningfully linked together. Because the New Critics favored complex, yet unified, works, they downgraded works that seemed simple or those that lacked unity. They preferred "difficult" works that contained apparently illogical and troubling material. They preferred works that stayed away from social and historical subject matter and that dealt rather with private, personal, and emotional experience.

As a method for teaching and interpretation, New Criticism was highly appealing. The New Critics believed that the language of great works of literature was accessible to modern readers. They were confident that well-trained interpreters could analyze, understand, and evaluate works of literature. Since to them great literature was one of civilization's proudest achievements, they imbued literary criticism with a noble, even priestly quality. Their method of analyzing literature—using literary elements to reveal artistry and meaning—was easy to understand and even "democratic"; anyone could appreciate and interpret great literature once they learned how. Finally, their method excused interpreters from having to master biographical and historical background. They believed that all that was needed was a careful and thorough scrutiny of the works themselves.

Two influential New Critical essays are "The Intentional Fallacy" and "The Affective Fallacy," both by W. K. Wimsatt and Monroe Beardsley, contained in Wimsatt's *The Verbal Icon* (1954). A stimulating work of New Criticism is Cleanth Brooks's *The Well Wrought Urn* (1947). See especially Chapter 1 ("The Language of Paradox") and Chapter 11 ("The Heresy of Paraphrase").

Structuralism

By the 1950s and 1960s, New Criticism had become the dominant theoretical approach that guided teaching and interpretation. New Critical textbooks, like those written by Cleanth Brooks and Robert Penn Warren, pervaded the classrooms. New Critical interpretations of literature filled the scholarly journals. College students who took introductory courses in literature were asked to learn the characteristics of fiction, drama, and poetry and tease out their implications from works published in anthologies. But at the peak of this dominance, a new generation of graduate students and teachers discovered structuralism, which had existed since the 1930s in Europe but was first translated into English in the 1960s. Although structuralism shared some of the methods of New Criticism—notably an emphasis on close reading and attention to the particularities of the text—it was diametrically opposed to it in fundamental ways and took the teaching and interpretation of literature in an entirely new direction.

Like New Criticism, *structuralism* denied the value of historical, social, and biographical information and concentrated on identifiable elements in works of literature. Unlike New Criticism, its theory and methodology were grounded in linguistics. Although some nineteenth-century thinkers anticipated structuralist principles, structuralism originated from the work of the Swiss linguist Ferdinand de Saussure (1857–1913). Early in the twentieth century, Saussure taught three innovative courses in linguistics. Because he left no notes on the content of these courses, his students pooled their notes and published a reconstruction of the courses called *Course in General Linguistics* (1916). This work is the basis of Saussure's fame and provides the theoretical underpinning of both structuralism and post-structuralism.

Saussure's key points about the nature of language broke new ground for studying literature. First, a language is a complete, self-contained system and deserves to be studied as such. Before Saussure, linguists investigated the history of languages (how languages evolved and changed through time) and the differences among languages; for this kind of study, Saussure coined the word *diachronic* (literally "through time"). Saussure argued that, instead of history of a language, linguists should also study how it functions in the present, how its parts interrelate to make up a whole system of communication. This kind of study Saussure called *synchronic* ("at the same time"). Second, Saussure claimed that a language is a system of signs. He defined a *sign* as consisting of a sound plus the thing the sound represents. He called the sound the *signifier* and the thing represented the *signified*. Third, Saussure said that the sounds that make up a language system are arbitrary. Any sound, it does not matter which one, could represent a given thing. The sound for the concept "tree" varies from language to language, yet users of each language know that that sound represents (signifies) "tree." Fourth, any given language is self-contained. The signs that make up a language have no meaning outside the system of that language. Finally, Saussure distinguished between the whole system, which he called *langue* (French for "language"), and one person's use of the system, which he called *parole* (French for "word" or "speech"). *Langue* consists of everything that makes the system work, such as words, syntax, and inflections. *Parole* consists of these same elements but with variations from user to user. Each speaker of a language uses the same system but does so in a slightly different way.

In the 1930s and 1940s, literary critics in Europe began applying Saussure's ideas and methods to the study of literature. This application took two different but often merging paths: literary criticism and cultural criticism. A term that describes both kinds of criticism is *semiotics*, the systematic study of signs. In most ways, the terms *structuralism* and *semiotics* are synonymous.

Structuralist literary critics attempt to show that literature is a form of language or that it functions like language. These critics saw the individual work of literature as similar to *parole*, and literary genres or literature in general as similar to *langue*. Just as linguists studied instances of *parole* in order to understand *langue*, literary critics studied works of literature in order to understand the system of signs that make up a genre or literature as a whole. They might study a Sherlock Holmes story in order to understand detective fiction, a specific poem in order to understand lyric poetry, a Shakespeare play in order to understand drama, a Louis L'Amour novel in order to understand westerns.

One kind of structuralist literary criticism is *stylistics*, the study of the linguistic form of texts. Stylistics can deal with both prose and poetry, but has dealt mainly with poetry, particularly with the qualities of language that distinguish poetry from prose. Some stylistic critics claim that it is *only* qualities of language that distinguish poetry from prose. By analyzing individual poems, these critics attempt to identify those qualities.

Structuralists who study entire cultures attempt to understand a culture's sign systems. The most prominent practitioner of this kind of criticism is the French anthropologist Claude Lévi-Strauss. Lévi-Strauss claims that a culture is bound together by systems of signs and that these systems are like language. He uses Saussurian linguistics as a way of describing the "grammar" of these systems. All aspects of a culture—technology, religion, tools, industry, food, ornaments, rituals— form sign systems. The people of the culture are unaware of these systems, so the structural anthropologist's task is to bring them to light. Lévi-Strauss is perhaps best known for his study of myth. He examines multiple versions of individual myths in order to isolate their essential structural units. Although Lévi-Strauss applies his theories to the study of tribal cultures, other critics, like the Frenchman Roland Barthes, use Lévi-Strauss's approach to "psychoanalyze" modern society. They look for the unconscious sign systems that underlie all aspects of Western culture, including food, furniture, cars, buildings, clothing fashions, business, advertising, and popular entertainment.

Structuralist analysis of culture and literature often merge because literature can be considered an artifact of culture. Literature is a system of signs that can be studied for itself and for its place in a given culture.

As a result, structuralist critics often shy away from complex and classic works and focus instead on popular literature. The Italian critic Umberto Eco writes essays on spy thrillers and comic book stories. He has even written a "semiotic" detective novel, *The Name of the Rose* (1983). Structuralist critics are also usually more interested in fitting a work within a culture or a tradition than in understanding the work itself.

Two readable book-length treatments of structuralism are Robert Scholes's *Structuralism in Literature: An Introduction* (1974) and Terence Hawkes's *Structuralism and Semiotics* (1977). Tzvetan Todorov's "The Grammar of Narrative" in *The Poetics of Prose* (1977) equates narrative structure to sentence structure. Umberto Eco's *The Role of the Reader: Explorations in the Semiotics of Texts* (1979) includes essays on Superman and James Bond. A collection of stylistic studies is *Linguistics and Literary Style*, edited by Donald C. Freeman (1970); see, for example, J. M. Sinclair's "Taking a Poem to Pieces."

Post-Structuralism

Post-structuralism evolved from Saussure's theories of language. It became the most influential and eye-opening application of structuralism to the interpretation of literature. It accepts Saussure's analysis of language and uses his methodology to examine the language of literary works, but it concerns itself with the relationship between language and meaning. Post-structuralism, in fact, offers a radical theory of reading that altogether rejects the certainty of meaning. The most influential post-structuralist critic is the Frenchman Jacques Derrida.

The basis of Derrida's radical skepticism is Saussure's distinction between signifier and signified. Theorists of language have long maintained that words (signifiers) represent identifiable objects (the signified). The word *tree* represents the object "tree." But Saussure questioned the pervasiveness of such one-to-one correspondences. Words, he said, refer not to objects but to "concepts," which are expressed by other words. It seems possible, then, that language, or at least parts of language, may not refer to anything in the sensuously apprehensible world. Saussure said that language is a self-contained system and that in order to function it does not need to reflect reality, it needs only to reflect itself. Signs gain meaning from other signs in the system, not necessarily from the real world.

Derrida and other post-structuralist critics conclude from Saussure's theories that there is a "gap" between signifier and signified. This gap blurs the meaning of the signifier so that we cannot know exactly what it refers to. The resulting ambiguity is multiplied by the connection of signifier to signifier in an endless chain, no part of which touches the real world. A literary text is equivalent to just such a chain. It is a self-contained system that exists independently from the real world. As we read, we absorb this system with our consciousness, which Derrida maintains is itself made up of language. Reading is the confrontation of one language system (our consciousness) with another (the text). Recovering meaning from texts, then, is impossible because interpretations of a text never point to the real world but only to more language. Our interaction with the text makes us *think* we are moving toward meaning, but we never get there.

The purpose of post-structuralist criticism is to expose the indeterminacy of meaning in texts. Derrida calls his critical method *deconstruction*. To "deconstruct" a work, the critic analyzes the text—especially its language—to show that whatever connection may seem to exist between the text and the real world is an illusion created by the author's clever manipulation of language. Whatever the author may have intended the work to mean or whatever a reader may think it means is always undercut by the ambiguity of the work's language. The gap between signifier and signified is symptomatic of a "space" of emptiness, nothingness, nonmeaning that lies at the heart of every text. The critic attempts to demonstrate that the presence of this space makes the text an "abyss" of limitless and contradictory meanings.

Post-structuralism may seem disquieting for those who want to understand the meaning of literature. Without question, nihilism pervades Derrida's theory of language and literature. But when post-structuralism became known in the United States and Great Britain in the 1970s, it seemed like a breath of fresh air to those who felt excluded by New Criticism. In the New Critics' certainty about how to interpret and evaluate literature, they downgraded many works and authors. Most of the New Critics—Brooks, Warren, Ransom, Tate—were from the American South and espoused traditional political and social values. But the next generation of critics came of age in the 1960s, a time of radical rethinking of social and political practices. They embraced post-structuralism as a means of expanding the literary canon to include previously "marginalized" groups of authors, especially women and persons of African descent, as well as genres the New Critics denigrated or ignored. Semiotics further made interpreting popular culture, not just "high" culture, especially appealing.

An accessible book-length study is Christopher Norris's *Deconstruction: Theory and Practice* (1982). The seminal text on deconstruction is Derrida's *Of Grammatology* (1976).

Archetypal Criticism

Although the post-structuralists may seem extreme in claiming that works never connect with the real world, only with other works, they made critics aware of how reliant authors are on the conventions and genres of all literature. We have already discussed this kind of intertextuality in Chapter 2. Another approach to intertextuality is *archetypal criticism*. Northrup Frye, the preeminent advocate of archetypal criticism, defined *archetype* as "the recurring use of certain images or image clusters" in literature (*Critical Path*, 23). But, more broadly, archetypes can be defined as any repeated patterns in literature, whether of plot, character, themes, settings, or images.

An example of a literary archetype is the hero. As outlined by Joseph Campbell in *The Hero with a Thousand Faces* (1949), the hero's career has three main parts. In the first, the "Departure," heroes receive a "call to adventure." By a seeming accident, someone or something invites the hero into "an unsuspected world," into "a relationship with forces that are not rightly understood" (51). Often heroes receive supernatural aid from a "protective figure" who helps them in their adventures (69). In the second part of the hero's story, the "Initiation," heroes cross a dangerous "threshold" into a strange, fluid, dreamlike world where they undergo a succession of trials (77, 97). The climax of these trials is the hero's victory over all opposition. Sometimes this victory is accompanied by a mystical vision that exposes the life-creating energy of all existence (40–41). The third part of the hero's story is the "Return." Because of their victory, heroes now have a boon to bestow upon those left behind (30). The trip back to their homeland can be arduous, but once back they have a choice: they can withhold or bestow the boon. They also face the problem of integrating their transcendental experiences with the "banalities and noisy obscenities" of their old world (218).

The hero is one of numerous archetypal characters. Others include such figures as the scapegoat, the outcast, the earth mother, the femme fatale, the rebel, the cruel stepmother, the "spiritual" woman, the tyrannical father, star-crossed lovers. These characters often find themselves in archetypal situations such as the quest, the initiation, the fall from innocence, death and rebirth, and the task. The more archetypal a work, the more it seems dominated by polarities, such as good versus evil, light versus darkness, water versus desert, heights versus depths.

What is the source of archetypes? Where do they come from? Some critics say that archetypes are merely structural elements in literature. They do not come from anywhere except literature itself. Other critics, like Northrup Frye, agree that this might be so, but suggest also that archetypes exist in real life and are incorporated into literature as part of its meaning. In his best-known work, *Anatomy of Criticism* (1957), Frye attempts to show that all of literature is bound together by a structure of archetypes, which arise from human experiences, wishes, and needs. Another possible source of archetypes is the human psyche. The Swiss psychologist Carl Jung argued that archetypes exist in the human "collective unconscious." Jung accepted Freud's concept of the unconscious mind but, whereas Freud held that each person's unconscious is unique, Jung argued that a part of the unconscious is linked by historical associations and communal "memories" to the unconscious minds of all people. To represent this phenomenon, he coined the phrase "collective unconscious." He believed that certain human products and activities— myth, symbols, ritual, literature—reproduced these memories in the form of "archetypes." Jung defined an *archetype* as any figure or pattern that recurred in works of the imagination from generation to generation. Still another source of archetypes is culture. Richard Slotkin, in his mammoth three-volume investigation of the influence of the frontier on American culture—*Regeneration Through Violence* (1973); *The Fatal Environment* (1985); and *Gunfighter Nation* (1992)—claims that numerous archetypes that influence American culture arose from the frontier experience. The most important of these, he said, is regeneration through violence, the concept that as a nation and as individuals, Americans must undergo violence in order to gain psychic wholeness and take possession of their rightful heritage. The "artifacts" of American culture—novels, films, legends, paintings, comic books, television shows—bear witness to this archetype's influence on American life. The title of the third volume—*Gunfighter Nation*—sums up Slotkin's belief about how this archetype continues to shape the American consciousness.

What meanings do archetypes impart to works of literature? The task of the archetypal critic, Frye says, is to help readers see the "structures" of what they read by identifying literature's "organizing patterns of convention, genre and archetype" (*Critical Path* 24). Like any other structural element, archetypes are potential but not inevitable places of meaning. But those critics who see archetypes as linked to real life—to universal human experience, the human psyche, or culture—claim that archetypes import powerful ideas to works of literature, ideas that resonate subliminally and emotionally with readers. Archetypes are thus equivalent to *myth*, as defined here by Alan Watts: "Myth is to be defined as a complex of stories—some no doubt fact, and some fantasy—which, for various reasons, human beings regard as demonstrations of the inner meaning of the universe and of human life" (7). "A mythology," Slotkin says, "is a complex of narratives that dramatizes the world vision and historical sense of a people or culture, reducing centuries of experience into a constellation of compelling metaphors" (*Regeneration* 6). Archetypal criticism—sometimes called myth criticism—strives to locate those larger meanings in works of literature.

The Author

Although not the only determiner of meaning in a literary work, authors are the most important. They choose the genres and conventions of their works. They craft their works to embody ideas. As readers, we arc drawn to certain works because we like the way authors write—their style, values, and artistic techniques. Most theoretical approaches to literature manifest at least some interest in the author. Three that focus largely on either the author or the author's time period are Historical Criticism, Biographical Criticism, and New Historicism.

Basic questions about how an author's life and times affect the meaning of a work include the following:

- What facts about the author's life suggest ideas in the work? Did anything that happened to the author affect his or her themes or choice of subject matter?

- What was the author's worldview? Which of the author's beliefs seem reflected in this work?

- What commentary on the work did the author make? Does it point to ideas in the work?

- What worldview was typical of the author's time? What aspects of this worldview seem prevalent in this work? Does the author seem to accept or rebel against this worldview?

- How did people respond to the author's work? What ideas did they find in it?

Historical and Biographical Criticism

Historical and *Biographical Criticism* are closely related and received their intellectual impetus from nineteenth-century ideas about science. Historical Critics believed they could illuminate works of literature by studying what gave birth to them: the intellectual and cultural environment from which they came, their sources and antecedents, authors' lives, authors' intentions, and authors' language. They believed that their approach was "scientific" because they were dealing with objective reality—historically verifiable facts—and were using a scientific method for collecting such facts. Two French philosophers influenced Historical and Biographical Criticism: Auguste Comte and especially Hippolyte Taine. Taine, in his *History of English Literature* (1863), held that all art is an expression of the environment and time in which the artist lived. Historical critics concentrated on authors they assumed were "great," not worrying much about why or what the works meant. A major emphasis of historical criticism was the historical periods and intellectual movements to which works belonged. Critics studied the conventions and ideas that characterized movements, such as blank verse during the Renaissance and an emphasis on free will during the Romantic period. They placed works within evolving traditions (the novel, Christian literature, allegory, political fiction, the epic) and compared them to the literature of other countries. In higher education today, a prevalent manifestation of historical criticism is the literature survey course, which links literature to authors' lives, historical periods, and intellectual movements. Literary histories, such as the *Columbia Literary History of the United States* (1988) and *The Literary History of England* (1967), owe their methodology and format to historical criticism. Although the meaning of individual works of literature was not explicit in such venerable historical studies as E. M. W. Tillyard's *The Elizabethan World Picture* (1943), M. I. Finley's *The World of Odysseus* (1978), and A. O. Lovejoy's *The Great Chain of Being* (1936), meaning was implicit. These Historical Critics assumed that the ideas associated with a particular age were manifested in the works of the age.

Samuel Johnson was the first great biographical critic. His *Lives of the Poets* (1779, 1781) provided truthful accounts of authors' lives and astute assessments of their literary achievements. Biographical Criticism became increasingly popular during the nineteenth and twentieth centuries and is still very much practiced. The assumption lying behind all literary biography is that the facts of authors' lives are important to their works. Some literary biographers make little overt connection between authors' lives and their works. But others, like the following, integrate facts about authors' lives with interpretations of their works: K. J. Fielding's *Charles Dickens: A Critical Introduction* (1964); F. W. Dupee's *Henry James: His Life and Writings* (1956); and Arthur Mizener's *The Far Side of Paradise: A Biography of F. Scott Fitzgerald* (1965).

The purpose of Historical and Biographical Criticism is well summed up by Douglass Bush, himself the author of outstanding examples of Historical Criticism: "Since the great mass of great literature belongs to the past, adequate criticism must grow out of historical knowledge, cultural and linguistic, as well as out of intuitive insight. Every work must be understood on its own terms as the product of a particular mind in a particular setting, and that mind and setting must be re-created through all the resources that learning and the historical imagination can muster—not excluding the author's intention, if that is known. The very pastness of a work . . . is part of its meaning for us and must be realized to the best of our power" (8). If we do not pay attention to authors and their historical context, Bush says, we run the risk of anachronistic misreadings and misunderstandings. We may be limited in our ability to "re-create the outward and inward conditions in which a work of art was engendered, but unless we try, we cannot distinguish between its local and temporal and its universal and timeless elements, indeed we may not be able to understand some works at all" (8).

New Historicist Criticism

New Historicism emerged in the late 1970s as a "new" way to use history to understand and evaluate works of literature. It shares "old" historicism's belief that the historical culture from which a work comes helps us understand the work. It differs drastically from the older historicism in its beliefs about the nature of literature, the nature of history, the ability of people to perceive "reality," and the purpose of literary studies. Its sympathy for disadvantaged—"marginalized"—peoples gives it a political slant lacking in older historicism. This sympathy, along with its other beliefs and methods, has profoundly influenced other, more narrowly focused theoretical approaches such as feminist, Marxist, and ethnic criticism. Its breadth of inclusion has made New Historicism highly visible today in the teaching and study of literature. The term *New Historicism* applies to the American version of "cultural studies." The British version, called Cultural Materialism, is more overtly Marxist than New Historicism, but both are heavily influenced by the French historian and philosopher Michel Foucault.

The key assumptions of New Historicism are embedded in its understanding of several related concepts: culture, text, discourse, ideology, the self, and history. These concepts, in turn, establish the New Historicist approach to the study of literature and are based on structuralist and post-structuralist theories of language. The first term, *culture*, is the most important. In an anthropological sense, "culture" is the total way of life of a particular society—its language, economy, art, religion, and attachment to a location. For New Historicists, culture is also a collection of codes that everyone in a society shares and that allows them to communicate, create artifacts, and act. These codes include not just language but every element of a culture—literature, dress, food, rituals, and games.

As a web of sign systems, culture is thus "textual." A *text*, traditionally defined, is a written document that employs a symbolic system (words, mathematical symbols, images, musical notation). The structuralists expand "text" to mean any system of codes. The post-structuralists go further by claiming that because everything we know is filtered through "language," *everything* is text. "There is nothing outside the text," Derrida says. New Historicists accept the structuralist concept of text but reject the post-structuralist concept that people cannot see the texts that surround them. Yes, they say, cultures consist of "texts," "discourses," and "ideologies," but people can analyze these texts and expose their weaknesses.

By *discourse*, the structuralists mean any system of signs, whether verbal or nonverbal. "Discourse," then, is analogous to language (Saussure's *langue*) and "text" to specific uses of language (*parole*). Foucault claims that groups of people, such as doctors, lawyers, priests, and athletes, create their own discourses. Each discourse has its own unique "discursive practice"—word choice, sentence structure, bodily movements, prejudices, rhetorical forms, and "rules" about where and when to use the discourse. Foucault claims that discourses are "political": People with power—social, economic, political, or artistic—use discourse to manipulate other people and maintain their own power.

Ideology is a system of beliefs that governs a group's actions, its view of reality, and its assumptions about what is "normal" and "natural." Ideology is communicated by discourse and represented by texts. New Historicists typically see ideology in political terms. One group of people unfairly imposes its ideology upon others, devaluing and exploiting those who fail to fit its definitions of the "normal" and "natural." Power elites can be persons within a society—wealthy persons, politicians, white people, males—or whole societies, such as countries that colonize and impose their ideology upon other regions. When an ideology becomes so pervasive that most people are unaware of its influence, it becomes "hegemonic." People assume that it represents the way things really are. However, no ideology is comprehensive enough to extend fair and equal treatment to all people. Thus, some people are "marginalized" and made vulnerable to exploitation.

If texts, discourse, and ideology are so dominant in society, how does the individual, the "self," fit in? New Historicists see the *self* as controlled by cultural codes and nearly blind to their existence. The self is a "subject." Like the subject of a sentence, it performs actions and relates to "objects" (physical things, other people, literary texts). But the self is also passive, "subject to" culture, to discourse, and to ideology. For this reason, people's ability to understand history is limited. They cannot see that *history*—the study and recounting of the past—is a social construct. Historians, Foucault says, can never know with certainty which events caused other events or which events are important. Human events are filled with inconsistencies, irregularities, and singularities that resist rational understanding. Historians may believe they are telling coherent stories about past events, but such constructs are always false. Even worse, to enhance their power, power elites create "official" histories, such as those taught in school and recounted in textbooks.

The New Historicist approach to literary study emerges from all of these concepts. Its beliefs about three things—literature, the author, and the reader—help distinguish it from other theoretical approaches. New Historicists claim that *literature* is merely a "text" indistinguishable in nature from all the other texts that constitute a culture. The concept "literature" is "socially constructed"; every society decides what "literature" is and what its conventions are, and these definitions always vary from society to society and age to age. Equally relative are judgments about literary value. No single author's works are better than those of other authors, no single work is better than others, no one culture's works are better than those of other cultures. Rather, *all* texts, literary and otherwise (including "popular" texts such as television shows, advertisements, and drugstore romances), are worthy of study.

The *author*, for the New Historicists, is far less noble and autonomous than in other approaches. Like everyone else, authors are "subjects" manufactured by culture. A culture "writes" an author who, in turn, transcribes cultural codes and discourses into literary texts. Authors' intentions about the form and meaning of their work merely reflect cultural codes and values. Likewise, culture "programs" the *reader* to respond to its codes and forms of discourse. When readers read works of literature, they respond automatically to the codes embodied by them.

Not all New Historicists are so deterministic and relativistic as this description would indicate. Some reject Foucault's pessimism about a person's ability to understand historical reality, to read texts objectively, and to make changes in society. However, New Historicists do tend to share beliefs about the purposes of literary study. First, they believe that literature must be studied within a cultural context. Old-style historicists see historical facts mainly as a means to clarify ideas, allusions, language, and details in literature. New Historicists believe that literature *is* history, is "enmeshed" in history. When New Historicists study literature, they examine such things as how the work was composed, what the author's intentions were, what events and ideas the work refers to, how readers have responded to the work, and what the work means for people today. They draw upon many disciplines—anthropology, sociology, law, psychology, history—to show what role literature has played in history, from the author's time to the present. Second, New Historicists focus on literature as cultural text. They study the relationship between literature and other texts, including nonliterary and popular texts. They identify the codes that constitute literary discourse and ascertain how people use such discourse to communicate with one another and to comment on society. Third, New Historicists scrutinize the relationship of literature to the power structures of society. They want to show how literature serves, opposes, and changes the wishes of the power elites and therefore what ideologies literature supports or undermines. Finally, many New Historicists see criticism itself as an "intervention" in society. By marking literature's cultural roles, its ideologies, its effects, and the biases readers have brought to it, New Historicists aspire to diminish the injustices of race, class, and gender.

Since New Historicism is a fairly new critical approach to literature, its concepts and methods continue to evolve. Some general studies include Jerome McGann's *Historical Studies and Literary Criticism* (1985) and Harold Veeser's *The New Historicism* (1989). Some of the best-known New Historicist criticism has focused on Renaissance literature, such as *Political Shakespeare: New Essays in Cultural Materialism* (1985), edited by Jonathan Dollimore and Alan Sinfield, and Stephen Greenblatt's *Renaissance Self-fashioning from More to Shakespeare* (1980). In *Orientalism* (1978), Edward Said offers a "post-colonial" version of New Historicism. He argues that Western culture has fabricated a distorted and unfair discourse about the East, manifested in countless works of literature and popular culture. Another post-colonial author is the Nigerian Chinua Achebe, who eloquently attacks the racism in Joseph Conrad's *Heart of Darkness* in "An Image of Africa: Racism in Conrad's *Heart of Darkness*." As for Michel Foucault, many of his works are excerpted in *The Foucault Reader* (1985). David R. Shumway's *Michel Fou-*

cault (1989) and Lois McNay's *Foucault: A Critical Introduction* (1994) are succinct critical overviews of Foucault's work and thought.

The Reader

As the "receiver" of works of literature, readers complete them. Their task is to make sense of them—to determine why they like the works and what ideas rest in them. Many theoretical approaches—Historical Criticism, New Criticism, structuralism, deconstruction—assume that readers are the same in their ability to understand literature. Any well-trained reader, they maintain, can perceive the properties of literature. But other approaches suggest that readers actually contribute to the meaning of works. In this section, we will look at the most notable of these approaches, reader-response criticism.

Basic questions about how readers find meaning in a work include the following:

- How do interpretations of the work vary from reader to reader? What beliefs and experiences lead readers to their interpretations?

- How have your own interpretations of the work varied from different times you have read it? What accounts for the difference?

- How have interpretations of the work differed from one historical period to another?

- What do you find appealing or unappealing about the work?

- What in your own life leads you to your interpretations of the work?

Reader-Response Criticism

Reader-response criticism studies the interaction of reader with text. Reader-response critics hold that the text is incomplete until it is read. Each reader brings something to the text that completes it and that makes each reading different. Reader-response critics vary on what that "something" is. Recent psychoanalytic critics, such as Jacques Lacan and Norman Holland, say that the something is the unconscious. Post-structuralist critics say that it is the "language" that constitutes the conscious mind. New Historicist critics say that it is the ideology of the dominant culture. All agree that the text has no life of its own without the reader.

Of all the post–World War II movements in literary theory, reader-response criticism perhaps most successfully challenges the dominance of New Criticism in the university classroom. It borrows methodology from New Criticism, structuralism, and post-structuralism, but rejects their contention that the work must be studied in isolation from its context. Context—historical, biographical, cultural, psychoanalytic—is relevant to the understanding of the text. Reader-response criticism furthermore rejects the post-structuralist claim that texts are meaningless. Texts may be incomplete in themselves, but the reading of them makes them potentially reflective of the real world—or at least the reader's experience of the real world.

Some reader-response critics, most notably the German critic Wolfgang Iser, agree with Derrida that works contain "gaps"—not necessarily because of the slippage between signifier and signified but because of the incompleteness of works. Authors always leave something unsaid or unexplained and thus invite readers to fill the resulting spaces with their own imaginative constructs. Iser argues, therefore, that many equally valid interpretations of a work are possible. Interpretations of a work will vary from person to person and even from reading to reading. Critics who agree with Iser often attempt to study how readers fill the gaps in works. These critics are more interested in mapping the process of reading than in explaining individual works.

Perhaps the most prominent group of reader-response critics focuses on how biographical and cultural contexts influence the interpretation of texts. These critics argue that reading is a collective enterprise. The American critic Stanley Fish states that a reader's understanding of what "literature" is and what works of literature mean is formed by "interpretive communities"—groups to which readers belong. These groups could be small (a circle of friends) or large (a region or cultural entity like "Western civilization"). Fish rejects the idea that a text has a core of meaning that everyone in any age would accept. Rather, shared understandings of a text's meaning come from the beliefs of a community of readers, not from the text. Each reader's preconceptions actually "create" the text. If, for example, a reader believes that a miscellaneous collection of words is a religious poem, the reader will perceive it as a religious poem. If a reader believes that the work fits a particular theory, the reader will find facts in the work to support that theory. The theory, in a sense, "creates" the facts.

Because of the influence and provocative nature of reader-response criticism, writings about it abound. *The Reader in the Text: Essays on Audience and Interpretation*, edited by Susan R. Suleiman and Inge Crosman (1980) provides an introduction to reader-response criticism as well as essays by prominent critics. Stanley Fish's *Is There a Text in This Class?: The Authority of Interpretive Communities* (1980) is a collection of lively essays.

All of Reality

As we said in Chapter 2, one of the pleasures of reading literature is noticing its reflection of reality, its claims to truth. Literary theorists vary in their faith that human beings can do this. The New Critics and traditional historicists were strongly confident that readers can do so. The deconstructionists are so skeptical about "truth" that, for them, all knowledge seems uncertain and relative. Most theoretical approaches make at least minimal claims about the nature of reality and urge readers to rely on those claims to interpret literature. But some approaches make their understanding of truth the sole or major basis for reading literature. No matter what the author may have intended, they examine works of literature for signs of their own version of truth. Three examples of such reality-based approaches are Marxist criticism, psychological criticism, and feminist and gender criticism.

Basic questions about making connection between a work and the real world include the following:

- How would different theories about the nature of reality change the interpretation of the work? For example, would one's religious beliefs—Muslim, Christian, Jewish, Buddhist—cause one to interpret the work differently?
- What have you learned about "reality" from the work—things you did not know before you read it?
- What are your own standards for assessing the "truth" in a work?
- What direct statements about reality does the work make?

Marxist Criticism

Fully developed *Marxist criticism* appeared early in the twentieth century, especially in the 1930s during the Great Depression. This "socialist" criticism applauded literature that depicted the difficulties of the poor and downtrodden, especially when they struggled against oppressive capitalist bosses. Examples of literature with such strong "proletarian" elements are works by Carl Sandburg, Émile Zola, Maxim Gorky,

Charles Dickens, Richard Wright, John Steinbeck, Theodore Dreiser, and John Dos Passos. Early Marxist critics approved of a socialist solution to the problems of the oppressed and judged the quality of works on the basis of their Marxist orientation. Granville Hicks's *The Great Tradition: An Interpretation of American Literature Since the Civil War* (1935) is a still-readable example of early Marxist criticism.

Since World War II, a new generation of critics has infused Marxist criticism with renewed vigor. An example is the Hungarian critic Georg Lukacs, who argues that literature should reflect the real world. Lukacs does not mean that literature should be a mirror image of society by, for example, giving detailed descriptions of its physical contents or its patterns of behavior. Rather, literature should represent the economic tensions in society as described in Marx's writings. Ironically, for Lukacs, works that accurately represent the real world may be less "real" than works that emphasize themes (ideas) over description. Lukacs believes that literature might even have to distort reality in order to represent the "truth" about society. To show the economic struggles caused by capitalism, for example, an author might have to create character types one would never meet in real life. Lukacs, therefore, prefers the novels of Balzac to those of Flaubert because, even though Balzac's plots and characters are less plausible than Flaubert's, Balzac reveals the economic pitfalls of capitalism as Marx saw them.

Most recently, Marxist criticism, like much late-twentieth-century literary theories, have been strongly influenced by structuralism. Structuralist Marxism overlaps with New Historicism (described above) and is often indistinguishable from it. Structuralist Marxists see authors and readers as enmeshed in a system of signifying codes. Authors and readers are shaped and determined by these codes. Although taken together the codes have no overall coherence, all are connected in some way to economic forces. Most people living in a society ascribe to its *ideology*, the false ideas about society's purposes and coherence promulgated by the power elites. Even though people are molded by society, they can nonetheless critique its ideology and change society for the better.

The purpose of Marxist's literary criticism is to expose how works of literature represent dominant ideologies. Some Marxist critics, like Louis Althusser, believe that literature helps readers see the contradictions and fault lines in ideology. Others, like Terry Eagleton, hold that literature furthers ideology by making it seem attractive and "natural." Eagleton's *Marxism and Literary Criticism* (1976) provides an overview of recent Marxist criticism. His *Literary Theory: An Introduction* (1983) surveys modern critical theory from a Marxist point of view. See also Althusser's essay "A Letter on Art."

Psychological Criticism

Psychological criticism applies modern psychological theories to authors and their works. Because Sigmund Freud's psychoanalytic theories dominated the field of psychology during the first half of the twentieth century, psychological critics found his ideas especially fruitful for interpreting literature. Although not all of Freud's ideas relate to literature, three seemed pertinent to early Freudian critics: the dominance of the unconscious mind over the conscious, the expression of the unconscious mind through symbols (most notably in dreams), and the primacy of sexuality as a motivating force in human behavior. These three ideas are related. Freud believed that sexual drives reside in the unconscious, that the conscious mind represses them, and that unconscious symbols usually represent this repressed sexual energy.

Early Freudian critics saw literature as a kind of "dream" and thus a source of insight into the authors themselves. Using works of literature as symbolic representations of an author's subconscious, Freudian critics created psychological portraits of authors. An example is Marie Bonaparte's *The Life and Works of Edgar Allan Poe: A Psychoanalytic Interpretation* (1949). Early Freudian critics also used psychoanalytic principles to analyze characters in works of literature. They looked upon characters as having motivations, conflicts, desires, and inclinations similar to those of real people. They sought psychological clues to the makeup of literary characters, especially the unconscious symbolic expressions found in dreams and repeated patterns of behavior. In Eugene O'Neill's *Long Day's Journey Into Night*, for example, whenever Mary Tyrone raises her hands to her hair, she unconsciously expresses anxiety about her wrecked youth, health, and innocence. Psychological critics were also drawn to works that are themselves dreamlike, such as Lewis Carroll's *Alice in Wonderland*, or that contain accounts of characters' dreams.

Authors themselves often imported psychological ideas to their works. Eugene O'Neill, D. H. Lawrence, Tennessee Williams and many others were well-read in Freudian psychology. Some writers employed structural devices based on psychological theories. Examples are the *stream of consciousness* technique, which conforms to William James's ideas about the workings of the conscious mind, and the surrealistic technique, which conforms to Freud's ideas about the undisciplined unconscious. Examples of stream-of-consciousness narration are James Joyce's *Portrait of the Artist as a Young Man* and *Ulysses*, William Faulkner's *The Sound and the Fury*, T. S. Eliot's "The Love Song of J. Alfred Prufrock," Virginia Woolf's *To the Lighthouse*, and Eugene O'Neill's *Strange Interlude*. Examples of surrealism are James Joyce's *Finnegans Wake* and the fiction of Franz Kafka.

Recent psychological critics continue to find Freud's theories a rich source of ideas about literature but, whereas earlier critics focused on authors and characters, recent critics have turned their attention to readers and texts. The critic Norman Holland, for example, argues that readers' psyches respond subconsciously to certain aspects of works of literature. The reader in effect "makes" the text, so that the text is different for every reader. Like Holland, the French critic Jacques Lacan posits ideas about how readers respond to literary texts. Lacan combines Freud's theories of the unconscious with Saussurian linguistics. He holds that the human psyche is made up of language. Our conscious and subconscious minds are born into language, a system of signifiers. From infancy to adulthood, we grow toward what we think is a secure and coherent identity. But at the heart of the psyche is an unbridgeable gap between signifier and signified. As a result, our psyche is never fully coherent, our identity never stable. His most famous application of this theory to literature is a long essay on Edgar Allan Poe's "The Purloined Letter." Lacan claims that the missing letter, which the detective Dupin has been commissioned to find, is equivalent to the signifier. But because it is missing it is a "symbol only of an absence" (Lacan, 38). It stands for the "lack" or emptiness that lies within all of us.

A well-known work of early psychological criticism is Ernest Jones's *Hamlet and Oedipus* (1949), in which Jones, a psychiatrist, argues that Hamlet's problems stem from Oedipal conflicts. An anthology of psychological criticism is *Literature and Psychoanalysis*, edited by Edith Kurzweil and William Phillips (1983). *The Purloined Poe*, cited in the previous paragraph, features psychoanalytic readings of Poe's story "The Purloined Letter."

Feminist and Gender Criticism

Feminist and gender criticism have much in common with reader-response and New Historicist criticism, especially with critics who, like

Stanley Fish, believe that interpretations of literature are influenced by communities of readers. We include it here under "All of Reality" because it bases its interpretations on ideas about the nature of females and female experience. With the rise of feminism in the 1950s and 1960s, feminist critics claimed that, over the years, men had controlled the most influential interpretive communities. Men decided which conventions made up "literature" and judged the quality of works. Men wrote the literary histories and drew up the lists of "great" works—the literary canon. Because works by and about women were omitted from the canon, women authors were ignored, and women characters misconstrued.

Since the 1960s, feminist literary critics have successfully challenged these circumstances. Far more women now teach, interpret, evaluate, and theorize about literature than ever before. Previously neglected works such as Zora Neale Hurston's *Their Eyes Were Watching God* (1937), Kate Chopin's *The Awakening* (1899), Charlotte Perkins Gilman's "The Yellow Wallpaper" (1892), and Rebecca Harding Davis's *Life in the Iron-Mills* (1861) are now widely read. Certain literary genres practiced by women, such as diaries, journals, and letters, have gained more respect. Numerous anthologies, literary histories, and interpretive studies explore women's contributions to literature. Recently, however, a new movement, "gender studies," has evolved out of feminist studies in order to address broader issues; notably, the nature of both femininity and masculinity, the differences within each sex, and the literary treatment of men and homosexuals. Gender studies "complicate" feminist studies because, although they share many interests, they are not exactly the same. Both, however, are political in that they argue for the fair representation and treatment of persons of all "genders."

A survey of the history of feminist and gender criticism helps spotlight their concerns. The first stage of feminist criticism began with two influential books: Simone de Beauvoir's *The Second Sex* (1949) and Kate Millet's *Sexual Politics* (1970). Both authors criticized the distorted representation of women by well-known male authors. Their work laid the foundation for the most prevalent approach of this stage, the "images of women" approach. Following de Beauvoir and Millet, feminist critics called attention to the unjust, distorted, and limited representation ("images") of females in works of literature, especially works authored by males. They celebrated realistic representations of women and brought to light neglected works by and about women. They sought to expose the "politics" of self-interest that led people to create stereotypical and false images of women.

In the second stage of feminist criticism, beginning in the early 1970s, critics shifted away from works by males to concentrate on works by females. Elaine Showalter, a prominent critic from this period, called this approach "gynocriticism." Especially influential was the work of French critics such as Luce Irigary, Julia Kristeva, and Hélène Cixous. Their criticism, called *écriture féminine* (female writing), argued for an "essential" (biological, genetic, psychological) difference between men and women that causes women to think and write differently from men. Gynocritics urged women to become familiar with female authors and to discover their own female "language," a language that supposedly enters the subconscious before the "patriarchal" language of the dominant culture. They tried to delineate a female poetics, a use of literary conventions and genres that seems typically "female." Some critics based feminist poetics on the possible connection between writing and the female body. Because women's bodies have more fluids than men's, they argued, women's writing is more "fluid." It is less structured, less unified, more inclusive of many points of view, less given to neat endings, and more open to fantasy than writing by men. It rejects or undermines the "marriage plot" and the "happy ending," in which a strong female protagonist "capitulates" to a male by marrying him. Female poetics seeks to understand why female authors tend to favor certain genres (lyric poetry, novel, short story, tale, letters, diaries, memoirs) over others (epic, martial romance, drama, satire).

The third stage of feminist criticism rebelled against the "essentialist" assumptions of gynocriticism and is closely allied with New Historicism in its focus on the cultural creation of identity. Gayle Rubin, in two influential essays—"The Traffic in Women" (1975) and "Thinking Sex" (1984)—distinguishes between "sex" and "gender." Whereas *sex* is the biological difference between males and females, *gender* is the cultural difference. Culture determines the traits and behavior that set masculinity apart from femininity and rules on "normal" and "natural" gender distinctions. Western culture, for example, has seen women as passive rather than active, irrational rather than rational, subjective rather than objective, at home rather than at "work," spiritual rather than material, and impractical rather than practical. It has ruled that certain kinds of behavior are "abnormal" and "unnatural" for females to practice, such as pursuing careers, doing construction work, being pastors or priests, wearing "male" clothes, or being assertive. Such gender distinctions, feminist critics claim, are arbitrary and almost always give women less power, status, and respect than men. In one sense, the feminist focus on gender is deterministic: Many women are "trapped" by the gender traits assigned to them by culture. In another sense, however, it offers hope. Culture, unlike biology, can be changed—through education, social action, and politics.

All three of these "stages" of feminist criticism have overlapped and coexisted. They continue to be practiced. But the focus on gender in the third stage led not only to a new stage of feminist criticism, it also helped to establish the broader movement of gender criticism. Until the mid-1980s, many feminist critics assumed that all women were the same in their biological nature, their gender traits, their shared history of oppression, and their aspirations. Most feminist critics, furthermore, wrote from the perspective of an elite group of people: women who were Western, politically liberal, middle class, and highly educated. Beginning around 1985, some feminist critics challenged these assumptions and this perspective. Feminist critics, they said, should look at the many ways in which women differ from one another. Factors other than gender, they said, give females identity. These factors include such things as race, ethnic background, and socioeconomic circumstances. Critics began studying the literary representation of women in minority cultures, in non–Western cultures, at various economic levels, and in different work situations. They began examining ways females themselves marginalize or "erase" other females. Perhaps most important, they began to pay attention to sex and gender differences among women, especially between heterosexuals and homosexuals.

Gender criticism, perhaps because it is so new, remains a nebulous, difficult-to-define approach to the study of literature. It covers almost anything having to do with "gender," including feminist criticism, theories of cultural influence, and crimes such as sexual abuse. One of the most important aspects of gender criticism is its exploration of the literary treatment of homosexuality. As with New Historicism, the theorist who most influences gender studies is Michel Foucault. The first volume of his three-volume study *The History of Sexuality* (1976) states his basic ideas about sexuality. The Western concept of "sexuality," Foucault maintains, is not a universal category but was invented in the late nineteenth century. Before then, there was no distinction between "homosexuality" and "heterosexuality." Although same-sex relationships occurred before that time, there was no concept of homosexuality as a "lifestyle." Modern Western views of sexuality constitute an "ideology" that benefits people in power, most notably bourgeois capitalists. This ideology, as with all ideologies, is manifested in discourses such as religion, science, politics, medicine, and literature. Although Foucault was himself apolitical, he was deeply sympathetic to "marginalized" people. He struggled with his own identity as a homosexual and felt personally marginalized. He attempted suicide in 1948 and died from an AIDS-related illness in 1984.

Some gender critics disagree with Foucault's heavy emphasis on cultural determinism. They believe that sexual identity, including homosexuality, results from biological rather than cultural causes. Gay criticism (which deals with men) and lesbian criticism (which deals with women) share certain goals, primarily the struggle to eliminate homophobia. They call into question the Western assumption that heterosexuality is the only "natural" sexual identity and attempt to expose the politics of gender—how certain groups manipulate concepts of sex and gender for their own benefit. Gay and lesbian critics analyze all discourses, including literature, that reinforce or destabilize conventional concepts of sex and gender. They study the works and lives of authors who were admitted homosexuals and bisexuals or who seemed to have suppressed homosexual tendencies.

Perhaps the best place to begin reading feminist criticism is with an anthology of essays such as *The New Feminist Criticism: Essays on Women, Literature, and Theory* (1985), edited by Elaine Showalter. Ellen Moers's *Literary Women* (1976); Sandra Gilbert and Susan Gubar's *The Madwoman in the Attic: The Woman Writer and the Nineteenth-Century Literary Imagination* (1979); and Kate Millett's *Sexual Politics* (1970), mentioned above, are among the best examples of "images of women" criticism. Virginia Woolf's *A Room of One's Own* (1929) and Hélène Cixous's "The Laugh of the Medusa" (1976) are well-known examples of gynocriticism. Gayle Rubin's essays, mentioned above, and Elaine Showalter's edited collection, *Speaking of Gender* (1989), represent the shift of interest toward gender. Two texts that deal with the broadening of feminist criticism are Barbara Smith's "Toward a Black Feminist Criticism" (1975) and *Wild Women in the Whirlwind: Afra-American Culture and the Contemporary Literary Renaissance*, edited by Joanne Braxton and Andree Nicola McLaughlin (1989). *The Gay and Lesbian Literary Heritage* (1995), edited by Claude J. Summers, is a one-volume encyclopedia featuring articles on authors, terms, and theoretical approaches. *The Gay and Lesbian Studies Reader*, edited by Henry Abelove (1993), is an anthology of essays. Eve Kosofsky Sedgwick's *Between Men: English Literature and Male Homosocial Desire* (1985) deals with heterosexuality and homosexuality in literature before the twentieth century. For works by and about Michel Foucault, see the discussion of New Historicism.

Works Cited

Literary Criticism and Theory

Culler, Jonathan. *Literary Theory: A Very Short Introduction.* New York: Oxford UP, 1999.

Graff, Gerald. *Professing Literature: An Institutional History.* Chicago: U of Chicago P, 1987.

Newton, K. M. *Interpreting the Text: A Critical Introduction to the Theory and Practice of Literary Interpretation.* New York: St. Martin's, 1990.

Selden, Raman, Peter Widdowson, and Peter Brooker. *A Reader's Guide to Contemporary Literary Theory.* 4th ed. New York: Prentice Hall, 1997.

Places for Interpretation

Abrams, M. H. *The Mirror and the Lamp: Romantic Theory and the Critical Tradition.* New York: Norton, 1958.

New Criticism

Brooks, Cleanth. *The Well Wrought Urn: Studies in the Structure of Poetry.* New York: Harcourt, 1947.

Ransom, John Crowe. *The New Criticism.* Norfolk, CT: New Directions, 1941.

Wimsatt, W. K., and Monroe Beardsley. "The Affective Fallacy." *The Verbal Icon: Studies in the Meaning of Poetry.* Lexington: U of Kentucky P, 1954. 21–39.

———. "The Intentional Fallacy." *The Verbal Icon: Studies in the Meaning of Poetry.* Lexington: U of Kentucky P, 1954. 3–18

Structuralism

Eco, Umberto. *The Name of the Rose.* San Diego: Harcourt, 1983.

———. *The Role of the Reader: Explorations in the Semiotics of Texts.* Bloomington: Indiana UP, 1979.

Freeman, Donald C, ed. *Linguistics and Literary Style.* New York: Holt, Rinehart and Winston, 1970.

Hawkes, Terence. *Structuralism and Semiotics.* Berkeley: U California P, 1977.

Saussure, Ferdinand de. *Course in General Linguistics.* LaSalle, IL: Open Court, 1986.

Scholes, Robert. *Structuralism in Literature: An Introduction.* New Haven: Yale UP, 1974.

Todorov, Tzvetan. *The Poetics of Prose.* Ithaca: Cornell UP, 1977.

Post-Structuralism

Derrida, Jacques. *Of Grammatology.* Baltimore: Johns Hopkins UP, 1976.

Norris, Christopher. *Deconstruction: Theory and Practice.* New York: Methuen, 1982.

Archetypal Criticism

Campbell, Joseph. *The Hero with a Thousand Faces.* New York: World, 1949.

Frye, Northrup. *Anatomy of Criticism.* Princeton: Princeton UP, 1957.

——. *The Critical Path.* Bloomington: Indiana UP, 1971.

Slotkin, Richard. *The Fatal Environment.* New York: Atheneum, 1985.

——. *Gunfighter Nation.* New York: Atheneum, 1992.

——. *Regeneration Through Violence.* Hanover: Wesleyan UP, 1973.

Watts, Alan. *Myth and Ritual in Christianity.* New York: Vanguard, 1954.

Historical and Biographical Criticism

Baugh, Albert C. *The Literary History of England.* 2nd ed. New York: Appleton, 1967.

Bush, Douglass. "Literary History and Literary Criticism." *Literary History and Literary Criticism,* ed. Leon Edel. New York: New York UP, 1965.

Dupee, F. W. *Henry James: His Life and Writings.* Garden City: Doubleday, 1956.

Elliot, Emory, et al. *Columbia Literary History of the United States.* New York: Columbia UP, 1988.

Fielding, K. J. *Charles Dickens: A Critical Introduction.* Boston: Houghton, 1964.

Finley, M. I. *The World of Odysseus.* Rev. ed. New York: Viking, 1978.

Lovejoy, Arthur O. *The Great Chain of Being: A Study of the History of an Idea.* New York: Harper, 1960.

Mizener, Arthur. *The Far Side of Paradise: A Biography of F. Scott Fitzgerald.* Boston: Houghton, 1965.

Tillyard, E. M. W. *The Elizabethan World Picture.* New York: Macmillan, 1944.

New Historicist Criticism

Achebe, Chinua. "An Image of Africa: Racism in Conrad's *Heart of Darkness.*" *Hopes and Impediments: Selected Essays.* New York: Anchor Books, 1990. 1–20.

Dollimore, Jonathan, and Alan Sinfield. *Political Shakespeare: New Essays in Cultural Materialism.* Manchester, Eng.: Manchester UP, 1985.

Foucault, Michel. *The Foucault Reader.* Ed. Paul Rabinow. New York: Pantheon, 1985.

Greenblatt, Stephen. *Renaissance Self-Fashioning from More to Shakespeare.* Chicago: U of Chicago P, 1980.

McGann, Jerome. *Historical Studies and Literary Criticism.* Madison: U of Wisconsin P, 1985.

McNay, Lois. *Foucault: A Critical Introduction.* New York: Continuum, 1994.

Said, Edward. *Orientalism.* New York: Pantheon, 1978.

Shumway, David R. *Michel Foucault.* Boston: Twayne, 1989.

Veeser, Harold. *The New Historicism.* New York: Routledge, 1989.

Reader-Response Criticism

Fish, Stanley Fish. *Is There a Text in This Class?: The Authority of Interpretive Communities* Cambridge: Harvard UP, 1980.

Suleiman, Susan. R, and Inge Crosman, eds. *The Reader in the Text: Essays on Audience and Interpretation.* Princeton: Princeton UP, 1980.

Marxist Criticism

Althusser, Louis. "A Letter on Art." *Lenin and Philosophy and Other Essays.* London: Verso, 1971. 221–27.

Eagleton, Terry. *Marxism and Literary Criticism*. Berkeley: University of California Press, 1976.

———. *Literary Theory: An Introduction*. Minneapolis: University of Minnesota Press, 1983.

Hicks, Granville. *The Great Tradition: An Interpretation of American Literature Since the Civil War*. New York: Macmillan, 1935.

Psychological Criticism

Bonaparte, Marie. *The Life and Works of Edgar Allan Poe: A Psychoanalytic Interpretation*. London: Imago Press, 1949.

Jones, Ernest. *Hamlet and Oedipus*. New York: Norton, 1949.

Kurzweil, Edith, and William Phillips. *Literature and Psychoanalysis*. New York: Columbia UP, 1983).

Lacan, Jacques. "Seminar on 'The Purloined Letter.'" *The Purloined Poe: Lacan, Derrida, and Psychoanalytic Reading*. Ed. John P. Muller and William J. Richardson Baltimore: Johns Hopkins UP, 1988. 28–54.

Muller, John P., and William J. Richardson, eds. *The Purloined Poe: Lacan, Derrida, and Psychoanalytic Reading*. Baltimore: Johns Hopkins UP, 1988.

Feminist and Gender Criticism

Abelove, Henry. *The Gay and Lesbian Studies Reader*. New York: Routledge, 1993.

Beauvoir, Simone de. *The Second Sex*. New York: Vintage, 1974.

Braxton, Joanne, and Andree Nicola McLaughlin, eds. *Wild Women in the Whirlwind: Afra-American Culture and the Contemporary Literary Renaissance*. New Brunswick: Rutgers UP, 1989.

Cixous, Hélène. "The Laugh of the Medusa." *Signs* 1 (1976): 875–94.

Foucault, Michel. *The History of Sexuality*. Vol. 1. New York: Vintage, 1980.

Gilbert, Sandra, and Susan Gubar. *The Madwoman in the Attic: The Woman Writer and the Nineteenth-Century Literary Imagination*. New Haven: Yale UP, 1979.

Millet, Kate. *Sexual Politics*. Garden City: Doubleday, 1970.

Moers, Ellen. *Literary Women*. New York: Oxford UP, 1976.

Rubin, Gayle Rubin. "The Traffic in Women." *Toward an Anthropology of Women.* Ed. Rayna R. Reiter. New York: Monthly Review, 1975.

———. "Thinking Sex." *Pleasure and Danger: Exploring Female Sexuality* Ed. Carole S. Vance. New York: Pandora, 1992.

Sedgwick, Eve Kosofsky. *Between Men: English Literature and Male Homosocial Desire.* New York: Columbia UP, 1985.

Showalter, Elaine. *The New Feminist Criticism: Essays on Women, Literature, and Theory.* New York: Pantheon, 1985.

———. *Speaking of Gender.* New York: Routledge, 1989.

Smith, Barbara. "Toward a Black Feminist Criticism." *The New Feminist Criticism: Essays on Women, Literature, and Theory.* Ed. Elaine Showalter. New York: Pantheon, 1985. 168–185.

Summers, Claude J., ed. *The Gay and Lesbian Literary Heritage.* New York: Henry Holt, 1995.

Woolf, Virginia. *A Room of One's Own.* New York: Harcourt, 1957.

PART TWO

Writing about Literature

Writing about Literature

Why Write about Literature?

The answer to this rests upon two considerations: your purpose and your audience. You may be so enthusiastic about a work that you e-mail friends, urging them to read it. Or you may be so confused by a work that you write down your thoughts just to clarify them for yourself. Or you may be so excited about your insights into a work that you want to share them with others. The common characteristic of such writings is that they require interpretation. Whoever your audience may be, they want to understand the works you write about. As a writer, your aim is to help them do so.

How Can You Write about Literature?

Writing about literature can take many forms: informal jottings, meant only for yourself; effusions of praise or condemnation; book-length studies of complex interpretive problems; and so on. The kind of writing we emphasize in this book is the essay about literature. An *essay* is a piece of writing that has the following characteristics:

1. Relative brevity—from about two to fifty pages.
2. Formality. It does not have to be stuffy and stilted, but it follows certain forms that have become conventional. It adheres, for example, to rules of usage—punctuation, spelling, syntax, diction—characteristic of mainstream publications (newspapers, magazines, and books).

It has a thesis that unifies the whole essay. It follows an organizational pattern that emphasizes intellectual coherence.

3. A "serious" audience, persons who care about the subject and will take time to consider what the author has to say.

4. Persuasiveness. Its purpose is to persuade readers that the author's ideas are worthy of consideration.

5. Give and take between author and readers. It usually responds to others who have written or spoken on the topic and assumes that its readers can talk back.

6. Argumentation. Although in common usage *argument* means a heated exchange between angry people, for writing it means reasoned discussion. Essays are "argumentative." They develop a line of thought (a logically related series of claims), they support a thesis and related claims with evidence, and they organize claims and evidence coherently and logically.

The essay is a versatile and elastic genre, applicable not just to literature but to all kinds of subject matter and circumstances. Take, for example, the crime scene we mentioned in Chapter 1. You, the detective, have examined the scene, sifted through the evidence, and decided who is guilty. Now you have to tell people your conclusions. Your "telling" could, of course, be aloud, but if you are like most police detectives, you will have to write it out as an essay. It may be called something else—a report, say—but it will have the characteristics of an essay: a thesis (so-and-so did the deed) and an orderly presentation of claims and evidence that support the thesis (*because* of what I learned at the crime scene and elsewhere, I conclude that so-and-so is guilty). Your essay's audience will be all those who must rely on it to render justice: other police officers, the district attorney, the defending attorney, the judge, the jury.

Or consider another scenario. For a year, you have worked amazingly well in a new job, but your immediate supervisor threatens to fire you. To keep your job, you write a letter to your supervisor's boss. Again, although this will not be called an essay, it really is. It will argue a thesis—that you have done outstanding work and should retain your job. You will defend your thesis with claims about your successes and with specific evidence to support your claims. The outcome, we can hope, is that your supervisor will be fired, not you.

In both of these examples, we can see a pattern of communication similar to that introduced in Chapter 1, only this time you are the author: author/work/reader. The same pattern applies to writing about literature and in its complete representation looks like this:

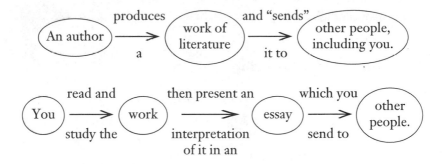

The purpose of your essay is to explain your interpretation to readers and persuade them that your interpretation is worthy of serious consideration. As a reader you were the receiver of an author's work of literature. Now you turn that situation around. You become an author *about* that same work of literature.

The Writing Process

When we write essays, we typically think and write through stages. Writers rarely follow this process rigidly—first one step, then another, then another. Rather, they go back and forth among stages and do many tasks simultaneously. But as they write essays, they inevitably follow the general outline of a process. Understanding this process—the writing process—helps us plan the task of writing. It also helps reduce "writer's anxiety," that dreadful feeling that we must come up with an essay all at once, produce it seemingly out of thin air. Like any involved building project, writing gets done in small steps. Knowing what the usual process is helps us relax and take steps one at a time. Even when we have to go back to earlier steps, as most writers do, we can feel sure we are moving toward completion. The writing process consists of four main sets of activities.

■ First Stage: Inventing

1. Studying the subject. For essays about literature, the "subject" is the work of literature.

2. Identifying your audience (its needs and interests).

3. Recognizing any limitations placed on your essay (length, time in which you have to write it, specifics of an assignment).

4. Generating topics.

■ Second Stage: Drafting

1. Determining a thesis and supporting claims.

2. Gathering facts from the work and, if helpful, from secondary sources to support claims.

3. Creating a plan of organization for a first draft.

4. Writing the first draft.

■ Third Stage: Revising

1. Reading your draft critically. If possible, getting others to read and comment on it.

2. Rethinking the topic, plan of organization, and line of reasoning.

3. Gathering more support for claims.

4. Writing further drafts.

■ Fourth Stage: Editing

1. Producing a final draft in the format expected by your audience.

2. "Publishing" the essay (by turning it in to your professor, by sending it to a circle of readers, by submitting it to a real publication, such as a magazine or newspaper).

The next chapter, Chapter 8, takes up the first stage of the writing process: inventing.

Choosing Topics

The most challenging question of the invention stage of the writing process is, "What can I write about?" For writers about literature, the answers are as varying as the people who write. People respond so differently to works of literature that it is hard to predict what they—and you—might choose to write about. For each of us, the most fruitful question for raising topics is probably, "What meanings do I find in the work?" Answer that for yourself and then write about one of those meanings. This chapter offers a number of more specific suggestions about how to search for topics and how to state them so that they are interesting and easy to discuss.

Preliminary Steps in Choosing a Topic

Be an Active Reader

We discussed this topic in Chapter 1 and throughout the first half of the book. Read actively rather than passively. Rather than just process works of literature, think about them as you read. Ask questions like the following:

- What don't I understand?
- Why is the author using this convention over other conventions?
- What ideas do the characters espouse?
- Can I detect the author's bias in favor of certain ideas?

- What interests me about the work?
- What do I dislike? What do I like?
- What experiences in my own life does the work reflect?

If it helps to skim parts of a work—even the whole work—and then reread, so as to get the whole picture, then do that. Consider the "places" to look for meaning we surveyed in Part One. Choose one or more of them to concentrate on as you read. Rather than let the work control you, use strategies of investigation and analysis to control it. You might object that such an "intellectual" approach to reading literature takes the fun out of it. Yes, there are times when we want to relax and not think much about what we are reading. But analyzing and interpreting works of literature, even when we read them for the first time, is pleasurable, too. In the long run, it is the most satisfying way of reading literature.

Identify Your Audience

This one is tricky.

A handy way to think about audiences for essays, no matter what the subject matter, is to imagine yourself in conversation with a friend. This person likes you and is interested in your ideas. One day you are having coffee with her at an outdoor café. You say, "The other day I was reading this strange story by Edgar Allan Poe, 'The Cask of Amontillado.' What puzzles me is that the narrator, Montresor, is not telling the story to us but to somebody else, someone in the story. But we never learn who it is. I think, though, that I can make a good guess." Your friend asks, "Who do you think it is?" You tell her. She then asks, "Why do you think so?" You explain, giving reasons and details from the story. She may disagree with some of your claims, maybe all of them. You respond to her challenges until you both come to agreement or get tired of the topic. Throughout your conversation with her, you tailor your comments for her—explaining what you think she needs to know, using language she can understand, anticipating questions she might have. Different friends would elicit different approaches from you. If your friend were eighty years old, you might speak to her differently than if she were twelve.

Such a dialogue between people who care about the topic under discussion and who respect one another is the basis of all essays. It is what makes them meaningful, productive, and enjoyable. When you write essays, your readers will not be right there in front of you, ready to speak back about every nuance of your argument. But they will respond to your surrogate, the words on the page. Inwardly, they will ask the same questions they would if you were there with them. Write, then, as if your readers are in a conversation with you and are eager to learn your ideas. Determine who they might be—their values, level of knowledge, facility with language, and so on, and adjust your writing for them accordingly. Sometimes, readers may not be friendly toward you. They might be skeptical about your subject, your ideas, or even your ability. If so, try to anticipate their questions. Ask yourself questions like these: To whom are you writing? What do they want from you? What information and explanation do they need from you in order to understand you? What effect do you want to have on them?

When you write for courses, however, identifying your audience becomes tricky. In such a case, isn't your professor your audience? Yes, of course. You want him or her to think well of your essay and to give it a high grade. It behooves you, then, to learn the professor's criteria for judging essays. Most professors want a well-crafted essay—such qualities as a clear statement of thesis, logical and coherent organization, fluent and correct prose, convincingly supported claims, thorough development of the topic. So far, so good. But professors often have a second audience in mind when they evaluate your essays—not just themselves but a "general" audience, one that is larger than the professor, one that includes the professor.

Who belongs to this audience? Two groups who do *not* belong, at least not solely, are (1) experts on your subject and (2) people intellectually incapable of grasping your reasoning (children, for example). You could write for both of these audiences, but if you wrote for an audience of experts, you would have to be an expert yourself and have something to tell them that they do not already know. Most students do not have enough time to master subjects that thoroughly. This, by the way, is another reason for not writing solely for your instructor. The instructor is an "expert" who, fortunately, rarely expects students to meet the needs of an audience of experts. On the other hand, if you wrote for the mentally immature, your essay would be too simpleminded for college courses.

Rather, a general audience consists of persons who are intelligent, who have read or can read the work you want to discuss, and who want to understand it better. It consists of individuals who are your equals, who form a community of which you are a part, to whom you can talk with equal authority. They share your interests and eagerly await your comments. If it will help, visualize people you know—classmates, friends, relatives, students at other campuses—as belonging to this audience. As with our conversation-over-coffee scenario, imagine yourself in a dialogue with them, saying things that would interest them, responding to their questions and comments. Project an image of yourself as the conscientious searcher for truth. Let your audience know that you are doing everything possible, within the limits of your time and ability, to answer the questions you have raised.

One reason professors may prefer you to write for a general audience is that you are more likely to include the facts and reasoning needed by *both* a general audience and your professors to understand and be convinced by you. When writing solely for professors, students often think, "The professor already knows this, so I won't include it." The professor usually *does* want you to include it. Professors cannot read your mind. In order to think well of your work, they need to see how you arrived at the claims you make. Professors know, furthermore, that writing for a general audience is the kind of writing you are most likely to do once you leave college. Your writing in the "real world" will usually be for groups of people, not just one person. Writing college essays for a general audience gives you practice in this kind of writing.

A third audience to write for is yourself. Writing essays is one way of satisfying your own intellectual needs and desires. Writing is not simply the product of thinking; it is a *way* of thinking. Some theorists argue that not until you write out your ideas can you be sure you have thought them through carefully. The process of writing essays, for example, underscores the need to use sound logic, to include all the steps in your reasoning, to state ideas precisely so your arguments will withstand scrutiny. It is easy *not* to do these things when you are just thinking to yourself or speaking to other people. Francis Bacon's maxim sums this point up well: "Reading maketh a full man, conference a ready man, and writing an exact man."

Perhaps the most important effect on you of writing is its ability to draw forth your ideas. One kind of essay about literature is the essay examination (discussed in Chapter 12). In writing essay examinations, students often discover ideas they never knew they had. The reason is that writing mates your knowledge of literature with the instructor's questions to give birth to new ideas. Essays about literature, then, can be journeys of self-discovery that lead you to new intellectual vistas. In this sense, you are part of your audience. You share your readers' curiosity and their desire to have puzzling questions answered. You write to convince them. But you write also to discover and clarify your own ideas and to convince yourself of their validity.

Raise Questions about the Work

Related to the identity and needs of your audience is the nature of your topic. Your audience wants to understand the work you wish to discuss. They want to know your interpretations of it. But what will you interpret—everything in the work or just some part of it? Since essays are relatively short, rarely can you interpret everything in a work. You have to limit yourself to some part of it. But which part?

The answer: Write about a specific problem of interpretation. The "problem" should be a question about the meaning (the coherence, the sense) of an aspect of the work. Your essay should identify that question and provide an answer to it. The topics of interpretive essays always refer to questions. You might announce your topic as "Hamlet's Indecision" or "Macbeth's Hunger for Power," but the audience knows that behind topics like these lie questions: Why does Hamlet hesitate to act? What propels Macbeth to seek power and to continue seeking it? The purpose of taking up such topics is to answer the questions that give rise to them. When you state your topic, you do not have to phrase it as a question, yet good topics always imply questions of interpretation.

Narrow Your Topic

What makes a topic good? One way to judge the quality of an essay topic is to ask yourself how easily your audience could answer the question that lies behind it. A useful criterion is that a topic is "good" if your readers could readily *not* answer the question after reading the work once. They could not answer it convincingly, either for themselves or for others, without reviewing and studying the work. The topic, in short, must be genuinely thought provoking.

A second consideration is the meaningfulness of your topic. As the author, you should care about the topic, and your audience should be interested in it. To assess your audience's interest, imagine yourself as part of your audience. What would you want to know if you were reading your own essay? Common sense should tell you that one of the *least* interesting questions is: What happened in the work? True, the events and details of works are sometimes hard to understand and need clarification, but usually readers can understand a work's details after reading it one time. You do not need to provide information your audience already knows.

A third way to assess the quality of a topic is to ask if it is focused narrowly enough for the confines of your essay. Most of the essays you write for college literature classes will run from three to ten typewritten pages (900 to 3,000 words). Your topic is good if you can deal with it thoroughly within those limits. For example, "Comedy in *Romeo and Juliet*" would probably be too broad for an essay topic; "The Nurse As Comic Figure" would be more specific and manageable. "Love in *Romeo and Juliet*" would be too broad; "Juliet's Mature Love versus Romeo's Adolescent Love" would be better. "Values in *Romeo and Juliet*"—too broad; "Shakespeare's Attitude Toward Suicide"—better. "Juliet As Character"—too broad; "Juliet's Change from Child to Young Woman"—better.

Charlotte Brontë's novel *Jane Eyre* provides an example of an essay topic that meets these three criteria. Brontë grew up absorbing the superstitions of the English north country. These superstitions included beliefs in fairies, elves, and demons, and we do not have to read far into *Jane Eyre* before encountering references to them. Jane, the narrator and main character, says that as a child she looked in vain for elves "under mushrooms and beneath the ground–ivy" and concluded that "they were all gone out of England to some savage country where the woods were wilder and thicker, and the population more scant" (53). After her first encounter with Mr. Rochester, he accuses her of being a fairy who "bewitched" his horse and caused it to fall. Her reply is that the fairies "all forsook England a hundred years ago" (153–154). Throughout her relationship, he calls her "elf," "fairy," "dream," "changeling," "sprite" (272, 302) After she returns at the end of the novel, he reverts to his epithets, once again calling her "fairy," "ghost," "changeling," "fairyborn and humanbred" (457–463).

If you spot this fairy lore motif in *Jane Eyre* you might think, "Aha, why not write an essay on that?" You could title the essay "Charlotte Brontë's Use of Fairy Lore in *Jane Eyre*." The question underlying the topic would be: What significance does this lore have in the novel? The purpose of the essay would be (1) to raise this question, (2) to show that the fairy lore actually does exist in the novel, and (3) to provide an answer to the question. This answer would be the "thesis" of the essay. The topic is meaningful because fairy lore is prominent in the work and is consistently associated with the main character; the topic promises to lead to an interpretation of the novel. Furthermore, the topic is complex enough so that most readers could not answer its implicit question fully and convincingly without rereading and studying the novel. And the topic is specific enough to be dealt with thoroughly in an essay of about six or so double-spaced pages. The topic, in short, is "good."

For some individuals, finding a good topic is easy and automatic. One person might happen to notice the references to fairies in *Jane Eyre*, and think, "Hey, that would be interesting to write about." For others, however, discovering good topics is difficult and frustrating, capable of inducing a severe case of writer's block. You or any writer can experience both situations. You might find that one work suggests all kinds of topics, whereas another leaves you at a total loss. If you ever find yourself in the latter situation, try a search strategy.

Search Strategies

A *search strategy* is a procedure for locating and examining important aspects of a work. It is a self-teaching device that helps you think about the work. As you examine the work, you become aware of areas you can raise questions about, questions that may lead to good topics. The following are brief descriptions of some well-known search strategies.

Focus on the Work's Conventions (Its Formal Qualities)

As we say in Part One of the book, the conventions of a work—such things as characterization, setting, plot, poetic style—make up its form and are "places" to locate meaning in works of literature. In your search for a topic, you may not want to examine *every* component of a work, but you can think about various ones until you hit on ideas that interest you. Systematically examining the standard conventions in a work, in other words, is a process of discovery, rather like shining a flashlight on different parts of a darkened room. You could even turn conventions of a work into essay topics: "Setting in Austen's *Pride and Prejudice*," "Meter and Rhyme in Shakespeare's Sonnet 116," "Characterization in O'Neill's *The Hairy Ape*," "Irony in Poe's 'The Cask of Amontillado.'" Your purpose would be to show how the author uses these conventions and how they are important to the overall scheme of the work. See, for example, the essay in Chapter 13 on the poem "Richard Cory."

Use Topoi (Traditional Patterns of Thinking)

Traditional patterns of thinking or *topoi*, such as definition, structure, process, comparison, and cause and effect, are useful for generating ideas about almost any subject, including literature, and for organizing essays. We take them up in Chapter 9 (pages 194–98).

Respond to Comments By Critics

Comments by literary critics are often a fruitful source of topics. Critics write about individual works, about an author's entire work, about the nature of literature itself, about a work's connection to society. Your purpose would be to make a critic's whole approach or an isolated comment by a critic the starting point of your essay. Chapter 6 outlines several well-known critical approaches to literature, but consider for the moment how you might use the following observation made by Terry Eagleton in *Literary Theory: An Introduction* (1983):

> Watching his grandson playing in his pram one day, Freud observed him throwing a toy out of the pram and exclaiming *fort!* (gone away), then hauling it in again on a string to the cry of *da!* (here). This, the famous *fort-da* game, Freud interpreted in *Beyond the Pleasure Principle* (1920) as the infant's symbolic mastery of its mother's absence; but it can also be read as the first glimmerings of narrative. *Fort da* is perhaps the shortest story we can imagine: an object is lost, and then recovered. But even the most complex narratives can be read as variants on this model: the pattern of classical narrative is that an original settlement is disrupted and ultimately restored (185).

Here, Eagleton states a quality in narrative that many people have probably not thought about consciously: that there is a lost-and-found pattern and variations on it in many narratives. Examples abound: Homer's *Odyssey*, Milton's *Paradise Lost*, Melville's *Moby-Dick*, Coleridge's *The Rime of the Ancient Mariner*, Keats's "La Belle Dame sans Merci," Shakespeare's *King Lear*, Jane Austen's *Pride and Prejudice*. You could make Eagleton's comment the basis for an essay about a particular narrative—a novel, a short story, a poem, a play. You would try to explain how the pattern or a variation on it operates in your work. You would begin your essay by explaining Eagleton's idea, giving proper credit to him. (For when and how to give credit in your essays, see

Chapter 11.) Then you would answer questions such as: What has been lost? How was it lost? How are the protagonists trying to recover it? Do they succeed? What qualities allow them to succeed or cause them to fail?

Eagleton's comment covers many works of literature, but critics also write extensively about individual works. You could use a critic's idea about a specific work as a starting point for an essay. You could write your essay in support of the idea or in disagreement with it. For an explanation of how to find critical interpretations of individual works, see the treatment of sources in Chapter 11, pages 233–35.

When you think of literary criticism, you may think only of published works, but do not forget your instructor and the other students in your class. Your instructor is a critic who "publishes" comments in class, aloud to you, and students often give interesting responses to the instructor and to one another. All of these comments can provide excellent starting points for essays.

Draw from Your Own Knowledge

People at all levels of achievement know a great deal and are learning all the time. If you are a student, you are most likely taking courses in a wide range of disciplines. All of this knowledge interconnects, even though for practical reasons colleges chop it up into schools, departments, and courses. You can bring this knowledge to bear on works of literature. Subject areas such as psychology, sociology, philosophy, design, art history, history of science, religious studies, cultural history, political history, even landscape gardening shine beams of light on authors and literature. Ibsen's Hedda Gabler (in the play *Hedda Gabler*) is a deeply troubled person. Can you find in your psychology textbooks theories that would help explain her problems? Ernest Hemingway said in an early version of "Big Two-Hearted River" that he wanted to write the way the Frenchman Paul Cézanne painted. Can you explain Hemingway's themes and methods by comparing his writing to Cézanne's pictures and theories of art? In the poem "Heritage," Countee Cullen conveys an ambivalent attitude toward Africa. How does the American understanding (or misunderstanding) of Africa at the time he wrote the poem (1925) both mirror his attitude and help explain his frustration? Anton Chekhov wrote plays at the turn of the twentieth century. What happened in Russia at that time, politically and socially, that reveals the intellectual currents in his plays?

Another kind of knowledge writers often overlook or discount is their own experience. Most students have developed expertise outside the academic world—through work, travel, family activities, personal experience of many kinds—and this expertise can illuminate works of literature. Have you done some sailing? If so, explain the complex maneuvers the young captain makes at the end of Joseph Conrad's "The Secret Sharer" and suggest what this knowledge tells us about the captain. (Is he taking a foolish, irresponsible risk?) Speaking of Conrad, have you been to the Congo River, the setting of *Heart of Darkness*? If so, are vestiges of the colonialism he condemns in that novel still there? What can you tell us about the landscape and atmosphere of the country that would help us better understand this puzzling novel? Have you seen any bullfights? If so, help us understand the symbolic meaning of bullfighting in Hemingway's fiction. Have you been the victim of prejudice? If so, provide insights into the dynamics of bigotry dramatized in Bernard Malamud's *The Assistant* or Richard Wright's *Black Boy*.

Talking and Writing Strategies

Talking and writing are themselves ways of generating ideas. When you talk with someone—or even to yourself—about a work, or when you write about it, you often come up with ideas you never knew you had. This is why the writing process often involves going back and forth among stages. As you write your first draft, you discover ideas that lead you to rethink your topic and major claims.

Talk Out Loud

Imagine yourself talking to a friend about the work you want to write about. Or, perhaps better, find a real person to talk to. Talk out loud. Keep your partner clearly in mind. You really want to explain this work to her. Say anything you want about the work—what you like and dislike about it, what interests you or does not interest you. Make claims about the work—what it means, what motivates the characters, what the setting is like—and support your claims with evidence. Try to get your listener to respond to you. Does she agree or disagree? Listen to her counterclaims and reasons. You might even summarize the work for her and ask if she understands and agrees with your summary. As you exchange ideas—or imagine that you are exchanging ideas—see if you can get at some of the themes of the work. What points does the writer seem to be making? By talking out loud, you get your mind working and push yourself toward developing interpretations of your own.

Make Outlines

Make an outline of the work. The outline need not be formal (complete sentences, Roman and Arabic numerals, and so forth); rather, it can be a list or a series of statements that indicate important aspects of the work. Write down the outline, mainly so you can remember everything you have put in it. The outline could focus on the whole work or one element of the work.

There are many possibilities for organizing outlines. The outline could follow the spatial order of the work; that is, it could show events in the order they appear in the work. Or it could follow a chronological organization; that is, the order in which the events occur in time. Another possibility is to outline the work according to the journalist's questions: who, what, when, where, why, how. The first four questions will help you get the facts straight. The last two will get you thinking about relationships among the facts. Who are the important characters in the work? What are they like? What has happened before the work begins? During what time period is the action set? Where does the action occur? Why does the action happen? At least one of the journalist's questions could lead you to other questions and more thorough development of an aspect of the work.

Freewrite

Choose a work or some aspect of a work and begin writing about it. Write for about ten minutes. During this time, do not stop writing. If you cannot think of anything new to say, repeat your last sentence over and over until something new occurs to you. Do not worry about sentence structure or correct usage. Write incomplete sentences if you wish. The benefit of freewriting is that writing generates thought, even if you repeat ideas or even write nonsense. You may find that a piece of freewriting provides not only the topic but a rough organization for a fullblown essay.

Brainstorm

To *brainstorm* is to think freely about particular works of literature—letting your mind flow where it will, but maintaining focus on the work and, after a point, on some aspect of the work. To brainstorm you need pen and paper—lots of paper. As ideas come to you, jot them down. Think of this activity as play, a game in which you talk to yourself. As you write, do not worry about spelling, constructing complete sentences, putting ideas in order. Include even your craziest ideas. Channel the flow of your thinking with questions such as these: Among the works I may write about, which do I like best? (Jot down the possibilities.) What interests me most about the work? (Jot down these.) What do I dislike about the work? (Jot down these.) Why do I like or dislike these particular things? (Jot down your reasons.) Are there aspects of the work I would like to write about? (Jot down these. For example, if you want to write about characterization, begin brainstorming about the characters in the narrative. Use the questions following "characterization" in Chapter 3 to get you started.) If your ideas about one aspect of the work seem uninspired, move on to another aspect and brainstorm about that.

At a certain stage of the brainstorming process, shift from a noncritical to a critical look at what you have done. Sort out, make connections, arrange your jottings into groups, and eliminate the unusable. Organization can be part of the play of brainstorming, even though it is a more controlled activity than the initial stages of brainstorming. Try certain arrangements and relationships, then discard them if they do not work. Try even the strangest, most unlikely connections and see if logical relationships emerge. If you have a list of ten items, see how you can group them. If you see connections between some but not others (perhaps five out of the ten), keep the ones that connect and cross out the others. Then brainstorm about the qualities linking the remaining items. Summarize these qualities in one phrase or apply one question to them. This phrase or question could be your topic, and the five items could provide the structure for a rough draft of the essay.

Make Notes

Notes are bits of writing you do for yourself. Write them wherever it is most convenient and helpful: in the margins of books you own, on little slips of paper, in a notebook. Since they are for yourself only, you need not worry about spelling, punctuation, or even coherence. Notes should almost always be short and pithy. Jotting down notes *as* you read stimulates interaction between you and the text. Writing notes *after* you read helps you think about the whole work, raise questions, state interpretations, and call attention to intriguing passages and details. The following are notes made by a student after she read Homer's *Odyssey:*

Notes on the <u>Odyssey</u>

Why does Odysseus want to leave Calypso's island?

He's got such a good deal there.

 If he loves Penelope, why does he sleep with

Calypso? And Circe? Is this being "faithful"? I won-

der what Penelope will think when he "confesses" (if

he ever does). Could she do the same thing--sleep

around--and get away with it? Double standard.

 Athene: Obsessed with tying up loose ends. Al-

though a goddess, power limited. Poseidon. Are

they rivals?

 Nausicaa: my favorite. "There slept a girl who

in form and feature was like the immortal goddesses"

(86). The "handsome girl" who, like Leto's daugh-

ter, is "the loveliest amid a whole bevy of beau-

ties" (89). Innocent but spunky.

 Zeus is patron of "strangers and foreigners in

distress" (92). Why doesn't Zeus just zap the

suitors?

 Odysseus: A Greek Woody Allen (always worrying

and down on himself).

 At the end, Odysseus's treatment of the servant

girls: horrible. Bloody and excessive. Sexist?

Keep a Journal

Journals are generally more coherent, more polished, and more developed than notes. You may be the sole audience for your own journals, but sometimes they are for others as well. The journals of authors like Ralph Waldo Emerson, Henry James, and F. Scott Fitzgerald provide fascinating insights into their lives and works. Like these authors, writers often use journals not only to try out lines of thought, but also to get other peoples' reactions to them. The root word for journal—*jour*, the French word for "day"—suggests that they are more systematic and regular than notes. Write in your journal, if not every day, then at least regularly. Take more time developing your ideas than for notes. The journal below is by the same student who wrote the previous notes on the *Odyssey*. Notice how her journal entry is more developed than her notes and less developed than her essay (which immediately follows the journal entry).

Journal Entry on the <u>Odyssey</u>

Two things bother me about the <u>Odyssey</u>. One is the way Homer presents women. Women are almost always more limited in what they can do than men and are treated as inferiors by the male characters. As a female I resent this attitude. I will admit that females in the <u>Odyssey</u> are stronger--more admirable and influential--than in some of the other things we have read this semester. If Athene weren't always helping Telemachus and Odysseus, where would they be? But Athene's femaleness seems unimportant. She isn't human, for one thing. And for another, when she takes human form, she almost always appears as a male. Penelope is admirable, I suppose, for being so loyal and patient, but she has to stay home and do domestic duties (for twenty years!) while her husband

---

gets to roam the world, have adventures, and sleep
with beautiful goddesses. What would the men of
Ithaca have thought had Penelope had similar adventures? Probably lynched her. Finally, at the end, I
think that Odysseus's treatment of the disloyal female servants is excessive. They are sentenced without a trial. Who knows, they might have been coerced
by the piglike suitors. They don't deserve to die,
especially in such a gruesome way. What threat to
Odysseus and Ithaca could they be if left alive?

    The other thing is Odysseus's attitude toward
Ogygia, Calypso's island. I keep wondering why he
wants to leave. Ogygia seems like paradise.
Odysseus says he loves Penelope and wants to return
to her, but is that the real reason? Ogygia strikes
me as being similar to Eden in the Bible. It even
has four rivers, just like Eden. In the Bible, Adam
and Eve are kicked out of Eden as punishment for
eating the apple. Yet, in the Odyssey, Odysseus
wants to leave. Why? I think I might want to stay.
Look at what he's got. He has a beautiful woman who
loves him and takes care of him. He could have immortality. (Calypso promises to make him immortal
if he will stay.) Ogygia is beautiful. All my life
I have thought that losing paradise, as Adam and Eve
did, would be terrible. Why would someone wish to
lose it? As a person (character), Odysseus seems
very restless. Maybe that's the reason. Once he
returns home, you wonder if he will stay long.

Sample Essay about Literature

The following essay is by the student whose notes and journal appear immediately above. It is a response to her reading of the *Odyssey*. Notice how her essay evolves out of her informal writing. In her notes she comments briefly on the "paradise" theme. She returns to it for more extended comment in her journal. She decides, finally, to focus an entire essay on this one theme. You can see from her notes and journal entry that she could have also written on other topics—the nature of the gods, Nausicaa, Athene, and gender equity. But she instead chose to write on this one.

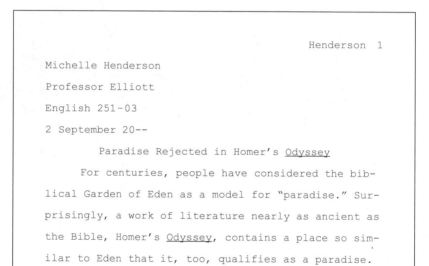

Henderson 1

Michelle Henderson

Professor Elliott

English 251-03

2 September 20--

   Paradise Rejected in Homer's Odyssey

       For centuries, people have considered the bib-

lical Garden of Eden as a model for "paradise." Sur-

prisingly, a work of literature nearly as ancient as

the Bible, Homer's Odyssey, contains a place so sim-

ilar to Eden that it, too, qualifies as a paradise.

This place is Calypso's island, Ogygia. Yet as

alike as Eden and Ogygia are, the mortals who dwell

there react to them very differently. Adam and Eve

want to remain in Eden, but because of their disobe-

dience they are expelled. In contrast, Odysseus

chooses to leave Ogygia. This choice is puzzling.

Why would he want to leave paradise?

       Ogygia is similar to Eden in at least four

ways. First, it looks and feels the same. The Gen-

esis account says that God caused trees to "spring
from the ground," trees that were "pleasant to look
at and good for food" (2:9). A river flows "from
Eden to water the garden" and branches into four
"streams," called Pishon, Gihon, Tigris, and Eu-
phrates (2:10-14). Eden is a "garden," a pleasant
place where all forms of vegetation and animal life
exist together in harmony (2:19-25). Homer's description of Calypso's Ogygia is almost the same,
complete with the four springs:

> Round her cave there was a thick wood of alder,
> poplar, and sweet smelling cypress trees,
> wherein all kinds of great birds had built
> their nests--owls, hawks, and chattering sea-
> crows that occupy their business in the waters.
> A vine loaded with grapes was trained and grew
> luxuriantly about the mouth of the cave; there
> were also four running rills of water in chan-
> nels cut pretty close together, and turned
> hither and thither so as to irrigate the beds
> of violets and luscious herbage over which they
> flowed. Even a god could not help being
> charmed with such a lovely spot [. . . .].
> (73-74)

Ogygia, furthermore, is fragrant: "There was a large
fire burning on the hearth, and one could smell from
far the fragrant reek of burning cedar and sandal
wood" (73).

Ogygia is like Eden in a second way: its inhab-
itants live in comfort and without pain. Adam, Eve,
and Odysseus hardly have to lift a finger to get the
necessities of life. Although God puts Adam "in the
garden of Eden to till it and care for it" (2:15),
Adam doesn't work. "Work" is what he has to do
after he is cast out of the garden: "You shall gain
your bread by the sweat of your brow until you return to the ground" (3:17). Adam and Eve are free
from pain in Eden. Only after they eat the apple
does God give them pain. He tells Eve that he "will
increase your labor and your groaning, and in labor
you shall bear children" (3:16). He says that Adam
will have to overcome the "thorns and thistles" of
the earth (3:17). As for Odysseus, Calypso seems to
provide all the food he could want: "Calypso set
meat and drink before him of the food that mortals
eat; but her maids brought ambrosia and nectar for
herself, and they laid their hands on the good
things that were before them" (77). We get the impression that, just as she provides food for
Odysseus, she can protect him from pain. "Good luck
go with you," she tells him, "but if you could only
know how much suffering is in store for you before
you get back to your own country, you would stay
where you are, keep house along with me, and let me
make you immortal [. . .] (77).

Third, like Eden, Ogygia provides loving companionship. After creating Adam, God worries that Adam
will be lonely, so God first creates the animals and
then Eve to keep him company. Adam and Eve are the
first married couple, becoming "one flesh" (2:18-25).
Odysseus, of course, yearns to be with his wife,
Penelope, but he has a loving companion in Calypso
and seems to enjoy her company: "Presently the sun
set and it became dark, whereon the pair retired into
the inner part of the cave and went to bed" (78).

Finally, in Ogygia as in Eden, there is no
death. God tells Adam and Eve that if they eat of
the tree of knowledge they will die (2:16-18). And,
sure enough, after they eat the apple God tells them,
"Dust you are, to dust you shall return" (3:19). We
can infer, then, that before they eat the apple, they
have eternal life. Odysseus is mortal, but he, too,
has the promise of immortality. Calypso tells Her-
mes, "I got fond of him and cherished him, and had
set my heart on making him immortal, so that he
should never grow old all his days" (75).

In sum, Adam, Eve, and Odysseus possess the
benefits of paradise: a beautiful environment, an
easy and painless life, loving companionship, and
eternal life.

Yet Odysseus rejects this paradise. Why?

The answer Odysseus himself gives is that he
loves Penelope and wants to be with her. His actions

support this statement. When we first see him, he is
"on the sea-shore as usual, looking out upon the bar-
ren ocean with tears in his eyes, groaning and break-
ing his heart for sorrow" (74). Odysseus admits that
Calypso is far more beautiful than Penelope. He
tells Calypso, "I am quite aware that my wife Penelope is nothing like so tall or so beautiful as yourself. She is only a woman, whereas you are an
immortal. Nevertheless, I want to get home, and can
think of nothing else" (77). At the end of the
Odyssey, after many hardships, he does just that.
The climax of the story occurs when Odysseus and
Penelope at last retire to bed to consummate their
long-awaited reunion.

A less obvious explanation for Odysseus's re-
jection of paradise, however, springs from his nature. He is incredibly creative and energetic and
thrives on meeting challenges and devising
stratagems. Early in the epic, Helen of Troy recounts the story of Odysseus's most famous
stratagem, the Trojan Horse (52–53). Odysseus later
tells with loving detail how he crafted his marriage
bed:

> [The bed] is a marvelous curiosity which I made
> with my very own hands. There was a young
> olive growing within the precincts of the
> house, in full vigor, and about as thick as a

and I made the doors strong and well-fitting.

Then I cut off the top boughs of the olive tree

and left the stump standing. This I dressed

roughly from the root upwards and then worked

with carpenter's tools well and skillfully,

straightening my work by drawing a line on the

wood, and making it into a bed-prop. I then

bored a hole down the middle, and made it the

center-post of my bed, at which I worked till I

had finished it, inlaying it with gold and sil-

ver; after this I stretched a hide of crimson

leather from one side of it to the other.

(354-55)

Homer gives a similarly detailed and admiring ac-

count of how Odysseus constructs the raft on which

he escapes from Ogygia (78-79).

Odysseus, in short, is a craftsman, a maker, a

builder. He crafts the stratagem of the Trojan

Horse. He crafts his escape from Polyphemus, the

Cyclops (135). He crafts his way past Scylla and

Charybdis (188-89). He crafts his artful speech to

Nausicaa that wins her help (90-91). He tells the

story of his adventures, Alcinous says, "as though

you were a practiced bard" (172). Finally, he

crafts the defeat of the suitors. He loves

stratagems so much that he invents them for the

sheer pleasure of it. After telling Athene one of

his elaborate lies, she says,

He must be indeed a shifty lying fellow who
could surpass you in all manner of craft even
though you had a god for your antagonist.
Dare-devil that you are, full of guile, un-
wearying in deceit, can you not drop your
tricks and your instinctive falsehood, even now
that you are in your own country again? (205)

How satisfied would Odysseus be in a place like
Ogygia? He would hate it. Ogygia, like the Garden
of Eden, provides everything one could possibly
want. That's the trouble with it. There are no
challenges, no obstacles to overcome. People whose
love for overcoming obstacles is "instinctual" would
be so bored and so restless they would go crazy.
That is the real reason Odysseus chooses to leave
Ogygia. He loves Penelope. But he loves, also, the
very things we usually think of as bad--the difficulty and pain of life. Athene tells Zeus at the
beginning that Odysseus "is tired of life" (2).
Odysseus would rather die than live forever in the
static eternity of "paradise."

Works Cited

Homer. The Odyssey. Trans. Samuel Butler. New
     York: E. P. Dutton, 1925.
The New English Bible. New York: Oxford UP, 1971.

Note: Normally, the "Works Cited" list would appear on a separate page, but we print it here,
right after the essay, to save space.

Comments on the Essay

This essay represents the interpretive and argumentative nature of essays about literature. The author begins by raising a question: Why does Odysseus leave Ogygia? This is her *topic*. She follows the question with claims about the nature of paradise and about Odysseus's motivation for leaving. She supports her claims with evidence. In her conclusion (final paragraph), she answers her question. This answer is her *thesis*. The essay deals with a serious issue that would interest thoughtful readers of the *Odyssey*. She shows them that the paradise theme is *meaningful* because of the light it sheds on Odysseus's values and motivations.

Works Cited

Brontë, Charlotte. *Jane Eyre*. New York: Penguin, 1966.

Eagleton, Terry. *Literary Theory: An Introduction*. Minneapoliis: U of Minnesota P, 1983.

Drafting the Essay

This chapter deals with the second stage of the writing process, drafting the essay. By the time you reach this stage, you should have chosen a topic and thought about what you want to say about it. Now your task is to draft the essay. How do you do this? To help you answer this question, we discuss the basic aspects of the interpretive essay and offer some guidelines for writing a first draft.

The Argumentative Nature of Interpretive Essays

Essays about literature are almost always argumentative. Although writings about literature can be purely informational (that is, just give information) or be purely expressive (that is, just state opinions), essays are argumentative. An *essay* has three main qualities. First, it persuades an audience of the validity of its ideas. Second, it uses evidence (facts, reasoning, and, when necessary, testimony) to explain and support its ideas. And third, it has a *thesis*, an overall claim supported by specific claims.

The argumentative nature of essays about literature emerges from the relationship between the work and its reader. Good literature is complex. It communicates on many levels of meaning and by many methods. A single work may exist as a system of sounds, of symbols, of ideas, of images, of analogies, of actions, of psychological portrayals, of moods, of grammatical structures—all of which are separate entities, yet all of which interrelate. Furthermore, literature also invites readers

181

to participate in creating the work. A work is not complete until it is read. The author leaves "gaps" in the work for readers to fill with their imagination. The completed work—the work that is read—is something more than the words on the page. It is a collaboration between text and reader. As a result, perceptions of a work vary from age to age, reader to reader, even reading to reading. This variability of perception occurs because no single reading, however careful, can take in all the elements of most works, or synthesize them into all their structural relationships, or include all the vantage points from which even one reader might experience a work.

Consequently, no single view of a work, whether your own or someone else's, can be the all-encompassing or final view. Cultures change, people change and, as a result, perception changes. It is a common experience for children to enjoy works—*Huckleberry Finn, Gulliver's Travels,* "Rip Van Winkle," *Alice in Wonderland*—and as adults to enjoy them again, but for very different reasons and with entirely new understandings of them. This does not mean that all interpretations of a work are equally valid. Interpretations of literature are subject to the same rules of human thought—accurate observation, sound reasoning, systematic procedure, thoroughness of treatment—as any other interpretive discourse. But no single interpretation can encompass the whole work.

Because literature is complex and can be perceived variously, essays about literature are arguments. You, the writer of the essay, cannot take for granted that your interpretation of the work is the same as your reader's. Your reader may have missed the very facts in the work you have found most compelling or most "obvious." Your reader may have a totally different understanding of the work than you do. If you want your reader to grasp your interpretation or accept it as valid, you must explain and persuade. You must write an argument.

The Structure of Essays about Literature

Argumentative essays have two interrelated structures: an *argumentative structure* based on logic and a *rhetorical structure* based on persuasion. The argumentative structure is really part of the rhetorical structure because argumentation is a means of persuasion. But the two structures are not exactly the same, so we will talk about them separately.

The Argumentative Structure

The argumentative structure of an essay consists of two kinds of reasoning: inductive and deductive. *Inductive reasoning* is the "scientific method" and consists of observing specific instances of something and then drawing conclusions about them. You might, for example, notice that in Act One of *Hamlet,* Hamlet exhibits melancholy behavior once. Then in Act Two, he is melancholy twice. In Act Three, he is melancholy four times. In Act Four, six times. And in Act Five, all the time. Having observed these instances of Hamlet's behavior, you could reasonably conclude that Hamlet is a melancholy fellow and that his melancholia increases dramatically throughout the play.

Inductive reasoning is essential for interpreting literature, but in itself it can seem like a dead end. So what if Hamlet is melancholy? To get beyond the "so what" question, you need a second kind of reasoning, deduction. What if, for example, you want to claim that Hamlet's melancholia is the cause of something or, that by Act Five, reaches crisis proportions? *Deductive reasoning* allows you to support such claims, to *do* something with your inductive conclusions.

Syllogisms are the basis of deductive reasoning. A *syllogism* is a unit of reasoning that consists of two claims that support a third claim. The two supporting claims are called *premises* and the third claim is called a *conclusion.* The *major premise* states a general concept. The *minor premise* is a specific instance of that concept. The *conclusion* connects the specific instance to the general concept:

MAJOR PREMISE: All complex characters are fascinating.

MINOR PREMISE: Anna Karenina is a complex character.

CONCLUSION: Therefore, Anna Karenina is fascinating.

Although in formal logic all three parts of a syllogism are stated, in argumentative essays parts of syllogisms are usually left unstated. The above syllogism would probably be stated something like this: "Anna Karenina is fascinating because she is so complex." Here, the major premise has been left out and is present only as an assumption. Such incompletely stated syllogisms are called *enthymemes.* Authors use enthymemes when they believe the unstated premises would seem "obvious" or readily acceptable to their readers. But just because an author uses enthymemes does not mean that the syllogisms are not present in the author's reasoning. Readers can recover all the parts of the syllogisms to examine critically an essay's reasoning.

The deductive reasoning of an essay consists of a series of syllogisms that support a thesis. Consider, for example, the deductive reasoning of the student essay on the *Odyssey* in the previous chapter (pp. 172–78). The student's thesis is that although Ogygia might seem like paradise to most people, Odysseus leaves it because to him it is not. She supports this thesis with two sets of syllogisms. In the first set she reasons why Ogygia seems like a paradise:

Many people believe that all places like Eden are paradises.

Ogygia is like Eden.

Therefore, many people would believe that Ogygia is a paradise.

In the second set of syllogisms, she reasons why Odysseus fails to find Ogygia a paradise.

1. All people who constantly scheme and love to overcome challenges are creative.

   Odysseus constantly schemes and loves to overcome challenges.

   Therefore, Odysseus is creative.

2. All creative people would hate living in a place that demands no creativity.

   Odysseus is a creative person.

   Therefore, Odysseus would hate living in a place that demands no creativity.

3. All places that anyone would hate are not paradise.

   Places that demand no creativity, like Ogygia and Eden, are places that some people (namely, Odysseus) would hate.

   Therefore, Ogygia is not, for Odysseus, a paradise.

These two sets of syllogisms—the syllogism about the nature of paradise and the ones about Odysseus—form the deductive framework of this student's essay. If you read her essay carefully, you will see that she leaves parts of her syllogisms unstated. She uses enthymemes. Such incompleteness is typical of essays. The point, however, is that the deductive reasoning of all essays consists of a chain of syllogisms, whether fully stated or not, that lead to and support a thesis.

But what about the inductive reasoning in her essay? We see inductive reasoning in two crucial places: (1) her claim that Ogygia is like Eden and (2) her claim that Odysseus is a craftsman. She arrived at these claims by noticing numerous related facts about Ogygia and Odysseus's behavior. Now, in her essay, she supports her claims with some of these facts. But had she done no more than this, we might be tempted to ask, "So what?" So what if Ogygia is like Eden? So what if Odysseus is crafty? She anticipates our "so what" questions by positioning her claims as minor premises in two key syllogisms. She thus joins inductive reasoning and deductive reasoning to establish the argumentative structure of her essay.

The Rhetorical Structure

Rhetoric, simply put, is the art of persuasion. It consists of all the devices writers use to make their claims attractive and convincing. For essays, the most important rhetorical device is argumentation—the reasoning that supports your thesis. Reasoning, however, is not the only rhetorical device you can use in an essay. Other rhetorical choices include how you organize the essay, where you put your thesis, what parts of your syllogisms you leave unstated, and which parts you emphasize and support with evidence from the text. All of these choices help create the rhetorical structure of the essay.

How should you organize your essay? The organization of any essay depends in part on the line of reasoning you develop, and this will vary from topic to topic. But the general structure of an argumentative essay is fairly standard and almost always contains the following units:

1. **Title.** The *title* should tell enough about the topic of the essay to capture the interest of readers and let them know the focus of the essay. It helps to include the author's name and the title of the work you are discussing: "The Jungle As Symbol in Joseph Conrad's *Heart of Darkness*."

2. **Introduction.** The *introduction* should state the topic of the essay and should be interesting enough to make the reader want to keep on reading. You may want to spell out your thesis here, but you could also announce it later in the essay. The introduction should be relatively short—one to three paragraphs.

3. **Body.** The *body* is the place where you develop your line of reasoning. It consists of a series of paragraphs that contain claims (usually one claim per paragraph) along with supporting evidence. The body should be as long as you need it to be in order to make your argument convincing.

4. **Conclusion.** The *conclusion* signals that the essay has come to an end. It should remind the reader of the problem posed at the beginning of the essay (the topic) and briefly summarize the solutions. It should state or restate the thesis. The conclusion should be brief, a paragraph or so.

The student essay on the *Odyssey* illustrates these structural principles. The title—"Paradise Rejected in Homer's *Odyssey*"—gives enough information about the topic for readers to know, and be intrigued by, the focus of the essay. The introduction (the first paragraph) presents the topic as a problem to be solved: Why does Odysseus leave "paradise"? The body of the essay consists of a series of paragraphs spelling out the chain of syllogisms that make up the author's reasoning. The conclusion—the last paragraph—answers the question raised in the beginning.

Where should you put the thesis?   You have three choices: You can put it in the introduction, you can put it in the conclusion, or you can leave it unstated but implicit. You have to decide which is rhetorically most effective for your topic. If you state the thesis at the beginning, readers have the comfort of knowing what to look for as they read the rest of the essay. If you withhold it until the end, you create a sense of suspense that is climaxed by the revelation of thesis. If you leave the thesis implicit, you allow readers to infer it for themselves and to participate with you in the process of discovery.

The author of the essay on the *Odyssey* puts her thesis at the end of the essay rather than at the beginning. Her rhetorical strategy is to open the essay with an intriguing question, then lead us toward an answer—her thesis—at the end.

Which premises of your syllogisms must be supported with evidence from the text?   Your syllogisms, and ultimately your thesis, are believable only if your audience accepts the premises of the syllogisms. You do not have time to support all your premises with evidence, and you do not really need to. Your audience will accept most of them as true, but you will have to support some of them to make your argument believable. Which ones? This, too, is a rhetorical question.

You have to decide which premises your audience will accept as true and which ones they will want supported with evidence. For essays about literature, "evidence" consists of anything in the text or outside it that bears on your topic.

The author of the student essay on the *Odyssey* leaves many of her premises and conclusions unstated. The ones she emphasizes and supports with evidence are (1) that Eden and Ogygia are similar and (2) that Odysseus is creative. Is she right to have supported these claims and not some others? Only she and her readers can answer that question for sure. Some readers might say no, that she needs to support other claims as well. Others may say yes, that these are the key claims needing support. Arguing effectively depends on your ability to choose for the benefit of your audience which claims to state and support. Where you present them—and how—becomes part of the rhetorical structure of your essay.

Guidelines for Writing First Drafts

You are now about to begin writing. The following guidelines are suggestions about what to think about and do as you write.

Keep in Mind the Needs of Your Audience

As you write the drafts of your essay, think of your audience and its needs. You will write better essays if you write for an audience that includes not just your instructor but anyone who enjoys literature and has ideas about it. Your goal is to convince them that your ideas have merit. Imagine yourself in conversation with your audience. In order to follow your line of thought, they will want to know certain things. Try to anticipate and supply their needs, just as you would if you were talking with them in person.

One of their needs is for clarity. They deserve a full and clear explanation of the points you are making. Your readers—including your instructor—cannot read your mind. Assume that they have already read the work or can read it; this means that you need only summarize and paraphrase those parts of the work that illustrate your points. But if you do not spell out your ideas, your readers may miss them altogether. In being fully clear, you may feel that you are being childishly obvious, but it is better to be obvious than risk having readers miss your points.

Your readers also need to be convinced. Assume that they want to learn from you, but do not expect them to surrender their views of the work just because you tell them to. Think of them as constantly asking, Why should we believe what you say? Your task is to explain and show them why.

Avoid Extreme Subjectivity (Overuse of "I")

Should you use "I" in essays about literature? Some teachers insist that students not use "I." One reason is that teachers want students to avoid stating their opinions without supporting them with facts and reasoning. We are used to asserting opinions in casual conversation: "The Harry Potter books are wonderful!" But the essay form demands proof and reasoning. Another reason is that if you fill your essays with phrases like "I feel," "I think," "I believe," "It seems to me," your essay, no matter how thorough and well reasoned, will sound overly opinionated. Notice how the author of the essay on the *Odyssey* uses "I" frequently in her notes and journal but eliminates it entirely from her essay.

Having said this, however, essays about literature are inevitably "subjective." Yes, you have to pay careful attention to details in the text. These are the basis for all your claims about it. Yes, you have to use sound logic to support claims. Yes, you have to be objective—willing to entertain understandings of a work other than your own. But nearly all works of literature are open to interpretation. That is why we write about them. Your interpretations are likely to be different from other people's. For this reason, it is standard practice for critics to use "I" when writing interpretations of literature, even in the most scholarly writing. Many essays, in fact, would sound stilted and strange if their authors did not use "I." An example is the student essay on George Eliot's *Adam Bede*, reprinted in Chapter 13. The author compares her own experiences to those of a character in the novel. Even in essays that do not, like this one, take a reader-response approach to literature, the inclusion of an occasional "I believe" makes rhetorical sense. It emphasizes where the author departs from others' opinions: "Scores of critics see Hetty as selfish and thoughtless, but I see her more sympathetically."

Two suggestions, then, pertain to the use of "I" in your essays. Use "I" helpfully but sparingly. Find out your teacher's preference about the use of "I" and write accordingly.

Draw Up a Rough Outline

Many people find rough outlines indispensable for drafting essays. A rough outline consists of the main points you want to make, including the thesis. If the author of the essay about the *Odyssey* had made a rough outline, it would look something like this:

```
                     Introduction
Raise this question: Why does Odysseus leave Ogygia,

which seems like paradise?
                        Body
Claim #1: Ogygia is a paradise.

Support this claim by comparing Ogygia to Eden (my

standard for what paradise is). Give facts from the

two texts.

Claim #2: Odysseus leaves Ogygia because he wants to

be with Penelope and because he is too creative to

be happy there.

Support these claims with facts from the Odyssey.

                     Conclusion
Claim #2 is the answer to my question and therefore

my thesis. I will make it my conclusion as well.
```

Rough outlines are just that—*rough*. They include only the main points of your draft, not all the nuances. Their usefulness is to give you a general sense of your line of thought and rhetorical strategy and to help you make sure that all claims relate to your topic. When you start writing, you may discover new ideas or run into dead ends. If so, redo your rough outline and go on from there.

Begin Writing

Don't bog down. If you have trouble with the introduction (as many people do), move on to the body of the paper. Work on stating your claims clearly and supporting the key ones with evidence. Tackle the claims that seem easiest to support first. Once you get a draft written, it is easier to rearrange claims, to fill in gaps, and to decide for sure what your thesis is.

Use Sound Deductive Reasoning

The deductive logic of your essay is made up of the syllogisms and chains of syllogisms that constitute your reasoning. If one or more of your syllogisms is invalid, the whole of your argument is undermined. Logic is a complex topic we do not have the space to discuss thoroughly here. But a general rule is to avoid *non sequiturs*. The Latin term *non sequitur* means, "It does not follow." A *non sequitur* results from the improper—that is, illogical—statement of a syllogism. For example, the conclusion of the following syllogism "does not follow" from the premises:

MAJOR PREMISE: All complex characters are fascinating.

MINOR PREMISE: Anna Karenina is fascinating.

CONCLUSION: Anna Karenina is complex.

Just because Anna is fascinating does not mean she is complex. She may be fascinating for many other reasons. The correct statement of this syllogism is as follows:

MAJOR PREMISE: All complex characters are fascinating.

MINOR PREMISE: Anna Karenina is a complex character.

CONCLUSION: Therefore, Anna is fascinating.

When you plan and write your essay, think about the validity of your most important syllogisms. After you finish the first draft, go back over it to make sure your syllogisms are valid. For practice, identify some of the key syllogisms in one of the essays in Chapter 13 or in an argumentative essay in a newspaper or news magazine. Write down the syllogisms and see if they are properly stated.

Support Key Claims with Facts

The believability of your argument rests not only on the validity of your reasoning but on the truth of your premises. The logic of your syllogisms may be perfectly valid, but if readers do not accept your premises as true, they will reject your conclusions, including your thesis. For example, look again at the correctly stated syllogism about Anna Karenina above. Is it true that "all complex characters are fascinating"? If not, the conclusion that Anna is fascinating is dubious.

One way of establishing the truth of premises is to support them with facts. Anything in the work is a "fact." Facts can be quotations, words, incidents, details of setting, descriptions of characters, conflicts within the plot, word sounds, punctuation—anything in the work. Facts need not be just quotations; sometimes your facts will be more compelling if you summarize scenes or events in your own words, emphasizing what is most salient to your point.

Notice, for example, how the author of the essay on the *Odyssey* combines summary and quotation to support her claim that Odysseus is a craftsman:

Odysseus is a craftsman, a maker, a builder. He

crafts the stratagem of the Trojan Horse. He crafts

his escape from Polyphemus, the Cyclops (135). He

crafts his way past Scylla and Charybdis (188-89).

He crafts his artful speech to Nausicaa that wins her

help (90-91). He tells the story of his adventures,

Alcinous says, "as though you were a practiced bard"

(172). Finally, he crafts the defeat of the suitors.

He loves stratagems so much that he invents them for

the sheer pleasure of it. After telling Athene one

of his elaborate lies, she says,

> He must be indeed a shifty lying fellow who
>
> could surpass you in all manner of craft even
>
> though you had a god for your antagonist.

> ```
> Dare-devil that you are, full of guile, un-
>
> wearying in deceit, can you not drop your
>
> tricks and your instinctive falsehood, even now
>
> that you are in your own country again?  (205)
> ```

The only "long" quotation in this paragraph is the one at the end. Otherwise, the paragraph consists of the author's summary of relevant facts as well as brief quotations she weaves into her own sentences. She also gives page references, so readers can check her facts or get a sense of their context. Page references have a rhetorical function as well. They say, in effect, "Reader, I know what I'm talking about. If you don't believe me, go check my references."

Use Sound Inductive Reasoning

When you reason inductively, you draw conclusions from facts in the work. Instances of Hamlet's melancholia, for example, lead you to conclude that he is melancholy. When you include inductive reasoning in an essay, you usually reverse this order. You state a claim (the conclusion of your inductive reasoning). Then you present facts that led you to it. To make your inductive reasoning convincing, keep in mind three rules of evidence. First, you need not report every fact that supports your claim, but give enough facts so readers can see for themselves that your claim is reasonable. Second, report facts that are representative of all the facts, not just isolated, atypical facts (the one and only time that Hamlet is melancholy). Third, account for facts that contradict your thesis. If there are incidents in which Hamlet is not melancholy, you need to explain why these do not nullify your claim that he is melancholy. Often, when you explain away negative examples of your claims, you make your overall argument more subtle and convincing. Hamlet's gaiety, you might argue, does not contradict his melancholia; rather, it is a cover for it, a mask he wears.

Define Key Terms

Learn the meaning of important words in primary sources. Look up words in a good dictionary when you have any doubts about their meaning. Doing so is especially necessary for poetry and earlier authors such as Shakespeare and Chaucer. For definitions of terms, the two most authoritative dictionaries are *The Oxford English Dictionary* (1989); and *Webster's Third New International Dictionary of the English Language* (1966). *The Oxford English Dictionary* (*OED*) is based on "historical principles"; it describes and gives examples of a word's use over the years. If you want to know what a word meant to Shakespeare or Chaucer, look it up in the *OED*. The *Merriam-Webster's Third International* is a "descriptive" dictionary; it describes how the word is used and spelled today. The college edition of the Merriam, abridged from the *Third New International*, is adequate for nearly all your needs, as are most hardcover "desk" dictionaries on the market. As of this writing, you can search *The American Heritage Dictionary* (3rd edition, 1996) online at <http://www.bartleby.com/61>. Also, your library may subscribe to the online version of the *OED*. A Website that includes a dictionary, a thesaurus, and other materials related to languages is <http://www.your dictionary.com>. For definitions of specialized literary terms, such as *gothic* and *Naturalism*, see M. H. Abrams's *A Glossary of Literary Terms* (1999).

Organize Evidence According to a Coherent Plan

Evidence consists of everything you offer in support of your claims and thesis. It includes both your reasoning and whatever facts you use to buttress your reasoning. The most important "coherent plan" for presenting evidence is your line of thought, the chain of enthymemes that lead to your thesis. These will vary from topic to topic. You will have to work out a different plan of reasoning for each essay.

Nonetheless, there are several ways of presenting facts from literature that make evidence easy to follow.

1. *Spatial organization* presents the facts as they appear in the work, from beginning to end.
2. *Chronological organization* takes up the facts in the order in which they occur in time. Often, spatial order is the same as chronological

but not always. Many works employ devices such as stream of consciousness and flashbacks that make spatial sequence different from chronological. Detective fiction, for example, depends on a gradual revelation of past events. Not until you finish reading a detective novel can you know the chronological order of events. One advantage of either organization is that you give the reader the sense that you are covering all the important details of the work.

3. *Organization by ascending order of importance* moves from the least important facts or claims to the most important. The primary advantage of this method is that it gives your essay an element of suspense by ushering readers toward a climax. Organizing from the least controversial claims to the most controversial is a variation on this plan.

The paragraph about Odysseus's craftsmanship (pp. 191–92) combines two of these plans of organization. The author arranges her facts *chronologically* by starting with the Trojan Horse and ending with the defeat of the suitors. Had she arranged them spatially—as they appear in the text—they would be out of chronological sequence. She also arranges her facts, at least roughly, in *ascending order of importance*. She ends with Odysseus's most important stratagem, the defeat of the suitors, and with his most surprising trait, his love of stratagems. This plan provides an orderly review of Odysseus's career, makes her facts easy to follow, and gives her presentation a measure of suspense.

Use Topoi to Generate Topics and Organize Your Essay

Generations of communicators have recognized that certain ways of thinking—patterns of thought—are helpful tools for examining subjects and developing ideas about them. In his *Rhetoric*, perhaps the greatest book about writing, Aristotle called these patterns *topoi*, which means "places." Aristotle seems to have meant that these patterns are "places" to look when you need to find ideas. Several of the traditional patterns are especially useful—at times inevitable—for coming up with ideas about literature and for explaining it. The following are descriptions of well-known *topoi*.

Definition—Definition is unavoidable in arguments because premises often contain terms that must be defined. Quite often, these terms are not controversial or ambiguous and therefore need no formal definitions. However, when you have controversial terms, you must define them, and you must use all key terms in such a way that your readers know what you mean by them.

Apart from the necessity of defining terms in your thesis, definition can be useful in two other ways. First, your claims about the facts may rest upon the definition of a particular word within the work. Second, you may want to focus your whole essay on a definition. You might, for example, show that "imagination" is Isabel Archer's most admirable trait in Henry James's novel *The Portrait of a Lady*. Your essay would attempt to explain what James means by the term. Or you might argue that Jane Austen in *Pride and Prejudice* distinguishes between "good pride" and "bad pride." Again, you would discuss the novel in order to define these terms. Finally, you might claim that Emily Brontë uses "gothic" elements in *Wuthering Heights*. You would need a reliable definition of *gothic* to make your case convincing, and to apply all parts of the definition to the work, showing which ones fit and which do not. A handbook of literary terms, such as M. H. Abrams's *A Glossary of Literary Terms* (1999) and the articles in encyclopedias such as *The Encyclopaedia Britannica*, are helpful starting points for finding definitions of literary and philosophical concepts.

Structure—Focus on structure helps identify an object's parts and how they contribute to the coherence and meaning of the whole. A structure is something that has a definite pattern of organization. Works of literature always have a structure, sometimes more than one structure. Some works conform to established structures like the sonnet form; other works establish their own structures. Your purpose in writing about a work's structure is to identify the structure and explain its relationship to other elements such as theme and characterization. You might, for example, claim that the passage of the seasons provides the structure of William Wordsworth's poem "The Ruined Cottage"; or that the rhyme scheme of his "I Wandered Lonely As a Cloud" emphasizes the narrator's shift from feeling isolated to feeling connected to nature. The less obvious the structure or its effect on the work, the more revealing your essay would be. You might even argue that the work has several structures— an obvious structure and a less-obvious structure.

Process—Tracking process identifies the stages in which things change—characters, states of mind, societies, settings, situations, conditions. Because literature often represents events occurring in time, it lends itself to process analysis: Characters change from weak to strong, societies from coherent to incoherent, settings from beautiful to ugly. When describing a process, avoid simply retelling the plot. Instead, explain and illustrate clear *steps* in the overall process. Present them in the order in which they occur in time. Each step would be a unit—probably a paragraph—of your paper. The claim of each unit would be your proposition about what characterizes the step.

Cause and effect—Examining cause and effect helps you investigate the causes and effects of things. When you investigate *causes*, you are always dealing with things in the past. Why does Goodman Brown go into the forest? Why does Hedda Gabler act the way she does? What causes Pip to change? Two kinds of causes usually figure in works of literature, the immediate or surface cause and the remote or deep cause. In Theodore Dreiser's *An American Tragedy*, the immediate cause of Roberta Alden's death is that she is pregnant. Clyde Griffiths kills her because he wants her out of the way so he can marry Sondra Finchley. The remote cause, however, is all those forces—childhood experiences, parental models, heredity, financial situation, cultural values, religious background, and accident—that have molded Clyde and that make the reasons he kills Roberta complex. When you investigate *effects*, you may deal with things in either the past or the future. In William Faulkner's fiction, you might examine the effect of slavery on Southern society and on his characters. These effects are part of the historical past in his work. You might also predict what the South will be like in the future, given the way he depicts it.

Because literature often deals with the actions of complex characters and societies, analyzing cause and effect is a fruitful source of essay topics. We constantly wonder why characters do what they do and what effects their actions have had or will have. Just as in real life, cause and effect in literature can be subtle. Your task is to discover and communicate those subtleties.

Comparison—Comparison means indicating both similarities and differences between two or more subjects. One use of comparison is to establish the value of something. You might argue that one of Shakespeare's comedies is not as good as the others, because it lacks some of the qualities the others have. Another use of comparison is to explain your insights about aspects of a work. A comparison of the two sets of lovers in Tolstoy's *Anna Karenina*, for example, helps us understand his distinction between sacred love and profane love. Comparing the themes of one work to another is also revealing. Sir Walter Raleigh's poem "The Nymph's Reply to the Shepherd" is a response to Christopher Marlowe's poem "The Passionate Shepherd to His Love." (See Chapter 2, pp. 27–28, for the texts of these poems.) Raleigh not only disagrees in general with the premise of Marlowe's poem, he also makes nearly every line of the poem respond to the parallel line in Marlowe's poem. A line-by-line comparison of the two poems helps make Raleigh's themes clear.

Comparison is revealing also when the author of a work contains allusions. An *allusion* is a reference to another work, a historical event, a myth, or an author. An allusion is always an invitation to compare the work at hand to the thing alluded to. Wordsworth, for example, in his long autobiographical poem *The Prelude* often alludes to Milton's *Paradise Lost*. One could compare *The Prelude* and *Paradise Lost* to clarify Wordsworth's methods and themes.

When you make extended comparisons, organize them so they are easy to follow. Cover the *same aspects* of all the things compared. If you compare two works and talk about metaphor, symbolism, and imagery in one work, you need to talk about these same things in the other work. Also, discuss the aspects *in the same order* for each thing compared. If you talk about metaphor, symbolism, and imagery in one work, keep this same order when you discuss the other work: metaphor first, symbolism second, imagery last. The outline for such a comparison would look like this:

Work #1
   Metaphor
   Symbolism
   Imagery
Work #2
   Metaphor
   Symbolism
   Imagery

For comparisons of more than two things or for long, complex comparisons, another method of organization may be easier for readers to follow:

Metaphor
    Work #1
    Work #2
    Work #3
Symbolism
    Work #1
    Work #2
    Work #3
Imagery
    Work #1
    Work #2
    Work #3

Notice how the student essay on the *Odyssey* uses this second plan of comparison:

Claim: Eden and Ogygia are similar.
    Reason #1: Their physical features are similar.
            A. Eden has certain physical features (described).
            B. Ogygia's physical features (described) are almost ex-
               actly the same.
    Reason #2: Their inhabitants live comfortable and painfree lives.
            A. Eden
            B. Ogygia
    Reason #3: The inhabitants have companionship.
            A. Eden
            B. Ogygia
    Reason #4: Both places are free from death.
            A. Eden
            B. Ogygia

There are other ways to organize comparisons. You could, for example, discuss all the similarities in one place and all the differences in
another. But the general rule is to make the comparison thorough and
orderly, so the reader can see all the lines of similarity and difference.
Doing this usually requires ample revisions of your outlines and drafts.
The next chapter, Chapter 10, deals with the revision and editing stages
of the writing process. It concludes with two drafts of a comparison

essay, illustrating how revision can improve the organizational structure of an extended comparison.

Works Cited

Abrams, M.H. *A Glossary of Literary Terms.* 7th ed. Fort Worth: Harcourt, 1999.

The American Heritage Dictionary. 3rd ed. Boston: Houghton Mifflin, 2000. <http://www.bartleby.com/61>.

Gove, Philip Babcock, ed. *Webster's Third New International Dictionary of the English Language.* Unabridged. Springfield: Merriam, 1966.

Simpson, J.A. , and E.S.C. Weiner. *Oxford English Dictionary.* 2nd ed. 20 vols. Oxford: Oxford UP, 1989.

yourDictionary.com . 2000. 24 October 2000 <http://www.yourdictionary.com>.

Revising and Editing

Revise Throughout the Writing Process

The third stage of the writing process is revision. The word *revision* means "to see again." Revision takes place throughout the writing process. You constantly see your work anew, and act upon that fresh understanding by rewriting. Assume that you will make several drafts of the essay, from scribbled lists to finished product—say, three to five drafts. Give yourself time—a week or so—to write the essay. You may be able to bring off an "all-nighter" every now and then, but few people can do so consistently. Work hard for a while, put your essay aside, let the ideas percolate, then come back to the essay fresh.

Revise for the Final Draft

Some people could go on revising forever, but most need to move quickly toward a final draft. The final draft differs from the earlier drafts because readers expect it to conform to "formal" rules that govern a particular format. To help yourself prepare the final draft, think about what your audience will expect from it. They will, of course, want the qualities of a good argument we have discussed: interesting topic, sound logic, thorough discussion of the works, good organization. But readers want also to feel that your writing is worth reading, that you are competent to talk about your topic, and that you can teach them something. Rhetoricians call this personal quality ethos. *Ethos* is the image that writers project of themselves. You cannot help doing this. Create, therefore, a compelling, trustworthy ethos.

The content and organization of the essay are the most important indicators of your ethos. By reasoning well and supporting claims with evidence, you make readers feel that you are conscientious and that your essay is intellectually sound. Other aspects of the final draft also help create a persuasive ethos. They are prose style, rules of usage, and physical format (the appearance of the essay). We treat these latter aspects in this chapter.

Write a Clear and Readable Prose Style

Style is the way writers put words together in units of thought—sentences—and the way they link sentences to make larger units—paragraphs, essays, books. Closely related to style is tone. *Tone* is a writer's attitude toward the material and the readers. You convey tone through style.

Adjust your style and tone to fit the occasion and audience. Sometimes the occasion and audience call for informal and humorous writing, such as for speeches made at parties or essays written for satirical magazines. At other times, they call for gravity and formality, such as for newspaper editorials and letters of application. The occasion and audience for essays about literature almost always require a measure of formality. Your audience is usually intelligent, literate, and serious. They take the trouble to read your essay because they want to learn. They might welcome some levity, some lightheartedness, but they mostly want you to get down to business and not waste their time. They want to learn from you economically, to get through your essay with pleasure but as effortlessly as possible.

Your style for this audience should meet these needs. Make your style clear, interesting, and readable: vary sentence structure, avoid the passive voice, emphasize active and concrete verbs, eliminate wordiness and unnecessary repetition, use words with precision, and base syntax on the natural rhythms of spoken English. Give your tone seriousness of purpose but avoid stiff formality: Stay away from incomprehensible words and long complex sentences. Because essays about literature involve personal judgment, use "I" to distinguish your ideas from those of others and to stress the individuality of your views. But use "I" sparingly, so you do not give the impression of being subjective and egotistical.

A well-known guide to writing graceful and clear prose is *The Elements of Style* by William Strunk, Jr., available at no charge on the Internet at <http://www.bartleby.com/141/index.html>.

Have Other People Read and Respond to Your Draft

In one sense, writing is an isolated, individualized task. We have to do it alone. In another sense, however, it can be collaborative. Other people's reactions to your writing can help you to improve. After all, your writing is *for* an audience. So, before you draw up a final draft, you might get someone else to read your essay. Ask them to answer such questions as these: Can you follow my line of thought? Do you agree with my reasoning? Can I support my claims more convincingly? Is my writing clear and fluent? Should I use different strategies of persuasion? Will my audience understand me? You may disagree with the answers you get, but even "wrong" answers can help you see "right" strategies. Your goal is to get fresh perceptions of your essay so you can make your final draft as good as it can be.

Edit the Final Draft

The final draft of your essay is the one you will "publish." Publishing can mean printing the essay in a journal, newspaper, magazine, or book. It can also mean distributing it yourself to a group of people. For university courses, it means turning in the essay to the professor or to the rest of the class. The "published" draft of the essay should follow a certain format. What should that format be? The format described in the following sections is typical of the writing done in a university setting and is based on the guidelines in the *MLA Handbook for Writers of Research Papers.*

Rules of Usage

Usage refers to the way English is applied in most published writing: in newspapers, magazines, books, advertisements, brochures, financial reports, and scholarly journals. Although some rules of usage are arbitrary and seem to serve no purpose other than convention, most serve important purposes. First, they often aid clarity. Punctuation, for example, represents parts of the sentence—pauses and inflections—that words do not. Marks of punctuation can be as important as the words. Misplace a comma, and you can change the meaning of a sentence. Second, rules of usage help communicate your ethos. Rules of usage are a form of etiquette; educated people are expected to follow them. By doing so, you communicate an image of competence and respect for your readers.

If you are not familiar with the basic rules of usage, they might at first seem bewildering. But they are not difficult to learn. Study and practice using them, and you will learn them quickly. Get a handbook of usage, such as *The Harbrace College Handbook*, and refer to it when you write. An online resource is *Guide to Grammar and Writing* at <http://ccc.commnet.edu/grammar>.

Although all rules of usage are important for your writing, in this book we concentrate on rules common to essays about literature. These include rules that govern documentary procedure, which we discuss in Chapter 11, as well as those that apply to such things as quotations, punctuation, capitalization, underlining, and the physical format of papers. In the following sections, we describe basic rules of usage. For a more thorough treatment of such rules, see the *MLA Handbook for Writers of Research Papers*. See, also, the sample essays in Chapters 8, 11, 13, and at the end of this chapter for examples of how these rules are used in practice.

Quotations

Quotations serve two key purposes in essays about literature: They help exemplify claims, and they reproduce the language of the source.

1. **Introduce your quotations.**
   a. For primary sources, identify the author, the work, and the context of quotations.

Incomplete information

```
The woman tells her lover that the world "isn't ours any-
more."
```

Complete information

Near the climax of the lovers' conversation in Hemingway's "Hills Like White Elephants," the woman tells the
man that the world "isn't ours anymore."

Readers need to know *where* in the text quotations occur. Otherwise, the quotation could seem meaningless.

b. Introduce quotations from secondary sources by giving the author's name or claim to authority.

Missing name

"A fully articulated pastoral idea of America did not
emerge until the end of the eighteenth century."

Included name

Leo Marx claims that a "fully articulated pastoral idea
of America did not emerge until the end of the eighteenth
century."

Included claim to authority

A prominent American critic claims that a "fully articulated pastoral idea of America did not emerge until the
end of the eighteenth century."

There are several reasons for this rule. One is that giving the
critic's name or claim to authority clearly distinguishes your ideas
from the other writer's. Quotation marks can of course help to
make this distinction, but introducing the quote by author makes
the distinction emphatic. A second reason is that when readers see
quotation marks, they are naturally curious about who said the
quoted passage. Also, as they read your essay, they may want to
note the different approaches of the critics you use. A third reason
is that, by giving the author's name, you distinguish between secondary and primary sources, a distinction that may not be clear
from the quotation alone. A final reason is that it is a matter of
courtesy to give credit in your text to the words and ideas of other
people. You are, in a way, thanking them for their help.

c. Introduce quotations with the correct mark of punctuation. Use a comma for brief, informal, grammatically incomplete introductions.

Missing comma

```
Prufrock thinks "I am no prophet--and here's no great
matter."
```

Included comma

```
Prufrock thinks, "I am no prophet--and here's no great
matter."
```

Use a colon to separate your own grammatically complete introductions or statements (complete sentences) from quotations.

```
Edith Hamilton describes Hera perfectly: "She was the
protector of marriage, and married women were her pecu-
liar care.  There is very little that is attractive in
the portrait the poets draw of her."
```

The purpose of these two rules is to separate your thoughts from those of the quotation; that is, to eliminate ambiguity. Thus, the first examples above mean two different things. Without the comma, the reader might see the whole sentence as one complete thought: "Prufrock thinks [that] 'I am no prophet—and here's no great matter.'" With the comma, the reader sees that "Prufrock thinks" is merely the introduction to the quotation; the quotation is the complete thought.

2. **Integrate quotations into your own sentences.**

```
Because of this increasing darkness, Brown cannot be
quite sure of what he does or hears.  The devil's walking
stick, for example, seems to turn into a snake, but this
may be "an ocular deception, assisted by the uncertain
light" (76).  He thinks he hears the voices of Deacon
Gookin and the minister, but "owing doubtless to the
```

```
depth of the gloom of that particular spot, neither the

travellers nor their steeds were visible" (81).
```

Once you introduce your source, you may want to integrate short quotations—words or phrases—from it into your own sentences, as in the above example. The quotations become part of your own thoughts rather than thoughts totally separate from yours. This technique allows you to summarize a source concisely and yet retain the language and authenticity of the source. If you use this method, you should obey several rules.

    a. As much as possible, make the tenses in the quotation correspond to the tenses of your sentences.

Awkward

```
While the legislators cringe at the sudden darkness, "all

eyes were turned to Abraham Davenport." [Cringe is pre-

sent tense; turned is past tense.]
```

Better

```
While the legislators cringe at the sudden darkness, "all

eyes [turn] to Abraham Davenport."
```

```
While the legislators cringe at the sudden darkness, "all

eyes" turn to Abraham Davenport.
```

    b. Be sure that sentences are complete.

Incomplete

```
Yeats asks if "before the indifferent beak." [Incomplete

sentence; makes no sense.]
```

Complete

```
Yeats asks if Leda "put on [the swan's] knowledge" before

his "indifferent beak could let her drop."
```

    c. Clarify pronouns that have no clear antecedents.

Unclear

Captain Wentworth says, "It had been my doing--solely
mine. She would not have been obstinate if I had not
been weak." [The antecedent of "she" is unclear.]

Clear

Captain Wentworth says, "It had been my doing--solely
mine. [Louisa] would not have been obstinate if I had
not been weak."

d. Be sure that subject and verb agree.

Disagreement

Wilfred Owen says that the only prayer said for those who
die in battle is war's noise, which "patter out their
hasty orisons." [Subject: <u>noise</u>; verb: <u>patter</u>. The subject is singular, the verb plural.]

Agreement

Wilfred Owen says that the only prayer said for those who
die in battle is the "rapid rattle" of guns, which "patter out their hasty orisons." [Subject: <u>guns</u>; verb: <u>pat-
ter</u>. Both subject and verb are now plural.]

In short, when you integrate a quotation into your sentence, make it a grammatical part of the sentence. The entire sentence, including the quotation, must conform to the standard rules of usage. See item 4 below for methods of altering (interpolating) quotations.

3. **Quote accurately.** Copy exactly what the author has written.

4. **Make editorial changes in quotations correctly.** You may legitimately change the quotation in two ways:

   a. By using *ellipses.* An ellipsis (three spaced periods) indicates omitted material. Writers often leave out sections of quotations for the sake of brevity or clarity. To indicate omitted material, use three periods surrounded by brackets. Put a space before and after the brackets. Put spaces between the periods. Here, for example, is a quoted sentence with omitted material *within* the sentence.

```
As one critic says, "Oedipus is guilty for two reasons:

because of the deeds he actually committed [ . . . ] and

because of his desire to commit them."
```

To indicate omitted material from the *end* of a sentence, follow this sequence: space after the last word, then put the bracketed periods, then a space, then a period, and finally the quotation mark.

```
In certain moods, Wordsworth confessed, he "was often un-

able to believe that material things can live forever

[ . . . ]."
```

If your *parenthetical reference* comes at the end of a quotation like the above, put the bracketed periods first, then the quotation mark, then the parenthetical reference, then the final period.

```
In certain moods, Wordsworth confessed, he "was often un-

able to believe that material things can live forever

[ . . . ]" (175).
```

You can also use bracketed periods to indicate the omission of whole sentences, a paragraph, or several paragraphs. The following example omits part of a long paragraph.

```
Ruskin gives two reasons for his belief that to demand per-

fection of art is to misunderstand it: "The first is that no

great man ever stops working till he has reached his point

of failure. [ . . . ] The second reason is that imperfection

is in some sort essential to all that we know of life."
```

In this example the period goes immediately after the final word of the sentence ("failure"), then a space, then the bracketed periods.

There is no need to place ellipses at the *beginning* of quotations:

> Even the commonest people, the duke says, would elicit
> from her "the approving speech, / Or blush, at least."

b. By using *brackets*. Brackets indicate editorial changes that *you*, not the author, make to clarify the quotation or to make it fit the grammatical structure of your sentence. Use brackets for *your* changes, not parentheses. Otherwise, your reader will construe them as part of the original quote.

Unclear

> Alceste says that "sins which cause the blood to freeze /
> Look innocent beside (Célimène's) treacheries."

Clear

> Alceste says that "sins which cause the blood to freeze /
> Look innocent beside [Célimène's] treacheries."

> Flaubert says that "she [has] an excess of energy."

5. **Indent long quotations.** A *long quotation* consists of more than four lines of poetry or prose. Usually, your introduction to a long quotation will be a complete sentence. Conclude your sentence, then, with a *colon* (not a comma or a period). Indent the quotation ten spaces (one inch) from the left margin. Do not use quotation marks for indented quotations.

> The duke is chagrined that his own name and presence were
> not the sole sources of her joy:
>
> > She had
> > A heart--how shall I say?--too soon made glad,
> > Too easily impressed; she liked whate'er
> > She looked on, and her looks went everywhere.
> > Sir, 'twas all one! My favour at her breast,
> > The dropping of the daylight in the West,

```
The bough of cherries some officious fool

Broke in the orchard for her, the white mule

She rode with round the terrace--all and each

Would draw from her alike the approving speech,

Or blush, at least.
```

As in this example, position the words of a quoted poem, especially in the first line, exactly where they appear in the line. If you are quoting a whole paragraph of prose, do not indent the first line. Instead, place it flush to the left margain of the quotation. If you quote more than one paragraph, indent the first line of each as you normally would.

6. **Punctuate quotations correctly.**
   a. Use *double quotation* marks (" ") for quotations. For quotations within quotations, use double quotation marks for the main quote and single quotation marks (the apostrophe mark) for the inner quote.

   ```
   After his interview with Hester, Dimmesdale sinks into

   self-doubt: "'Have I then sold myself,' thought the min-

   ister, 'to the fiend whom, it men say true, this yellow-

   starched and velveted old hag has chosen for her prince

   and master!'"
   ```

   b. Always put *periods* and *commas* inside quotation marks.

   ```
   After performing her "duties to God," as she called them,

   she was ready for her "duty to man."
   ```

   c. Always put *colons* and *semicolons* outside of quotation marks, unless they are part of the original text being quoted.

   ```
   She had the "exquisite pleasure of art"; her husband had

   only envy and hatred.
   ```

   d. Put *other marks of punctuation* (question marks, dashes, exclamation points) inside quotation marks when they are part of the quoted material, outside when they are not.

```
One critic asked, "Could the Pearl Poet really be the au-
thor of Sir Gawain and the Green Knight?"

But can it be, as one critic claims, that "the Pearl Poet
really [is] the author of Sir Gawain and the Green
Knight"?
```

e. *When quoting a line of poetry or part of a line,* make the quotation part of your sentence. Use a slash mark (also called a solidus or virgule [/]), with a space before and after it, to indicate line divisions.

```
Hopkins describes God's grandeur as gathering "to a
greatness, like the ooze of oil / crushed."
```

When quoting more than four lines of poetry, or, if you prefer not to use slash marks, indent the quotation ten spaces (one inch) from the left margin. Indented quotations of poetry do not need quotation marks, nor do they need slashes to mark line divisions. Some people prefer not to use slash marks when quoting poetry. Instead, they indent the quotation, even if it is short. Type the lines and words in exactly the same position as in the original. For examples of indented quotations from poems, see item 5 on page 210 and the sample essay at the end of this chapter.

Other Rules of Usage Related to Essays about Literature

Essays about literature obey the same rules of usage as other essays. Several rules deserve special mention.

1. **Tense.** Describe fictional events, whether in drama, poetry, or prose fiction, in the present tense. For examples of this practice, see the student essays in this and other chapters.
2. **Authors' names.** Use either the full name (Charles Dickens) or the last name (Dickens). Some exceptions are Lord Byron, Mrs. Browning, and Dr. Johnson.
3. **Underlining versus italicizing.** For student papers, the *MLA Handbook* recommends underlining instead of italicizing because underlining is easier to see.

4. **Words used as words.** Underline words used as words.

> In England the word <u>honor</u> is spelled with a <u>u</u>: <u>honour</u>.

5. **Titles**
   a. Capitalize the first letter of the title, plus the first letter of all words except articles, short prepositions, conjunctions, and the preposition *to* in infinitives ("First to Go"). Capitalize the first letter after a colon.

> "How I Won the World but Lost My Soul to the Devil's Wiles"
>
> <u>Exile's Return: A Narrative of Ideas</u>

In the second example, the colon indicates the subtitle of the book.
   b. Use quotation marks for titles of works included within larger works. Examples are short stories; short poems; songs; chapter titles; articles in journals, magazines, and newspapers; and unpublished works such as dissertations and master's theses.
   c. Underline the titles of works published independently, such as books, plays, long poems published as books, periodicals, pamphlets, novels, movies, compact discs, works of art, works of music, and radio and television programs. An exception is sacred writings such as the Bible, books of the Bible, the Koran, and the Talmud.
   d. Do not underline, italicize, or put in quotation marks the titles of your own essays.
   e. Many instructors prefer that your essay titles include full names of authors and works.

Incomplete

> The Four Stages of Knowledge in <u>Huck Finn</u>

Complete

> The Four Stages of Knowledge in Mark Twain's
>
> <u>The Adventures of Huckleberry Finn</u>

   f. If your instructor approves, in the text of your essay you may use shortened titles for works you frequently cite: "Prufrock" for

"The Love Song of J. Alfred Prufrock" or *Huck Finn* for *The Adventures of Huckleberry Finn.*

6. **Foreign language terms**
   a. Underline foreign words used in an English text, such as *sans doute, et tu Brute, amor vincit omnia.*

   ```
   She objected to her son-in-law's behavior because it was
   not comme il faut.
   ```

   Reproduce, either by hand or in type, all marks and accents as they appear in the original language: *étude, à propos, même, übermensch, año, leçon.*
   b. Some foreign words, like *cliché, laissez-faire,* and *genre,* have been naturalized—that is incorporated into—English usage and need not be underlined. Use your dictionary to determine whether the word or phrase needs underlining. Foreign words in dictionaries are either italicized or placed at the back of the book in a separate section.

   ```
   Adam Smith advocated a laissez-faire economic policy.
   ```

   c. Do not underline quotations that are entirely in another language.

   ```
   Louis XIV once said, "L'état, c'est moi."
   ```

Physical Format

As with rules of usage, the appearance of your essay also affects your argument. Readers want an essay that is easy to read, pleasant to hold, and attractive to view. The more care you take with the appearance of the essay, the more competent your readers will think you are. Although your instructor may have specific preferences, the following are standard guidelines.

1. **Typewritten and handwritten essays.** Some instructors may prefer that you type or print all your work, but sometimes you may also handwrite college essays. Whether you handwrite, type, or print your essay, use only one side of each sheet of paper. For *hand-*

written essays, use black or blue ink (which, unlike pencil, will not smear or rub off). Use lined paper. Write on every other line. Write legibly.

2. **Paper.** Use standard-size paper (8 1/2 × 11″), not legal-pad size or notepad size. Use a sturdy weight of paper. Avoid "erasable" paper and paper that has been ripped out of a spiral-bound notebook.

3. **Spacing.** Double-space everything, including indented quotations and works cited entries.

4. **Pagination.** Number *all* pages, beginning with the first page. Number pages consecutively, including pages for endnotes and works cited. Put the page numbers in the upper right-hand corner of each page. To avoid having pages misplaced, put your last name before each page number, with a space between the two. Example:

Caraway 16

5. **Margins.** For typewritten essays, leave one-inch margins at the top, bottom, and sides. This gives the page a "frame" and a place for corrections and comments. For handwritten essays, leave margins at the top, bottom, and left side.

6. **First page.** One inch from the top of the first page, on the left-hand side, put your name, the instructor's name, the course title, and the date, each on a separate line. Double-space between the lines. After the last line (the date), double-space again and center your title. If your title has more than one line, double-space between lines. Double-space between the title and the first line of text.

   Title pages for college essays—even research essays—are usually unnecessary; but if your instructor expects a title page, check with him or her for its content and form.

7. **Corrections.** You may write corrections on final copies of essays— if the corrections are few and inconspicuous. In typed essays, white out incorrect letters and write or type in the correct letters. In handwritten essays, draw a vertical line through unwanted words and write the correct words just *above* the line. Separate run-together words with vertical lines (for example, made ׀ a ׀ mistake). To delete words, phrases, and clauses, draw a single horizontal line through them. Add words, phrases, and clauses by writing them in above the line. Use a caret (∧) below the line to show where inserted material should go.

8. **Putting the essay pages together.** Avoid covers or binders. Join the pages of your essay with a paperclip, unless your instructor specifies some other method.

9. **Copies.** Make a photocopy of your essay. If your instructor loses your essay, you can immediately present him or her with a copy. If your instructor keeps your essay indefinitely, you will have a copy for your files.

10. **To fold or not to fold.** Leave your essay unfolded unless your instructor specifies otherwise.

Sample Essay in Two Drafts

The student essay that follows the poem below gives a brief idea of how the revising process works. Nearly all writers, no matter how experienced, go through several drafts of an essay before they produce the final draft. Printed here are an early draft of the essay and, after considerable revision, a final draft. Since the essay is about a poem by Robert Frost, we reprint the poem here. The poem first appeared in *North of Boston*, published by Henry Holt in 1914.

THE DEATH OF THE HIRED MAN

Mary sat musing on the lamp-flame at the table
Waiting for Warren. When she heard his step,
She ran on tip-toe down the darkened passage
To meet him in the doorway with the news
And put him on his guard. "Silas is back."
She pushed him outward with her through the door
And shut it after her. "Be kind," she said.
She took the market things from Warren's arms
And set them on the porch, then drew him down
To sit beside her on the wooden steps.   10

"When was I ever anything but kind to him?
But I'll not have the fellow back," he said.
"I told him so last haying, didn't I?
'If he left then,' I said, 'that ended it.'
What good is he? Who else will harbor him
At his age for the little he can do?
What help he is there's no depending on.
Off he goes always when I need him most.

'He thinks he ought to earn a little pay,
Enough at least to buy tobacco with,   20
So he won't have to beg and be beholden.'
'All right,' I say, 'I can't afford to pay
Any fixed wages, though I wish I could.'
'Someone else can.' 'Then someone else will have to.'
I shouldn't mind his bettering himself
If that was what it was. You can be certain,
When he begins like that, there's someone at him
Trying to coax him off with pocket-money,—
In haying time, when any help is scarce.
In winter he comes back to us. I'm done."   30

"Sh! not so loud: he'll hear you," Mary said.

"I want him to: he'll have to soon or late."

"He's worn out. He's asleep beside the stove.
When I came up from Rowe's I found him here,
Huddled against the barn-door fast asleep,
A miserable sight, and frightening, too—
You needn't smile—I didn't recognize him—
I wasn't looking for him—and he's changed.
Wait till you see."

         "Where did you say he'd been?"

"He didn't say. I dragged him to the house,   40
And gave him tea and tried to make him smoke.
I tried to make him talk about his travels.
Nothing would do: he just kept nodding off."

"What did he say? Did he say anything?"

"But little."

         "Anything? Mary, confess
He said he'd come to ditch the meadow for me."

"Warren?"

         "But did he? I just want to know."

"Of course he did. What would you have him say?
Surely you wouldn't grudge the poor old man
Some humble way to save his self-respect.   50
He added, if you really care to know,

He meant to clear the upper pasture, too.
That sounds like something you have heard before?
Warren, I wish you could have heard the way
He jumbled everything. I stopped to look
Two or three times—he made me feel so queer—
To see if he was talking in his sleep.
He ran on Harold Wilson—you remember—
The boy you had in haying four years since.
He's finished school, and teaching in his college.   60
Silas declares you'll have to get him back.
He says they two will make a team for work:
Between them they will lay this farm as smooth!
The way he mixed that in with other things.
He thinks young Wilson a likely lad, though daft
On education—you know how they fought
All through July under the blazing sun,
Silas up on the cart to build the load,
Harold along beside to pitch it on."

"Yes, I took care to keep well out of earshot."   70

"Well, those days trouble Silas like a dream.
You wouldn't think they would. How some things linger!
Harold's young college boy's assurance piqued him.
After so many years he still keeps finding
Good arguments he sees he might have used.
I sympathize. I know just how it feels
To think of the right thing to say too late.
Harold's associated in his mind with Latin.
He asked me what I thought of Harold's saying
He studied Latin like the violin   80
Because he liked it—that an argument!
He said he couldn't make the boy believe
He could find water with a hazel prong—
Which showed how much good school had ever done him.
He wanted to go over that. But most of all
He thinks if he could have another chance
To teach him how to build a load of hay—"

"I know, that's Silas' one accomplishment.
He bundles every forkful in its place,
And tags and numbers it for future reference,   90
So he can find and easily dislodge it

In the unloading. Silas does that well.
He takes it out in bunches like big birds' nests.
You never see him standing on the hay
He's trying to lift, straining to lift himself."

"He thinks if he could teach him that, he'd be
Some good perhaps to someone in the world.
He hates to see a boy the fool of books.
Poor Silas, so concerned for other folk,
And nothing to look backward to with pride,   100
And nothing to look forward to with hope.
So now and never any different."

Part of a moon was falling down the west,
Dragging the whole sky with it to the hills.
Its light poured softly in her lap. She saw
And spread her apron to it. She put out her hand
Among the harp-like morning-glory strings,
Taut with the dew from garden bed eaves,
As if she played unheard the tenderness
That wrought on him beside her in the night.   110
"Warren," she said, "he has come home to die:
You needn't be afraid he'll leave you this time."

"Home," he mocked gently.

                   "Yes, what else but home?
It all depends on what you mean by home.
Of course he's nothing to us, any more
Than was the hound that came a stranger to us
Out of the woods, worn out upon the trail."

"Home is the place where, when you have to go there,
They have to take you in."

                    "I should have called it
Something you somehow haven't to deserve."   120

Warren leaned out and took a step or two,
Picked up a little stick, and brought it back
And broke it in his hand and tossed it by.
"Silas has better claim on us you think
Than on his brother? Thirteen little miles
As the road winds would bring him to his door.
Silas has walked that far no doubt to-day.

Why didn't he go there? His brother's rich,
A somebody—director in the bank."

"He never told us that."

                        "We know it though."   130

"I think his brother ought to help, of course.
I'll see to that if there is need. He ought of right
To take him in, and might be willing to—
He may be better than appearances.
But have some pity on Silas. Do you think
If he'd had any pride in claiming kin
Or anything he looked for from his brother,
He'd keep so still about him all this time?"

"I wonder what's between them."

                              "I can tell you.
Silas is what he is—we wouldn't mind him—   140
But just the kind that kinsfolk can't abide.
He never did a thing so very bad.
He don't know why he isn't quite as good
As anyone. He won't be made ashamed
To please his brother, worthless though he is."

"*I* can't think Si ever hurt anyone."

"No, but he hurt my heart the way he lay
And rolled his old head on that sharp-edged chair-back.
He wouldn't let me put him on the lounge.   150
You must go in and see what you can do.
I made the bed up for him there to-night.
You'll be surprised at him—how much he's broken.
His working days are done; I'm sure of it."

"I'd not be in a hurry to say that."

"I haven't been. Go, look, see for yourself.
But, Warren, please remember how it is:
He's come to help you ditch the meadow.
He has a plan. You mustn't laugh at him.
He may not speak of it, and then he may.
I'll sit and see if that small sailing cloud
Will hit or miss the moon."   160

It hit the moon.
Then there were three there, making a dim row,
The moon, the little silver cloud, and she.
Warren returned—too soon, it seemed to her,
Slipped to her side, caught up her hand and waited.

"Warren," she questioned.

"Dead," was all he answered.

Early Draft

Jennifer Hargrove

Professor Bell

English 105-13

14 April 20

A Comparison of Mary and Warren in Robert Frost's

"The Death of the Hired Man"

Robert Frost in "The Death of the Hired Man"
presents two different views of how to respond to
human need. Into the home of Mary and Warren comes
the derelict hired hand, Silas. Mary and Warren
disagree over how to treat him.

Mary tells Warren to "Be kind" (7) to Silas.
Warren, however, is upset with Silas for having run
out on him the year before, when he needed him most.
"There's no depending on [him]," Warren says (17).
Mary shushes Warren so Silas will not hear him, but
Warren does not care if Silas hears or not: "I want
him to: he'll have to soon or late" (32).

In my opinion, Mary understands Silas much
better than Warren. She is also much more sympathetic than Warren. Her sympathy is like that extended to all people by the Virgin Mary. This may
be why Frost chose Mary's name, to underscore this
quality. She reminds Warren, for example, of Silas's
longstanding argument with the college student
Harold Wilson. Warren agrees that Silas is proud of
his one accomplishment, building a load of hay:

>   He bundles every forkful in its place,
>
>   And tags and numbers it for future reference,
>
>   So he can find and easily dislodge it
>
>   In the unloading. (89-92)

Mary then tells Warren that Silas has come home to
die: "You needn't be afraid he'll leave you this
time" (112).

One of the things that most upsets Warren is
that Silas comes to them rather than going to
Silas's brother for help:

>   Why didn't he go there? His brother's rich
>
>   A somebody--director in the bank. (128-129)

But Mary explains that probably there is some misunderstanding between Silas and his brother. Also,
she says that Silas is "just the kind that kinsfolk
can't abide" (141). He may be "worthless," she argues, but he "won't be made ashamed / To please his
brother" (144-145).

Hargrove 3

The climax of the poem comes when Warren seems
to agree reluctantly with Mary that Silas should
stay. She tells him to go inside and check on him.
He quietly returns and catches up her hand. When she
asks him what happened, he replies, simply, "Dead."

In sum, Warren has many qualities that Mary
does not have. He is quick to blame, cynical, and
even a little stingy. But most of all he lacks the
sympathy, the kindness, and the understanding that
Mary has. She seems also to be more imaginative
than he. Finally, though, her kindness wins him
over to her side. Even though Silas dies, Warren
seems ready to do what Mary wants.

Comments on the Early Draft

This draft was one of several the author wrote before she produced the final draft. You can see in the first few paragraphs that she is moving toward a concept of how Mary and Warren are different. In the final paragraph she even states some specific ways in which they are different. You can see, also, how the details and quotations she gives between the beginning and end of the essay *might* be relevant to her claims about difference. But notice how almost all the paragraphs in the body of the paper lack topic ideas (topic sentences). Notice also how she never connects any of the poem's details to specific claims. As a result, although the paper begins and ends promisingly, it is more like a summary of the poem than an argument in support of a thesis. To make the paper better, the author needs to do several things. In the introduction, she needs to clarify and emphasize her thesis. If she put the thesis at the end of the introduction rather than at the beginning, she could better show how all the sentences in the introduction relate to the thesis. In the body of the paper, she needs to state her claims about how Mary and Warren are different and support each with evidence from the text. Each claim could be the topic sentence of a paragraph, followed by supporting evidence. In the conclusion, she needs to restate her thesis, summarize her reasoning, and offer some generalizing idea that pulls the entire essay together.

Final Draft

Hargrove 1

Jennifer Hargrove

Professor Bell

English 105-13

14 April 20--

A Comparison of Mary and Warren in Robert Frost's

"The Death of the Hired Man"

When Silas, the unreliable hired hand, returns to the farm owned by Mary and Warren in Robert Frost's "The Death of the Hired Man," Mary and Warren immediately disagree about what to do with him. Warren wants to send him packing. Mary wants to keep him on and care for him. In recounting their disagreement about how to treat Silas, the poem reveals fundamental differences between them.

The most obvious difference is that Mary is compassionate and Warren is not. The poem continually reveals Mary's pity for the sick and troubled Silas. She tells Warren that she discovered him

Huddled against the barn-door fast asleep,

A miserable sight, and frightening, too--.

(35-36)

His physical weakness

hurt my heart the way he lay

And rolled his old head on that sharp-edged

chair-back.   (147-48)

She says that his prospects are bleak:

Poor Silas, so concerned for other folk,

And nothing to look backward to with pride,

And nothing to look forward to with hope.

So now and never any different.   (99-102)

Mary's pity leads her to certain moral conclusions. She feels that they should not just take
Silas in, but should try to protect his pride as
well. "Be kind," she tells Warren (7). Warren, in
contrast, resists hints that he has not done right
by Silas. Mary's gentle request to be kind elicits
an almost angry response: "When was I ever anything
but kind to him?" (11). He is impatient with
Silas's shortcomings and unforgivingly judgmental:

"I told him so last haying, didn't I?

'If he left then,' I said, 'that ended it.'"

(13-14)

Not caring if Silas hears, he loudly expresses his
bitterness (32). He dismisses Silas's plans to
"ditch the meadow" as the foolish promises of an in-
sincere old man (44-46).

Underlying their disagreement about how to
treat Silas are more fundamental differences. One
is that they value people differently. Warren values people for their usefulness and wants to cast
them off when they are no longer useful:

> What good is he [Silas]? Who else will
>> harbor him
> At his age for the little he can do?
> What help he is there's no depending on.
>
>   (15-17)

Even one of Warren's few positive comments about
Silas concerns a useful skill, Silas's ability to
load hay: "Silas does that well" (92). Warren believes, then, that one should be kind to people only
if they are useful. Mary's compassion for Silas reveals a different view of people. She sees them as
good in themselves. She admits that Silas may be
"worthless" (145) as a hired hand:

> You'll be surprised at him--how much he's
>> broken.
> His working days are done; I'm sure of it.
>
>   (152-53)

But she insists that their farm is his "home," and
it is their responsibility to receive him. Warren's
definition of home is in keeping with his attitude
toward people:

> "Home is the place where, when you have to
>> go there,

Hargrove 4

They have to take you in." (118-19)

At "home," in other words, people take care of you
out of duty, not love. Mary's counter definition is
in keeping with her belief that people are valuable
in themselves:

> I should have called it
> Something you somehow haven't to deserve.
>
> (119-20)

People at home give you tenderness no matter what
you've done.

Another fundamental difference between them is
that Mary is imaginative and Warren is not. Frost
suggests this quality in the opening line of the
poem: "Mary sat musing on the lamp-flame at the
table." The word muse means "to ponder or meditate,"
"to consider reflectively." The word is associated
with the Muses of Greek mythology, "each of whom
presided over a different art or science." Because
of this association, the noun muse means "the spirit
or power regarded as inspiring and watching over
poets, musicians, and artists; a source of inspiration" (American Heritage Dictionary). Frost's use
of the term presents Mary as something of a poet.
Her imagination allows her to "understand" Silas.
She guesses why he says he wants to ditch the
meadow, even though he probably knows he cannot:

Hargrove   5

Surely you wouldn't grudge the poor old man

Some humble way to save his self-respect.

(49-50)

She recognizes why Silas remains troubled by his ar-

guments with the college boy Harold Wilson:

I sympathize. I know just how it feels

To think of the right thing to say too late.

(75-76)

She realizes that "he has come home to die" (111).

Warren, in contrast, lacks the imagination to see

past his own practical needs. This limited vision

causes him to be unsympathetic to people who hinder

them. When Warren asks why Silas's brother (a

"somebody--director in the bank," [129]) cannot take

care of Silas, Mary has to tell him that the banker

brother may not want to take Silas in. When Warren

wonders why, Mary uses her imagination to guess what

the trouble may be:

He don't know why he isn't quite as good

As anyone. He won't be made ashamed

To please his brother, worthless though he

is. (143-45)

Their different imaginative capacities lead them to

different moral conclusions. Warren wants to get as

much as he gives. Mary's ability to put herself in

the place of troubled people leads her to want to

help them.

Hargrove 6

A final difference between them is that Mary is allied to nature and Warren is not. Frost connects Mary to nature twice. Just before Mary and Warren exchange definitions of <u>home</u>, Frost describes nature in metaphoric terms:

> Part of a moon was falling down the west,
>
> Dragging the whole sky with it to the hills.
>
> Its light poured softly in her lap.
>
> (103-05)

Mary's sympathetic response to this fanciful and beautiful quality in nature fortifies her compassionate impulses:

> She saw
>
> And spread her apron to it. She put out
>
>   her hand
>
> Among the harp-like morning-glory strings,
>
> Taut with the dew from the garden bed eaves,
>
> As if she played unheard the tenderness
>
> That wrought on him beside her in the night.
>
> (105-10)

At the end, Mary sends Warren to check on Silas and again urges him to be kind. While she waits, she says, she will

> see if that small sailing cloud
>
> Will hit or miss the moon. (160-61)

Frost blends her in with nature: The cloud

> hit the moon.

Then there were three there, making a
   dim row,
The moon, the little silver cloud, and she.

(161-63)

Mary's sympathy with nature, like her view of people
and her imagination, also leads to moral conclusions:

Of course he's nothing to us, any more
Than was the hound that came a stranger to us
Out of the woods, worn out upon the trail.

(115-17)

They should care for Silas for the same reason they
cared for the stray dog: Both are living creatures.
Frost does not say anything about Warren's attitude
toward nature, but Warren's not responding suggests
that he lacks Mary's poetic love for nature. He is
a farmer who has reduced nature to its economic
value, just as he has done with people.

We might wonder why, if Warren and Mary are so
different, they ever got married. But as it turns
out, Warren is not quite so different from Mary as
he at first seems. Who knows, he may have married
Mary just for her imaginative and compassionate
qualities. By the end of their conversation he has
come around to her view. He is now sympathetic to
Silas and takes his side against the status-minded
brother: "I can't think Si ever hurt anyone" (146).
He even asserts that maybe Silas's working days are

Hargrove 8

not over after all (154). When he brings news of

Silas's death, he does so as Mary would have done,

with solemnity and tenderness.

Works Cited

The American Heritage Dictionary of the English Lan-

guage. New College Edition. New York:

Houghton, 1981.

Frost, Robert. "The Death of the Hired Man." North

of Boston. New York: Henry Holt, 1914. 14-23.

Note: Normally, the "Works Cited" list would appear on a separate page, but we print it here, right after the essay, to save space.

Comments on the Final Draft

The final draft is much better than the early draft. The author opens with just enough information to give readers their bearings and get quickly to her thesis. In the body of the paper, each of the paragraphs has an unmistakable topic sentence. Each of the topic sentences is supported with reasoning and facts from the poem. The last paragraph closes the essay with a summary of the differences between Mary and Warren and an explanation of how, at the end of the poem, they reach harmony. Notice how the final draft is more complex in its interpretation of the poem than the early draft. The rewriting process often brings about this enhancement. Good argumentative essays have a necessary structure: thesis clearly stated, claims supporting the thesis, evidence supporting claims, conclusion tying everything together. If there is a problem with an essay's structure—as there was in the early draft of this essay—it usually reflects problems with reasoning and organization. Most writers struggle just to get ideas on the page. Their early drafts typically have gaps and inconsistencies. But during the rewriting process, writers force themselves to pay attention to the necessary structures of the essay. By doing so, they make their ideas, reasoning, and organization better.

Documentation and Research

D
ocumentation, or "giving credit," means identifying the sources
you consult when you prepare your essays. Two kinds of sources
are relevant to writing about literature: primary sources and
secondary sources.

Primary Sources

Primary sources are the works of literature themselves. If your essay is
about *Hamlet*, then *Hamlet* is your primary source. If you are writing
about all of Shakespeare's sonnets, then all of these comprise your primary source. Primary sources are crucial for essays about literature.
After all, they are what your essays are about, what you want to interpret. Your most important facts, the ones that support your claims, will
come from primary sources.

Secondary Sources

For many of your essays, primary sources will be the only ones you will
need. But if you want to include facts from outside the work or commentary from people outside the work, then you will need to use secondary sources. Facts from *secondary sources* include such things as
information about the author's life, the period in which the author
lived, the author's philosophy, literary history, other authors, the original audience, the work's influence, similarities to other works. Secondary

sources are valuable for what they teach us about the work. They give information that helps us form our own opinions. When we study Hawthorne's fiction, our perception of his themes sharpens when we learn that he was ashamed of his Puritan ancestors' dire deeds. When we learn that Jane Austen used an actual calendar to plot the events of *Pride and Prejudice*, we appreciate the care with which she crafted her fiction. When we compare Shakespeare's sources to his plays, we see his genius for deepening characterization and philosophical themes.

Employ secondary sources, then, to learn as much as you can about a work. Use reliable secondary sources—accurate histories, biographies, autobiographies, memoirs, and interviews. When you include facts from secondary sources, cite them and your sources for them. Keep in mind, though, that secondary sources must be backed up by facts from primary sources. When you quote or summarize critics, make it a practice to buttress their claims with your own analysis of the works themselves.

In addition to facts, secondary sources also contain *testimony*, interpretation by critics. You can find testimony in such places as introductions to individual works, head notes in anthologies, opinion columns on Websites, articles in professional journals, chapters in books, and book-length studies.

Although testimony is no substitute for your own skillful argumentation, it can add to the persuasive power of your essays. If you show that certain literary critics agree with your interpretation, readers may more readily accept your claims. Furthermore, testimony indicates that your argument is part of an ongoing debate about the work. Testimony signals that you are aware of the debate and, therefore, of the different solutions already proposed to your problem. By explaining other solutions, you can highlight the one that seems most reasonable or offer new solutions of your own.

Use testimony, then, as a complement to your reasoning and facts. If critics make especially good points or give especially good analyses, summarize their ideas and include particularly apt or telling quotations from their writings. Think of critics as witnesses on your behalf or points of departure for your own ideas.

Research Papers and the Use of Secondary Sources

Most people associate the use of secondary sources with "research" and "research papers," so it is appropriate here to address just what research papers are. Although research papers about literature sometimes deliver information for its own sake, they usually are interpretive. They use information to develop interpretations of one or more works of literature. The writer searches through secondary sources to find facts and opinions that lead to an interpretation. Some research papers begin with summaries of different interpretations before settling on one. Others use only a few secondary sources, either to support and illustrate the author's own ideas or as springboards for alternative interpretations. The sample essay on E. A. Robinson's "Richard Cory" in Chapter 13, for example, takes issue with one critic's opinion in order to present another view.

Interpretive research papers are essays. Here, the terms *research paper* and *research essay* are synonymous. Like all essays, research essays present opinions about a subject. They synthesize *your* discoveries about a topic and *your* evaluation of those discoveries. The reader should hear *your* voice speaking throughout the paper and should be constantly aware of *your* intelligence and consciousness. Research essays are not mere anthologies of facts or of other people's ideas. They have the same qualities of all essays: a unifying idea expressed directly and emphatically in a thesis, an introduction and a conclusion, and paragraphs that relate to the essay's thesis and that follow a logical plan. The sample essay at the end of this chapter exemplifies these traits.

How to Find Information and Opinions about Literature

How do you find information and opinion about literature? Where do you start? In the next four sections, we present a plan for learning about and gaining access to secondary sources. Since most secondary sources are located in libraries, we base this plan on three major places typical of university libraries: the stacks, the reference room, and the periodicals room. We conclude with a fourth "place," one that exists outside libraries, the Internet.

I. Library Catalogs and Stacks

Your research needs will vary from writing project to writing project. Some projects will require minimal research, others more elaborate research. Let's say, however, that you want to write an essay about one work, "Porphyria's Lover," a well-known poem by Robert Browning.

Your instructor asks only that you use the primary source (the poem), but you want to read some secondary sources to get yourself thinking about the poem. Go to the *card catalog* or *online catalog* of your college library, find where the author's works are located in the *stacks*—the shelves where books are stored—and browse among the books in that section. Most college libraries have many books about well-known authors. For Browning, choose several books. Look up "Porphyria's Lover" in the indexes, and read what each book has to say about the work. This should not take long, a few minutes per book.

By doing this kind of exploratory reading, you familiarize yourself with critics' ideas about the work. Sometimes, no matter how carefully you read a work, you may be at a loss for what it means. Doing some introductory reading in secondary sources can clue you in to issues critics have been debating about the work. In your own writing, you can join the discussion by seizing upon one of these issues as your topic. If it turns out you want to incorporate some of this material in your essay, then you need to read the sources carefully, take notes, and give credit for the sources you use.

II. Library Reference Room

What if there is little in the stacks on your author, or what if your teacher asks you to do a full-fledged research paper? You can supplement material you find in the stacks with what you turn up in a second place in the library, the *reference room*. The reference room is especially helpful when books are missing from the stacks (lost or checked out) or when your library's collection on an author is small.

The reference room of a college library typically includes several kinds of materials. First, it contains books with background information, such as encyclopedias, literary histories, brief biographies, books that describe and illustrate critical reactions to authors, handbooks to literary terms, surveys of contemporary authors, and guides to works by ethnic minorities. Consider beginning your writing project with one of these. They can tell you when and what your author wrote, the author's cultural context, and how critics have interpreted and evaluated the author's work. Some examples are as follows:

Benson, Eugene, and William Toye. The Oxford Companion to

Canadian Literature. 2nd ed. New York: Oxford UP, 1997.

Dictionary of Literary Biography. Detroit: Gale, 1978– .

Drabble, Margaret, ed. The Oxford Companion to English Literature. Rev. ed. New York: Oxford UP, 1998.

Hart, James D., and Phillip W. Leininger. The Oxford Companion to American Literature. 6th ed. New York: Oxford UP, 1995.

Howatson, M. C., ed. The Oxford Companion to Classical Literature. 2nd ed. New York: Oxford UP, 1989.

Magill, Frank N., ed. Cyclopedia of World Authors. Rev. 3rd ed. 5 vols. Pasadena: Salem, 1997.

Merriam-Webster's Encyclopedia of Literature. Springfield, MA: Merriam-Webster, 1995.

The New Encyclopaedia Britannica. Chicago: Encyclopaedia Britannica, 1998.

Scott-Kilvert, Ian, ed. British Writers. 8 vols. plus supplements. New York: Scribner's, 1979–99.

Stade, George, ed. European Writers. 14 vols. New York: Scribner's, 1983.

Unger, Leonard, ed. American Writers: A Collection of Literary Biographies. 4 vols. plus supplements. New York: Scribner's, 1974–98.

Second, the reference room contains books that give specific and specialized information about primary sources. These include concordances and indexes to standard authors like Tennyson, Milton, and Shakespeare as well as books dealing with specialized qualities of works, such as author's use of allusions, Greek mythology, or the Bible.

A third kind of material found in reference rooms is bibliographies. With these, you can make your research systematic and thorough. There are many kinds of bibliographies for the study of language and literature, but for the sake of simplicity they are here divided into five categories.

A. General Reference

Baker, Nancy L. A Research Guide for Undergraduate Students: English and American Literature. 4th ed. New York: MLA, 1995.

Book Review Digest. New York: Wilson, 1905- . Also available online.

Book Review Index. Detroit: Gale, 1965-69, 1972- . Also available online.

The Essay and General Literature Index. New York: Wilson, 1931- . Also available online.

Harner, James L. Literary Research Guide: An Annotated Listing of Sources in English Literary Studies. 3rd ed. New York: MLA, 1998.

Humanities Index. New York: Wilson, 1975- . Also available online as Humanities Abstracts.

MLA International Bibliography of Books and Articles on the Modern Languages and Literatures. New York: MLA, 1922- . Also available online.

Readers' Guide to Periodical Literature: An Author and Subject Index. New York: Wilson, 1901- . Also available online.

The best place to begin your quest for secondary sources on an author or work is the *MLA International Bibliography* (*MLAIB*). The *MLAIB* is the most comprehensive bibliography of books and articles on authors and their works. In fact, it is so comprehensive that it may give you *too* much material, so much that you feel overwhelmed. If that is the case, try some of the more selective bibliographies listed in the next few sections. The *MLAIB* is published annually and covers nearly everything published each year on modern languages, literature, folklore, and linguistics. Since 1981 the bibliography has been published in five parts: Part 1 (British Isles, British Commonwealth, English Caribbean, and American Literatures); Part 2 (European, Asian, African, and South American); Part 3 (Linguistics); Part 4 (General Literature and Related

Topics); and Part 5 (Folklore). Most libraries will have all five parts bound together in a single volume. A very helpful feature of the bibliography since 1981 is a subject index for each of the five parts. You can use these subject indexes to locate works about topics and authors. Before 1981, you have to look up an author by country and period and look up topics under a limited number of headings. The online version of the *MLAIB*, available by subscription, covers editions from 1963 to the present and is much easier to search than the print version.

Harner is a selective but comprehensive guide to reference works for the study of literature in English. He covers just about every area of the study of literature, with chapters on, among other things, research methods, libraries, manuscript collections, databases, biographical sources, genres, national literatures in English (English, Irish, American, and so forth), and foreign language literature. Harner is most valuable for accessing *areas* of study rather than specific authors. If, for example, you are interested in the English Renaissance, find the section on the Renaissance and locate the reference works—encyclopedias and bibliographies—that will lead you to the information you need. The book's index is very helpful for locating topics.

Baker is an excellent brief introduction to research methods in English and American literature. The author, a reference librarian, provides a guide to the basic tools of the library. She discusses, among other things, research strategies and how to use bibliographies, library catalogs, and computer databases.

The *Humanities Index* (the online version is called *Humanities Abstracts*) lists articles about all the humanities (including literature) in nearly 300 periodicals. It is organized alphabetically by topic and author and is issued four times a year. Its title from 1920 to 1965 was *International Index to Periodicals* and from 1965 to 1974 was *Social Sciences and Humanities Index*. (In 1975 the index was separated into two individual indexes: *Social Sciences Index* and *Humanities Index*.)

The *Essay and General Literature Index* lists essays that appear in books. Library catalogs and many bibliographies do not do this. Someone, for example, might have written an essay on Robert Browning's "Porphyria's Lover" for an anthology of essays titled *Psychotics in Literature*. If you were doing a paper on this poem, you might overlook this essay because it is "hidden" by the title of the book. The *Essay and General Literature Index*, however, would have it. This bibliography comes out twice a year and is easy to use. Authors and topics are listed alphabetically.

The *Readers' Guide to Periodical Literature*, the *Book Review Digest* and the *Book Review Index* list articles and reviews in newspapers and popular journals.

B. Genres

Drama

Breed, Paul F., and Florence M. Sniderman, comps. Dramatic Criticism Index: A Bibliography of Commentaries on Playwrights from Ibsen to the Avant-Garde. Detroit: Gale, 1972.

Eddleman, Floyd Eugene, comp. American Drama Criticism: Interpretations 1890–1977. 2nd ed. Hamden, CT: Shoe String, 1979. Supplement 1 (1984). Supplement 2 (1989).

Palmer, Helen H., comp. European Drama Criticism: 1900 to 1975. Hamden, CT: Shoe String, 1977.

Salem, James, comp. A Guide to Critical Reviews: Part I: American Drama, 1909–1982. 3rd ed. Metuchen, NJ: Scarecrow, 1984. Part II: The Musical, 1909–1989, 3rd ed. (1991). Part III: Foreign Drama, 1909–1977, 2nd ed. (1979). Part IV: Screenplays from The Jazz Singer to Dr. Strangelove (1971). Part IV, Supplement 1: Screenplays 1963–1980 (1982).

Fiction

Adelman, Irving, comp. The Contemporary Novel: A Checklist of Critical Literature on the English Language Novel since 1945. 2nd ed. Lanham, MD: Scarecrow, 1997.

Beene, Lynndianne. Guide to British Prose Fiction Explication: Nineteenth and Twentieth Centuries. New York: G. K. Hall, 1997.

Kearney, E. I., and L. S. Fitzgerald, comps. The Continental Novel: A Checklist of Criticism in English 1900–1966. Metuchen, NJ: Scarecrow, 1983.

———. The Continental Novel: A Checklist of Criticism in English 1967–1980. Metuchen, NJ: Scarecrow, 1983.

Palmer, Helen H., and Anne Jane Dysen, comps. English Novel

Explication: Criticism to 1972. Hamden, CT: Shoe String,

1973. Supplement 1 (1976). Supplement 2 (1981). Supple-

ment 3 (1986). Supplement 4 (1990). Supplement 5 (1994).

Walker, Warren S., comp. Twentieth-Century Short Story Expli-

cation: Interpretations 1900-1975, of Short Fiction since

1800. 3rd ed. Hamden, CT: Shoe String, 1977. Supplement

1 (1980). Supplement 2 (1984). Supplement 3 (1987). Sup-

plement 4 (1989). Supplement 5 (1991). Index to Supple-

ments 1-5 (1992). New Series Vol. 1 (1993). New Series

Vol. 2 (1995). New Series Vol. 3 (1993-94). New Series

Vol. 4 (1995-96).

Poetry

Kuntz, Joseph, and Nancy Martinez, comps. Poetry Explication:

A Checklist of Interpretation since 1925 of British and

American Poems Past and Present. 3rd ed. Boston, MA:

G.K.Hall 1980.

Martinez, Nancy C., Joseph G. R. Martinez, and Erland Ander-

son. Guide to British Poetry Explication. 4 vols. New

York: G. K. Hall, 1991.

Ruppert, James, and John R. Leo. Guide to American Poetry Ex-

plication. 4 vols. Boston, MA: G. K. Hall, 1989.

If the *MLAIB* seems too daunting, you might try more selective bibliographies, like those that focus on genres of literature—drama, novel, poetry, short story. These bibliographies provide lists of books and essays about authors and works that the editors deem important. Their disadvantage is that they may leave out works on the very topics you want to research. To use these bibliographies, look up the author and the work in the appropriate bibliography; there you will find a list of critical essays on the work you are studying. These bibliographies undergo constant revision, so check for supplements that bring them up to date. You can bring them up to date yourself with the *MLAIB*. The works listed above are only a few of the ones available. Your library may carry these or others like them.

C. Regions and Countries

World

Contemporary Authors. Detroit: Gale Research, 1962- .

Fister, Barbara. Third World Women's Literature: A Dictionary and Guide to Materials in English. Westport, CT: Greenwood, 1995.

Henderson, Lesley. Reference Guide to World Literature. 2nd ed. 2 vols. Farmington Hills, MI: St. James, 1995.

Serafin, Steven R, ed. Encyclopedia of World Literature in the Twentieth Century. 3rd ed. 4 vols. Farmington Hills, MI: St. James, 1999.

Africa and the African Diaspora

Cox, C. Brian, ed. African Writers. 2 vols. New York: Scribner's, 1997.

Valade, Roger M., III, ed. The Schomburg Center Guide to Black Literature: From the Eighteenth Century to the Present. New York: Gale, 1996.

Ancient Greece and Rome

Gwinup, Thomas, and Fidelia Dickinson. Greek and Roman Authors: A Checklist of Criticism. Metuchen, NJ: Scarecrow, 1982.

Luce, T. James, ed. Ancient Writers: Greece and Rome. 2 vols. New York: Scribner's, 1982.

Eastern

Lang, David M. A Guide to Eastern Literatures. New York: Praeger, 1971.

Nienhauser, William H., et al. The Indiana Companion to Traditional Chinese Literature. Bloomington: Indiana UP, 1986.

English Language

Hawkins-Dady, Mark, ed. Reader's Guide to Literature in English. Chicago: Fitzroy-Dearborn, 1996.

Shattock, Joanne, ed. The Cambridge Bibliography of English
Literature. 3rd ed. Vol. 4 (1800-1900). New York: Cambridge UP, 1999. (This is the first available volume of a
new edition of The New Cambridge Bibliography of English
Literature, listed below.)

Spiller, Robert E., et al., eds. Literary History of the
United States. 4th ed. rev. Vol. 2. New York: Macmillan,
1974. 2 vols. (Vol. 1 is the literary history; Vol. 2 is
the bibliography.)

Watson, George, ed. The New Cambridge Bibliography of English
Literature. 5 vols. Cambridge: Cambridge UP, 1969-77.

Europe

Stade, George, ed. European Writers. 14 vols. New York:
Scribner's, 1983.

Native America

Marken, Jack W. The American Indian Language and Literature.
Arlington Heights, IL: AHM, 1978.

Latin America

Fenwick, M. J. Writers of the Caribbean and Central America: A
Bibliography. 2 vols. New York: Garland, 1992.

Sole, Carlos A., ed. Latin American Writers, 3 vols. New
York: Scribner's, 1989.

Like the bibliographies on genres, these bibliographies provide *selected* lists of sources on regional literatures and on specific authors within regions. The *Literary History of the United States, The New Cambridge Bibliography of English Literature*, and the emerging *Cambridge Bibliography of English Literature* are especially helpful in pointing to important studies done on American and English literature up to their dates of publication. Many of these bibliographies are more like encyclopedias in that they combine biography with bibliography. They provide information about regional literature and authors as well as a brief list of secondary studies on them.

The above list is itself a short selection. Your library may have these bibliographies as well as others that are equally useful. New bibliographies come out regularly, and many existing ones are updated periodically. You can supplement and update any of these bibliographies with the *MLAIB*.

D. Authors

Weiner, Alan R, and Spencer Means. Literary Criticism Index.

2nd ed. Metuchen, NJ: Scarecrow, 1994.

Literary Criticism Index is a bibliography of bibliographies. It is organized alphabetically by authors, and keys their works to specific bibliographies. If, for example, you wanted to know where to find critical studies of Browning's "Porphyria's Lover," you would look for the title of the poem under "Browning, Robert." The entry would tell you which bibliographies contain lists of works on the poem.

For the most thorough bibliographies of works by and about authors, seek out bibliographies devoted solely to individual authors. In contrast to the bibliographies listed above, these bibliographies usually contain *complete* listings of works by and about an author. These listings are complete—up to the publication date of the bibliography. For anything after that date, consult the *MLAIB*.

E. Computer Databases Available through Purchase or Subscription

Computer databases can save you enormous amounts of time. Using a bibliography database, for example, is the same as going through hardbound print bibliographies, only the computer does it for you and much faster. Computer databases are available on compact disc (CD-ROM), magnetic tape, diskette, and the Internet. Most college and university libraries subscribe to various databases. Ask your librarian for guidance in choosing and using databases pertinent to your projects.

Of all the bibliography databases, the most useful for discovering secondary sources about literature is the *MLAIB* (1963–present). Its coverage is very comprehensive. Like most bibliography databases, you can search it by author, title, and subject as well as by key words. Several interdisciplinary databases that cover nonliterary subjects and their connection with literature are *Essay and General Literature Index, Humanities Abstracts,* and *Arts and Humanities Search.* These allow you to research interdisciplinary topics (art and literature, psychology and literature, science and literature, and so forth). Some excellent content databases are *Literature Resource Center, The Encyclopaedia Britannica Online,* and *DiscLit,* all of which provide information about authors and movements as well as historical background. *The Literary Resource Center* includes various reference works published by Gale: *Contemporary Authors, Dictionary of Literary Biography,* and *Contemporary Literary Criticism. DiscLit* reproduces the introductory books published by Twayne Publishers. These books cover major American, British, and world authors.

Several other databases may help as well: *Reader's Guide to Periodical Literature, New York Times, Book Review Digest, America: History and Life, American National Biography, Biography Index,* and the *Oxford English Dictionary.* Databases are constantly being created, expanded, renamed, and incorporated into other databases, so check your library's resources to see which ones it shelves that might pertain to your area of research.

One more database is worthy of mention here: the online catalog of your library. Many online catalogs have the capacity to perform sophisticated and thorough searches of authors and topics. Your library's online catalog may be limited to only the material in that library, but it may be all you need. Many online catalogs link to other databases: to the Internet and to catalogs of nearby libraries, of newspapers, scholarly journals, and popular magazines.

III. Library Periodicals Room and Stacks

Now that you have drawn up a list of resources for your project—by consulting bibliographies and databases—your next step is to locate these resources in the library. Does your library own them or provide access to them? To find out, use your library's online catalog to see which books the library owns. Then locate them in the stacks. For computer databases and Internet resources, use either the computers on campus (in the library or labs) or your own computer. For journal articles, look up the title of the journal in the online catalog or in a "serials holding catalog." Either should tell you whether or not the library subscribes to it and, if so, where it is located. Recent issues of journals are usually stored in the *periodicals room* of the library, and back issues are kept in the stacks. To save space, some libraries also store past issues of journals on microfilm. If you have difficulty finding the journal articles you need, ask the librarian in the periodicals room for help.

This discussion of how to find information is basic. If you want more thorough guidance on a particular project, see Nancy L. Baker's *A Research Guide for Undergraduate Students: English and American Literature*, listed above under "General Reference." Perhaps the most valuable resource for doing research is the reference librarian. Reference librarians are experts on locating sources of information and opinion. They are usually eager to help and can save you time.

IV. Information and Opinion on the Internet

The Internet is an enormous, constantly changing, continuously growing collection of documents. It is an "ocean" we have to "navigate." This ocean is so vast and changes so fast that almost anything published about it is dated as soon as it is released. What follows, then, are a few observations about how to use the Internet for conducting research about literature. Once you get the hang of using the Internet, you can catch up with new developments on your own.

More than anything, the emergence of the World Wide Web in 1993 has made the Internet easier to search than ever before. Most Web documents are hypertexts. *Hypertext* is a document containing *links* (also known as *hyperlinks* or *embedded links*), highlighted phrases that take you to other portions of the document or other hypertexts. Click on a link, and you are whisked to another place within the document or to a completely new Website. That site will have links of its own, which take you to other sites, which in turn connect to new sites—many of which may link back to your original site. You can see why the World Wide Web is called a "web."

Because of the Web's ease of use, it has just about subsumed everything else on the Internet. You can gain access to the Web through *online services* such as America Online, Prodigy, Earthlink. You can also log onto the Internet by means of a *browser* such as Microsoft Explorer or Netscape Navigator. These are available through companies known as *Internet Service Providers* (or *ISPs*). If your college or university already subscribes to a service, you may be able to log on from your dorm room or computer lab. Once on the Internet, you can use a *search engine* such as Alta Vista, Webcrawler, or Yahoo to scan Websites. Most services offer a choice of search engines. Whichever one you choose, it will typically have a box, located near the beginning of the document, that allows you to search by typing in *keywords*. Doing this is one of the most effective ways of finding things on the Internet. Type in any terms or combination of terms you want: an author's name ("William Shakespeare"), a literary movement ("English Romanticism"), a geographical or national region ("Canadian literature"). The search engine will find documents related to your keywords, tell you how many documents it has found, and arrange them in descending order of relevance: the most relevant documents first, the least relevant last. If one search engine fails to turn up what you want, try another. Some are more detailed and comprehensive than others. A useful feature of most Web browsers is the *Bookmark* option, located at the top of the screen. If you find a site you want to keep for future reference, click on "Bookmark" to store the Web address or Uniform Resource Locator (URL). When you want to get to that site quickly, open your Bookmark file and go directly to the addresses stored there. Bookmarks save you from having to retrace steps to get back to sites you want.

You can also go directly to any site on the Web if you know its address. Look for a box at the top of the screen that contains the address of the site where you are. The address for the search engine Yahoo, for example, is http://www.yahoo.com. The "http" part of the address stands for Hypertext Transfer Protocol, the program that establishes a common language between computers and accommodates the transmission of all documents on the Web. Click on the address, delete all or part of it, type in a new address, and press Enter. The browser takes you to the site of the new address. Two publications that describe Internet sites are *Gale Guide to Internet Databases* (Detroit: Gale) and *The Book Lover's Guide to the Internet* by Evan Morris (2nd ed., New York: Fawcett Columbine, 1998). Published annually, the *Gale Guide* has a subject index at the back and descriptions of databases in the main body of the book. Far more comprehensive on matters relating to literature is *The Book Lover's Guide to the Internet*. Morris gives an excellent, nontechnical introduction to the Internet: a brief history, definitions of terms, how to hook up, pathways through the Internet (Gopher, File Transfer Protocol [FTP] sites, Telnet, Internet Relay Chat [IRC]), and different ways of using the Internet (discussion/news groups, mailing lists, self-publication, e-mail, online resources). Especially valuable is his long list of addresses, arranged by category (authors, cultural studies, poetry, mystery literature, science fiction, humor, hypertext literature, magazines, bookstores, and so forth).

General databases

Four databases should be especially helpful for starting literary research on the Web. The first two survey and provide links to sites having to do with all areas of English studies.

Literary Resources on the Net, maintained by Jack Lynch.
　http://andromeda.rutgers.edu/~jlynch/Lit/
Literature Resources for the High School and College Student, maintained
　by Michael Lee Groves
　http://www.teleport.com/~mgroves/

　　Both of these sites contain links to literary periods, literary movements, language study, women's studies, ethnic studies, literary theory, research materials, and much more. Lynch's site allows you to search by keyword. Lynch, who teaches at Rutgers University, seems to aim his site at undergraduates and graduate students. Groves, a high school teacher, slants his toward high school students and undergraduates. The third site covers all the humanities, not just literature:

Voice of the Shuttle: Electronic Resources for the Humanities, maintained by
　Alan Liu
　http://vos.ucsb.edu/

Finally, the fourth site provides access to all of knowledge:

The Internet Public Library
　http://www.ipl.org/

　　These four sites are the best places to begin your quest for research materials on the Web. The following is a very selected list of more narrowly focused sites:

Literary criticism of authors and works
Online Literary Criticism Collection
http://www.ipl.org/ref/litcrit/

Author sites
Jane Austen Information Page
http://pemberley.com/janeinfo/janeinfo.html/
Mr. William Shakespeare and the Internet
http://daphne.palomar.edu/shakespeare/
Shakespeare Resource Center
http://www.bardweb.net/index.html/

Multi-author sites
American Studies Web
http://www.georgetown.edu/crossroads/asw/
Latina/o Literature and Literature of the Americas
http://asweb.unco.edu/latina/
OzLit [Australian literature]
http://www.ozlit.org/
Postcolonial Studies
http://www.emory.edu/ENGLISH/Bahri/
Romantic Circles [the Romantic movement]
http://www.rc.und.edu/indexjava.html/
Storytellers: Native American Authors Online
http://hanksville.org/storytellers/
The Victorian Web
http://landow.stg.brown.edu/victorian/vicov.html/
Voices from the Gaps: Women Writers of Color
http://vlices.cla.umn.edu/

Electronic texts
Bartleby.com
http://www.bartleby.com/
English Online Resources
http://etext.lib.virginia.edu/eng-on.html/
The On-Line Books Page
http://digital.library.upenn.edu/books/

Project Gutenberg
http://www.gutenberg.net/

Hypertexts and annotated texts

Pride and Prejudice (by Jane Austen), a hypertext
http://www.pemberley.com/janeinfo/janeinfo.html/

A Midsummer Night's Dream (by William Shakespeare), an annotated text
http://cmc.uib.no/dream/

The Complete Works of William Shakespeare (hypertexts)
http://tech-two.mit.edu/Shakespeare/works.html/

Robert Browning and Others (hypertexts, some illustrated with paintings)
http://fmc.utm.edu/~geverett/465/rb.htm/

Grammar, style, documentary guidelines

The Elements of Style (by William Strunk, Jr.)
http://www.bartleby.com/141/index.html/

Guide to Grammar and Writing
http://ccc.commnet.edu/grammar/

MLA Style (Modern Language Association guidelines for citing sources)
http://www.mla.org/style/

Poetic techniques

Poetry: Meter, Form, and Rhythm
http://www.uncg.edu/~htkirbys/

Online journals

Domestic Goddesses: AKA "Scribbling Women"

"A moderated E-journal devoted to women writers, beginning in
the 19th century, who wrote 'domestic fiction.'"
http://www.womenwriters.net/domesticgoddess/

Other Voices: The (e)Journal of Cultural Criticism
http://dept.english.upenn.edu/~ov/index2.html/

Renaissance Forum
http://www.hull.ac.uk:80/Hull/EL_Web/renforum/

Newsletters, discussion groups, and electronic mail

Interpersonal communication by means of newsletters, discussion groups,
and e-mail is a wonderful opportunity for people doing research. You can

exchange opinions, share information, and keep up with trends. Jack Lynch's Website, mentioned on page 248, includes a directory of literary discussion lists. Bear in mind that newsletters and discussion lists are most valuable for researchers who have *long-term* projects. They are less helpful for people who need to get research papers done quickly, say within a semester. It is, for example, a breach of "Netiquette" (etiquette for using the Internet) for someone to send out a message on a discussion list saying something like, "I have a paper due in three weeks on *Beowulf.* Can anyone out there help me think of a topic?"

Evaluating the Quality of Websites

How do you know if a Website is good? In contrast to scholarly books and journals, which are published by reputable publishers with high standards of acceptance, Websites can be created by anyone with an Internet address. One way to evaluate the quality of Websites is to read reviews of them. The online version of *Forbes* magazine, for example, maintains a list of the 300 best Web sites. Among these are *Mr. William Shakespeare and the Internet* and Jack Lynch's *Literary Resources on the Net.* See the complete list and reviews at

Forbes.com
   http://www.forbesbest.com/index.asp/

But as valuable as *Forbes* and other organizations are that review Websites, most of the sites you visit will probably not be reviewed anywhere. You should then evaluate them yourself. Ask questions like the following:

1. **Who is the developer of the site?** How trustworthy is this person? Is the developer a scholar, well-versed in the subject, or an amateur who may be enthusiastic but have limited knowledge? Does the developer give his or her name (something other than "Webmaster")? Can you get in touch with the developer?

2. **How authoritative is the site?** Who publishes the site? Does it originate from a school (university, college, high school) or from a single individual? How commercial is it? Does it seem more interested in selling you things than in presenting information and interpretation?

3. **Is the site well maintained?** Has the site been updated recently? How thorough, thoughtful, and careful is the site? Does the developer

seem active in maintaining the site? Are the links current? (How many dead links are there?) Does the information on the site seem dated?

4. **How knowledgeable are the authors who write for the site?** Do the writers document their information and opinions? Are their references to one or two sources or to many? Do they seem well-read in their subject, familiar with the groundbreaking and essential treatments of their subject? How detailed is the treatment of the subject? Is the information accurate?

5. **For e-texts, how reliable are they?** Are the e-texts well-edited? Are they accurate? Is the source of the text given? How trustworthy is the source?

In general, Websites are best when they meet the following criteria:

- The developers are scholars in the field.
- The developers are accountable. They tell you who they are and how to get in touch with them.
- They constantly and thoughtfully maintain the site, keeping information and links current.
- The site is noncommercial and is associated with a school or press. Be wary of the .com sites. More reliable are the nonprofit domains: .edu, .gov, .org, and .net.
- Information and interpretation is well-documented and gives evidence of sound knowledge of the subject.
- E-texts are edited recently by scholars.

Giving Credit to Sources

Why Should You Give Credit?

First, give credit so readers can find and read the same material you read. They may also want to check the reliability of your sources or your ability to use them fairly and accurately. Giving credit, to put it positively, is one more means of arguing. The more careful and honest you are in giving credit, the stronger your argument will be. Second, give credit to distinguish your ideas from those of others. The purpose of the essay, after all, is to express *your* ideas, to argue *your* position. You may use facts, ideas, and words from other sources to clarify and support your ideas, but readers are interested, finally, in knowing what *you* think. That is why they are reading your paper. By giving credit, you show them exactly where your ideas begin and where other writers' ideas leave off.

Finally, give credit to be ethical. Honor policies stress this reason heavily. Although the ethical principle is obvious, it is not always simple. The usual definition of *plagiarism* is "the presentation of someone else's ideas, work, or facts as your own." The moral judgment that follows is, "Plagiarism is stealing and therefore wrong." These judgments are apt when applied to blatant plagiarism, cases in which someone copies the work of someone else and claims it as his or her own. Most cases of student plagiarism, however, are not so egregiously criminal. The issue of plagiarism is clouded with some uncertainties. Everything you know comes from a "source." When is what you know "yours" and not someone else's? Another uncertainty is that when you summarize someone else's ideas, you will probably use some of that writer's words. How many and what kind of words can you use without plagiarizing? A third uncertainty is the nature of facts. Some facts, even when they appear in a source, do not need documentation. But which ones? Because of uncertainties like these, most students who "plagiarize" do so unintentionally. The following are principles and guidelines that anyone using sources in essays about literature should follow. They can help you use sources meaningfully, clearly, and ethically.

When Should You Give Credit?

Give credit for primary sources Whenever you make a specific reference to an incident or words in a work and whenever you quote from a work, you need to cite the source (give credit) from which you obtained the information. This is as true for primary as for secondary sources. You must do this for several reasons. Works of literature, especially famous ones, often go through many editions. Readers need to know which edition you used so they can find the parts of the work you discuss. You document your primary source, then, for their convenience. Another reason is that the edition you use may affect the validity of your argument. If the edition is unscholarly and contains misprints or omissions, your interpretations will be suspect. A well-known example is Emily Dickinson's poetry. After her death in 1886, Thomas Wentworth Higginson and Mabel Loomis Todd edited Dickinson's poetry for publication. They published it (or some of it) in four volumes throughout the 1890s. Instead of printing it as Dickinson had written it, they "regularized" it for the tastes of nineteenth-century readers. They changed the meter to make it more conventional, changed words to make them rhyme, normalized punctuation, and altered metaphors that seemed illogical. Not until Thomas H. Johnson published a new edition of Dickinson's poems in 1955 did we have versions of her poetry as she had written it. If you write an essay about her poetry, your readers will want to know that you used Johnson's edition (or reprints therefrom). By giving full information about the editions you use, you enhance the reliability of your essay.

Often the nature of college courses allows you to omit complete citations for primary sources. If you write about a work assigned for a course, page numbers may be the only documentation you need. Check with your professor to be sure this practice is acceptable. If so, follow each quotation or reference with appropriate page numbers in parentheses, placing your final mark of punctuation after the closing parenthesis.

Quotation

    Lawrence says that when she is with her children she feels
    "the center of her heart go hard" (125).

A specific reference but not a quotation

    When she returns home from the party, she finds Paul rid-
    ing the rocking horse. Lawrence contrasts her elegant,
    icy dress to Paul's frenzied and exhausted state (134-35).

More formal usage requires a complete citation for the edition you are using. Complete citations are necessary when you use a book that is not a basic text in your course.

Give credit for facts that are not common knowledge

"Common knowledge" facts are those the average well-read person would likely know: very basic facts about history (that Woodrow Wilson was president of the United States during World War I, that the United States entered the war several years after it began), birth and death dates, occupations, publication dates, basic biographical facts about famous people (that Ernest Hemingway began his writing career as a newspaper reporter, that he entered World War I as an ambulance driver, that in 1929 he published a famous novel, *A Farewell to Arms*, based on his wartime experiences, that just before the outbreak of World War II he published a novel, *For Whom the Bell Tolls*, about the

Spanish Civil War). Facts that are not common knowledge (what Hemingway's parents thought of his newspaper career, where he saw action during the war, how he was wounded, the identity of the nurse he fell in love with while recuperating, what he actually said to people about the war) come from secondary sources and must be cited. Also, controversial facts need to be documented. If you claim that Theodore Roosevelt was a secret Marxist, or had an affair with Emma Goldman, or conspired to assassinate President McKinley, you must give sources for such outlandish assertions; otherwise readers will write you off as ignorant and irresponsible.

Give credit for all direct quotes This kind of documentation is crucial, whether you quote from primary or secondary sources.

Give credit for summaries or paraphrases of someone else's ideas Even when you do not quote directly from the work, you must provide documentation when you repeat someone else's ideas. This includes ideas held by other writers, by your instructor, or even by other students. It also includes ideas you arrive at on your own and then find expressed in print.

Give credit for ideas not "assimilated" by you Once you have absorbed someone's ideas, thought about them over a period of time, added ideas of your own or of others, you can assume that these ideas are now "yours." If, however, your memory is so good that these ideas remain in your mind exactly as they were when you read and heard them, then you must give credit to the original author.

A final word about when to give credit The dividing line between facts that are common knowledge and those that are not is sometimes frustratingly vague. So too is the line between ideas assimilated by you and those that are not. *When in doubt about where that line is, give credit.* Doing so takes a little extra time and trouble, but the trouble and time are worth it to protect yourself against charges of plagiarism and to provide curious readers with enough information to check your facts.

Where Should You Give Credit?

Give credit by introducing your source in your text
When you use the ideas and specialized or controversial facts of another

person, introduce them *in your own text,* not just in parenthetical references. To do this, use introductory phrases like the following:

```
As Jane Tompkins says, "The ground for complaint . . ."

One critic has called attention to "the absurdity of

Huck's shore experience."

Annette Kolodny suggests . . .

Tuchman's second point is . . .

Judith Butler sees Queer theory as . . .
```

All of these introduce paraphrases, summaries, and short quotations. The following example introduces an indented or blocked quotation (that is, a long quotation moved right ten spaces [1 inch] from the established left margin).

```
Friedman's definition of plot focuses on the changes the

protagonist undergoes:

        The end of plot, then, is to represent some com-

        pleted process of change in the protagonist.
```

Acknowledgments for facts are also necessary when the facts are very specialized or controversial. For example, details about F. Scott Fitzgerald's love life in Hollywood during his last years can come from only a few people. You must mention such people *in your text* when you use them:

```
Sheilah Graham claims that . . .

Budd Schulberg saw that Fitzgerald was . . .

Nathanael West said that at the party Fitzgerald concen-

trated his attention on . . .
```

Note, however, that facts available from many sources do not have to be introduced in your text. Details about English history, for example, are available in many textbooks and are not associated with any one person or group. You do, however, need to provide parenthetical references for such information and to cite your sources in the "Works Cited" list.

> Anarchism was such a compelling theory at the turn of the
> century that six heads of state—of France, Austria,
> Italy, the United States, and two of Spain—were executed
> by anarchists (Tuchman 72).

Give credit in the text of your essay by making parenthetical citations to the works contained in your "Works Cited" list See Guidelines for Parenthetical Citations on page 258.

Give credit in a "Works Cited" list at the end of your essay. The parenthetical citations and "Works Cited" list work together to give readers complete information about your sources and how you use them. In your parenthetical citations, give enough information so readers can find the sources in the "Works Cited" list. The "Works Cited" list enables readers to check out the sources themselves.

Correct Documentary Form

Documentary form varies from discipline to discipline. For people writing about literature, the authoritative guide to documentary form is the *MLA Handbook for Writers of Research Papers, Theses, and Dissertations.* (*MLA* stands for Modern Language Association, the preeminent scholarly organization devoted to the study of modern languages and literature.) In 1984 the MLA created a new documentary format, one that resembles the formats of the social and natural sciences. The guidelines in this chapter are from the most recent edition of the *MLA Handbook:*

The MLA Handbook for Writers of Research Papers. Joseph Gibaldi. 5th ed. New York: MLA, 1999.

You can get an abbreviated set of these guidelines from the MLA Website:

MLA Style
http://www.mla.org

Although this site is not nearly as thorough as the *MLA Handbook*, it does provide the basic formula for citing sources on the Web. To gain access to this formula, go to the MLA Website, click on "MLA Style," then click on "Frequently Asked Questions about MLA Style." Several of these questions address how to cite Web documents. For a comparison of various documentary styles (MLA, APA, Chicago), see the following site:

The Columbia Guide to Online Style
   http://www.columbia.edu/cu/cup/cgos/index.html

Guidelines for Parenthetical Citations

The purpose of parenthetical citations   Your main goal in making parenthetical citations is to give readers enough information so they can do two things: find the work in the "Works Cited" list and find the exact location of your references *in* the work.
   Make a parenthetical citation whenever you

- refer directly to a particular part of a source
- use facts that are not common knowledge
- use direct quotations
- summarize or paraphrase someone else's ideas.

Basic information: single author books   For most parenthetical references, especially for books, it is usually enough to give the author's last name and the page number or numbers of the reference:

> Long historical poems, such as The Battle of Maldon, pro-
> vide "the soundest evidence we have" for recreating the
> Europe of 1000 years ago (Reston 5).

An alternative way of giving this information is to mention the author's name in your text. In this case, only the page number need appear in the parenthetical reference.

> James Reston, Jr. says that poetic depictions of histori-
> cal events, such as The Battle of Maldon, provide "the
> soundest evidence we have" for recreating he Europe of
> 1000 years ago (5).

In both instances, the author's name points to the work in the "Works Cited" list, and the page number points to the citation in the work itself. The above citation is to the following work in the "Works Cited" list:

Reston, James, Jr. The Last Apocalypse: Europe at the Year
    1000 A.D. New York: Anchor Books, 1998.

Several works by the same author Give more information than just the author's last name and page number when necessary. For example, if you use several works by the same author, give the author's last name, a portion of the title, and the page number.

> Reston claims that Olaf Trygvesson's conversion to Chris-
> tianity in 994 AD diminished Viking hostility in southern
> England (Last Apocalypse 18).

When you use more than one work by the same author, be sure the reader knows which work you are discussing.

> Lawrence describes the two mothers differently. Eliza-
> beth Bates is "a tall woman of imperious mien, handsome,
> with definite black eyebrows" ("Odour of Chrysanthemums"
> 248), whereas Paul's mother is simply "a woman who was
> beautiful" ("The Rocking-Horse Winner" 271).

> Lawrence describes the two mothers differently. Eliza-
> beth Bates in "Odour of Chrysanthemums" is "a tall woman
> of imperious mien, handsome, with definite black eye-
> brows" (248), whereas Paul's mother in "The Rocking-
> Horse Winner" is simply "a woman who was beautiful"
> (271).

Authors with the same last name If you have several authors with the same last name, give initials or the whole name to distinguish among them:

> (J. Reston 58-60)

Internet sources   Some works, like many on the Internet, may not have page numbers. If so, give other information to mark the location of references.

> Diane Elam worries that because a university education is
> becoming more of "a vocational exercise," the value of
> reading literature "is no longer a self-evident proposi-
> tion in market-driven universities" (par. 4).

If you refer to more than one paragraph, use the abbreviation "pars.": for example, (pars. 15–18).

Magazines and newspapers   Like Internet sources, magazine and newspaper articles may have unusual page indicators. As always, give enough information so readers can find your references. The following example is from a newspaper article:

> Kunitz said that one of the advantages of being so old is
> that "I encountered a good portion of the best poets of
> the twentieth century" (C5).

Whole works   When you refer to an entire work (not some part of it), you may omit a parenthetical reference to it if you identify the author and the title of the work in your text:

> E. M. W. Tillyard devotes a short book to explaining how
> the Elizabethans saw the structure of the cosmos.

If readers are interested in Tillyard's book, they can find it in the "Works Cited" list.

Works of literature: prose   When referring to primary sources, use page numbers for prose works.

> In Shirley Jackson's "The Lottery" the people are at
> first reluctant to participate in the lottery. The men
> standing around waiting are subdued: "Their jokes were
> quiet and they smiled rather than laughed" (219). The

children, when called, come "reluctantly, having to be
called four or five times" (220). Once the black box is
brought out, the villagers keep "their distance" (221).

Works of literature: verse drama   For plays written in poetry, use act, scene, and line numbers.

In Hamlet the queen bids farewell to Ophelia by saying, "I
hoped thou shouldst have been my Hamlet's wife" (V.i.211).

Here the reference is to act five, scene one, line 211. You may also use arabic numbers instead of roman numerals to cite acts and scenes.

In Hamlet the queen bids farewell to Ophelia by saying, "I
hoped thou shouldst have been my Hamlet's wife" (5.1.211).

Works of literature: poetry   For poems, especially long ones (more than about twenty lines), cite line numbers.

In commenting on our growing distance from heaven,
Wordsworth says in "Intimations of Immortality,"
    Heaven lies about us in our infancy!
    Shades of the prison-house begin to close
    Upon the growing Boy. (66-68)

The Bible   Refer to the Bible by indicating chapter and verse numbers:

When Solomon became old, his many wives "turned away his
heart after other gods." He worshiped the goddess Ashtoreth
and "did evil in the sight of the Lord" (1 Kings 11.4-6).

More than one page   Use hyphens between line or page numbers to indicate material that lies within a continuous sequence of lines or pages.

(231-33).

Use commas between line or page numbers to indicate interruptions in sequence.

```
(200, 219).
```

Multivolume works   If your reference is to a work with more than one volume, indicate in your parenthetical reference the volume to which you refer. Separate volume and page numbers with a colon. Insert a space between the colon and the page number.

```
Even on the point of death, Clarissa writes to her father

asking his forgiveness. She begs him "on her knees" to

forgive her for "all her faults and follies," especially

"that fatal error which threw her out of [his] protec-

tion" (4: 359).
```

Here the reference is to the fourth volume, page 359. If you use only one volume from a multivolume work, you need not give the volume number in the parenthetical reference. Instead, include the volume number in the "Works Cited" listing.

Anonymous works   If the author of a work is anonymous, give the complete title or the first few words of the title, plus the page number. (Anonymous works are alphabetized by title in the "Works Cited" list.)

```
Unlike the pilgrims, the Puritans remained members of the

Anglican church. But like the Pilgrims, they adhered to

a Calvinistic theology ("Early American Literature" 2).
```

More than one work   You may refer to more than one work in a single parenthetical reference by separating the works with semicolons.

```
At least two critics have seen the similarity between

Voltaire's character Candide and the young Benjamin

Franklin in the Autobiography (Orkney 13; Scott 151-52).
```

If, however, you want to refer to more than two or three works, use a footnote or endnote instead of a parenthetical reference. (See the discussion of footnotes and endnotes below.)

Two or three authors   When referring to a work by two or three authors, give all their names in the text and in the reference.

> One work makes the useful distinction between "representational" and "illustrative" narrative (Scholes and Kellogg 84).

> Scholes and Kellogg make the useful distinction between "representational" and "illustrative" narrative (84).

More than three authors   When referring to a work by more than three authors, give all their names or, more simply, give the first name and "et al." (abbreviation for Latin *et alii*, "and others").

> The trickster has been a traditional folk hero not just of American "Yankee" narrative but of American Indian and African-American narrative as well (Spiller et al. 729).

Works quoted in other works   If you find a quotation in a book or article but cannot find the original source for the quotation, rather than abandon the quotation, cite the place where you found it. Use "qtd. in" ("quoted in").

> When Dreiser was a magazine editor, he would write on rejection slips, "We like realism, but it must be tinged with sufficient idealism to make it all a truly uplifting character" (qtd. in Fiedler 46).

Placing parenthetical references   Place the reference immediately after the material that needs referencing. Usually this is at the end of a sentence or paragraph, but sometimes it can be within a sentence as well. Put the reference before the closing punctuation of the phrase or sentence (comma, period, semicolon, colon, exclamation point).

```
James Joyce, as Arnold Kettle notes, was consistent about
employing his artistic principles (301), but that does
not mean his works are all the same.
```

```
John H. Arnold points out that although Herodotus seems
strikingly modern to us, his histories cannot be fully
trusted (17).
```

Indented quotations   The exception to the above punctuation rule occurs when a quotation is indented (1 inch/10 spaces). Then the reference goes outside the closing punctuation.

```
Near the climax of the story, Wells has Nunez recognize
the pleasing qualities of life in the Country of the
Blind:
        They led a simple, laborious life, these people, with
        all the elements of virtue and happiness, as these
        things can be understood by men. They toiled, but
        not oppressively; they had food and clothing suffi-
        cient for their needs; they had days and seasons of
        rest; they made much of music and singing, and there
        was love among them, and little children. (15)
```

Guidelines for Using Footnotes and Endnotes

You can place explanatory notes either at the foot of pages (footnotes) or on separate sheets at the end of the paper (endnotes).

Use footnotes or endnotes for citing several sources (more than two or three) all at once

Text

```
A host of critics agrees that Swift does not share Gul-
liver's condemnation of human beings at the end of Gul-
liver's Travels.¹
```

Note

¹Abrams 23-28; Converse 55-70; Portnoy 150-65; Clore and
Barchester 300-05; Kellerman 83; Soles 15-20.

Use footnotes or endnotes for comments or information relating to something in your text

These comments or facts are not necessary to your line of thought, but you may want to include them because you think your readers would find them interesting.

Text

Irving adopts the stance of the ironic narrator in his
comic masterpiece "The Legend of Sleepy Hollow."²

Note

²The ironic narrator was a common fictional device in
eighteenth-century English fiction and was most notably present in one of Irving's favorite authors, Henry Fielding.

To set up a footnote or endnote, do the following:

- In the text of your essay where you want the reference to appear, place a number raised slightly above the line (*superscript;* note the examples above).
- Place a corresponding superscript number just before the note itself (note the examples above).
- Indent the note five spaces (one-half inch).
- Number the notes sequentially throughout the paper. In other words, do not restart your numbering (with "1") when you come to a new page. Rather, go from "1" to the final number all the way through the paper.
- Place your notes either at the bottom of the page (footnotes) or on a new page at the end of the paper (endnotes). Many people place them at the end of the text and before the "Works Cited" list because it is easier to format the paper that way.
- Single-space footnotes and place them four lines below your text (two double spaces from the text) and begin the footnote. Double-space (one single line of space) between footnotes.

- If you use endnotes rather than footnotes, begin them on a separate page or pages and position them between the text of your essay and the "Works Cited" page. Center the title "Notes" one inch from the top of the page.

- Indent the first line of each note. The rest of the note goes all the way to the left margin. Double-space within and between endnotes. For a "real life" example of the use of endnotes, see the sample paper at the end of this chapter.

Guidelines and Form for the "Works Cited" List: General Rules

The "Works Cited" list, placed at the end of the paper, contains citations for all the resources—primary and secondary—to which you refer in the body of your paper. Be sure that every source you referred to is included in your "Works Cited" list. Your goal here is to give enough information so readers can find these same sources and verify their content and reliability. Follow the guidelines below. Use the sample entries as models for each guideline or category.

1. **Arrange entries alphabetically by author.** If the author is anonymous, list the entry alphabetically by its title. For the purpose of alphabetizing, ignore *A, An,* and *The* at the beginning of titles.

2. **Do not number entries.**

3. **In each entry, put the author's last name first.** (The author's last name appears first because the list is in alphabetical order.) If there is more than one author in an entry, put the last name first for the first author: Rochester, Henry. Put the names of the other authors in regular order: Rochester, Henry, Roch Small, and Leonard Handy.

4. **Put the first line flush with the left margin.** Indent any subsequent (turnover) lines of the entry five spaces (one-half inch) from the left-hand margin.

5. **Include without exception every source—primary or secondary—cited in your paper.**

6. **Divide your entries into three main sections:**
   - author's name (last name first)
   - the name of the article or book
   - information about publication

Sometimes more sections are necessary—information about editors, about volume numbers, or about reprinted editions. But these three divisions are essential for all entries. Punctuate citations as indicated in the sample entries below.

7. **If information seems missing from a source, don't panic.** Provide as much information as you can.

8. **Put the "Works Cited" list at the end of your paper, on sheets separate from your text.** Double-space the entire list, both between and within entries.

Sample Entries for Books

A book with one author

```
Lewis, C. S. The Allegory of Love: A Study in Medieval Tradi-

    tion. New York: Oxford UP, 1936.
```

You can usually find the date of publication of books on the copyright page (the reverse of the title page) or, for some books published outside the United States, at the back of the book. If there is more than one date, choose the most recent one. If several cities are listed as places of publication, use the first one. The "UP" after "Oxford" in the above entry represents "University Press."

More than one work by an author

```
Jewett, Sarah Orne. A Country Doctor. New York: Garret, 1970.

---. A White Heron and Other Stories. Boston: Houghton,

    1886.
```

When you include more than one work by an author, substitute three hyphens for the author's name after the first citation. Arrange the works in alphabetical order by title.

A book with two or three authors

```
Berry, Lester V., and Melvin Van den Bark. The American The-

    saurus of Slang: With Supplement. New York: Crowell, 1947.
```

Reverse the name of the first author only.

A translation

Salih, Tayeb. Season of Migration to the North. Trans.

Denys Johnson-Davies. London: Heinemann, 1969.

A book that has more than three authors, has gone through several editions, and is one of several volumes in a set

Spiller, Robert E., et al. Literary History of the United

States. 4th ed. rev. Vol. 1. New York: Macmillan, 1974.

2 vols.

Using "et al." saves you from listing all the other authors of the work.

Multivolume work

Richardson, Samuel. Clarissa; or, the History of a Young

Lady. Vol. 4. London: Everyman, 1932. 4 vols.

An introduction or an afterword to a primary source

Charvat, William. Introduction. The Last of the Mohicans.

By James Fenimore Cooper. Boston: Riverside, 1958.

iii-xiv.

Magarshack, David. Afterword. The Death of Ivan Ilych and

Other Stories. By Leo Tolstoy. New York: Signet, 1960.

295-304.

An edition of an author's work

Trollope, Anthony. The Last Chronicle of Barset. Ed. Arthur

Mizener. Boston: Riverside, 1964.

In this example, Arthur Mizener is the editor of this edition of Trollope's *The Last Chronicle of Barset.*

An article in an encyclopedia

"La Fontaine, Jean de." The New Encyclopaedia Britannica:

Macropaedia. 15th ed. 1987.

For familiar reference works, especially ones that undergo frequent revision, give the author's name (if known), the title of the article, the title of the reference work (underlined or italicized), the edition number, and the date of publication. If the entries are listed alphabetically, there is no need to give volume or page numbers.

An anonymous introduction or article in an anthology of literature

"The Middle Ages to ca. 1485." <u>Norton Anthology of English</u>

<u>Literature</u>. Ed. M. H. Abrams et al. 7th ed. Vol. 1. New

York: Norton, 2000. 1-22.

Here the reference is to the first volume, pages 1–22. Note that when you cite sections of books, you usually give numbers for the whole section. The abbreviation "Ed." after the titles in the examples above means "edited by"; no need to add an "s" to the abbreviation if the book is edited by more than one person.

A work from an anthology

Christie, Agatha. "The Dream." <u>Detective Stories from the</u>

<u>Strand Magazine</u>. Ed. Jack Adrian. New York: Oxford UP,

1992. 21-43.

Jackson, Shirley. "The Lottery." <u>Literature: Reading, React-</u>

<u>ing, Writing</u>. Ed. Laurie G. Kirszner and Stephen R. Man-

dell. Compact 3rd ed. Fort Worth: Harcourt, 1997.

261-69.

Lyon, Thomas J. "The Literary West." <u>The Oxford History of the</u>

<u>American West</u>. Ed. Clyde A. Milner, II, Carol A. O'Con-

nor, and Martha A. Sandweiss. New York: Oxford UP, 1994.

707-41.

A book with one or more editors

Drabble, Margaret, ed. <u>The Oxford Companion to English Liter-</u>

<u>ature</u>. Rev. ed. New York: Oxford UP, 1995.

Suleiman, Susan R., and Inge Crosman, eds. The Reader in the
   Text: Essays on Audience and Interpretation. Princeton:
   Princeton UP, 1980.

The abbreviation "ed." above means "editor." Add an "s" to the abbreviation if the book is edited by more than one person.

Sample Entry for Articles in Scholarly Journals

Leverenz, David. "The Last Real Man in America: From Natty
   Bumppo to Batman." American Literary History 3 (1991):
   753-81.

In this entry, *American Literary History* is the journal, 3 is the volume
number, 1991 is the year of publication, and 753–81 are the page numbers. Note that you give page numbers not just for the pages you cite
but for the entire article.

Sample Entries for Articles in Popular Publications

A weekly magazine

Dubos, Andre. "Witness." New Yorker 21 July 1997: 33-36.

A monthly magazine

Malone, Michael. "Books in Brief." Harper's June 1977: 82-84.

A book review in a weekly magazine

Blake, Patricia. "Gingerly Removing the Veil." Rev. of
   Josephine Herbst, by Elinor Langer. Newsweek 3 Sept.
   1984: 80.

An article in a newspaper

Coneroy, Herman. "David Copperfield Revisited." New York
   Times 19 Aug. 1962, late ed.: F23.

Weeks, Linton. "Stanley Kunitz, 95, Becomes Poet Laureate for
a New Century." The Washington Post 29 July 2000: C1+.

When citing newspaper articles, indicate if possible the edition of the paper ("late edition," "national edition," "city edition"). The reason is that the content of articles may vary from edition to edition. The edition is usually indicated in the newspaper's masthead.

Sample Entries for Computer Databases

The documentary format for computer resources continues to evolve along with the resources themselves. The fifth edition of the *MLA Handbook for Writers of Research Papers* is the source for the guidelines below, but even these will change as technology evolves. For the most up-to-date MLA guidelines for documenting online resources, check the *MLA Style* Website at http://www.mla.org. (At the Website, click on "MLA Style" and then "Frequently Asked Questions.)

When you are faced with the sometimes puzzling problem of documenting electronic resources, keep in mind the reasons to document *anything:* You want to verify the existence and reliability of your re sources. You want to help readers find these resources. You want to show that you have conscientiously sifted through the relevant evidence and opinion. So, if you are confused about how to document a resource, use common sense. Give the information necessary to accomplish the above goals. Since databases often cease publication, especially on the Internet, you might want to print out the relevant sections of documents you cite, in case you have to show readers they really existed.

Portable databases published periodically For CD-ROMs, diskettes, and magnetic tapes that are continually updated, use the following format:

Dolan, Marc. "The (Hi)story of Their Lives: Mythic Autobiog-
raphy and 'The Lost Generation.'" Journal of American Studies. 27 (1993): 35–56. America: History and Life on Disc.
CD-ROM. ABC-Clio. 1996.

Earthman, Elise Ann. "Creating the Virtual Work: Readers'
Processes in Understanding Literary Texts." Conference on

```
College Composition and Communication.  Seattle, Washing-
   ton, 17 March 1989.  ERIC.  CD-ROM. SilverPlatter.  June
   1996.
```

Your citations should include as much of the following information as you can find:

- Author's name—if the work is anonymous, omit the name.
- Publication information—if the work appears in print (for example, in a scholarly journal), use the same format for giving publication information as you would for the printed version. (See the above sample entries for books, scholarly journals, and popular publications.)
- Title of the database (underlined).
- Publication medium (CD-ROM, diskette, magnetic tape)
- Name of the vender—you can usually spot the name of the vender somewhere on the first screen. If it is not there, check to see if you can click on "information about this database." If that does not work, leave out the information and move on.
- Electronic publication date (when the database was released)—the sources of information just mentioned should give you this date.

The first example above is an abstract of an article in a scholarly journal. If you wanted to summarize or quote from this abstract, you would cite the computer database (*America: History and Life on Disc*) that provides it. The second entry is a lecture available only from the computer database *ERIC*. If you wanted to use it, you would cite the database.

Portable databases not published periodically These are CD-ROMs, diskettes, and magnetic tapes published only once, like a book.

```
Hallam, Walker.  Molière.  Boston: Twayne, 1990.  CD-
   ROM. Boston: DiscLit, 1992.

"Mingle."  The Oxford English Dictionary.  2nd ed.  CD-ROM. Ox-
   ford: Oxford UP, 1992.
```

For these databases, include the following information:

- Author's name—If the work is anonymous, omit the name. If the name is for an editor, translator, or compiler, indicate that with the appropriate abbreviation (ed., comp., trans.).
- Title of the publication (underlined)
- Name of the editor, translator, or compiler. This is relevant if the work is not in its original published form.
- Publication medium (CD-ROM, diskette, magnetic tape)
- Place of publication
- Name of the publisher
- Date of publication

The first example is a book from the Twayne Publishers series of books about authors. For this entry, publication information about the printed book is followed by information about the CD-ROM. The second example is the definition of a word from *The Oxford English Dictionary*.

Online databases accessed through a computer service and featuring material published in print Such databases are available over the Internet, usually through subscription. You typically gain access to them through your college or library computer network.

Halberstam, Judith. "Technologies of Monstrosity: Bram
    Stoker's <u>Dracula</u>." <u>Victorian Studies</u> 36 (1993): 20. <u>Ex-</u>
    <u>panded Academic ASAP</u>. Infotrac Online. Jackson Library,
    UNC at Greensboro. 5 July 2000.

Hutchinson, Mark. "In Defense of Fiction." <u>New York Times</u> 22
    October 1995, late ed., sec. 7:30. <u>New York Times</u>. First
    Search. Jackson Library, UNC at Greensboro. 20 May 2000.

For these databases, supply the following information:

- Name of the author (if given).
- Publication information for the printed source. Use the same format as described above for printed material. See the sample entries for books, scholarly journals, and popular publications.
- Title of the database (underlined or italicized)

- Name of the computer service
- Name of the library that gave you access to the database
- Date of access (the date you used the service to read or print this material)

In the first example on page 273, the computer service, Infotrac Online, provides an abstract and the full text of an article that appeared in a printed scholarly journal. There are no page numbers in this document, but the information about it includes the number of pages (twenty) of the printed essay. In the second example, the service gives an abstract of a newspaper article.

Online databases accessed via a computer service and featuring material with no printed source

"Courtly Love." 1994-2000. Britannica Online. CompuServe.

Jackson Library, UNC at Greensboro. 12 June 2000.

For these databases, supply the following information:

- Author's name (if available)
- Title of the article or chapter (in quotation marks)
- Date of the material (if given)
- Title of the database (underlined)
- Name of the computer service
- Name of the library through which you accessed the database
- Date of access (the date you used the service).

In the example on page 275, the author is unknown (so not included) and the article was accessed from the Internet via subscription to *Britannica Online*. Were you to look up "courtly love" in the printed version of the *Encyclopaedia Britannica*, you might find the same article as the one cited above, but the editors of *Britannica Online* claim that they update their entries regularly, so their version of the article might be different from the printed version.

Articles in online periodicals and Websites

Cohen, Rachel. "A Private History: Moments in the Friendship

of Mark Twain and Ulysses S. Grant." Doubletake 21 (Summer

    2000). 12 September 2000 <http://www.doubletakemagazine.org
    /issues/21/cohen/index.html>.

Elam, Diane. "Why Read?" Culture Machine. 2 (2000). 3 August
    2000 <http://culturemachine.tees.ac.uk/frm_fl/htm>.

Many essays and commentaries are published only on the Internet in such places as Websites, journals, magazines (e-zines), and newsletters. For these resources, give as much of the following information as you can:

- Author's name (if available)
- Title of the article (in quotation marks)
- Title of the Website or publication (underlined)
- Volume number, issue number, or other identifying number (if available)
- Date of publication (if available)
- Date of access
- Electronic address of the site (URL), contained within angle brackets (< >).

Professional and personal Websites

Churchyard, Henry. Jane Austen Information Page. 29 Sept.
    2000 <http://pemberley.com/janeinfo/janeinfo.html>.

When you cite the Website itself, not an article within the Website, give as much of the following information as you can:

- Name of the person who created or maintains the site
- Title of the site (underlined)
- If there is no title, a description such as "Home Page" (not underlined or in quotation marks)
- Name of any institution or organization connected with the site
- Date of access
- Electronic address (URL), contained within angle brackets

Electronic texts

Keats, John. "La Belle Dame sans Merci." The Poetical Works

of John Keats. London: Macmillan, 1884. 28 Aug. 2000

<http://bartleby.com/126/55.html>.

Milton, John. Paradise Lost. Ed. Joseph Raben. 1965. 27

Mar. 2000 <ftp://metalab.unc.edu/pub/docs/books/gutenberg

/etext92/plrabn12.txt>.

For e-texts, give the following information:

- Author's name (if given)
- Title of the text—if the title is a work within a larger work, such as a poem or short story, put it within quotation marks; if the title is a self-contained work, such as a novel, play, or collection, underline it.
- Name of editor, translator, or compiler (if available)
- Publication information about the printed source (to the extent available)
- Date of access
- Electronic address (URL), contained within angle brackets

The first example above is a poem by John Keats located in a collection of his poems published in 1884. Information about the printed source for the poem is made clear at the beginning of the site. The second example is the complete version of John Milton's *Paradise Lost.* The publisher of the text, Project Gutenberg, provides an introduction to this edition that indicates who created it and what the edition is like.

Online discussion groups and news groups

Foner, Heather. "Time Travel Fiction." Online posting. 10

June 1999. Weird Science Discussion Group. 12 June 1999

<darwin-1@_uconnaix.cc.uconn.edu>.

Grayfield, John. "Two Years Before the Mast." Online posting.

3 June 1999. Naval Science News Group. 12 Aug. 1999

<sci.military.naval.rec.ships>.

Discussion groups abound on the Internet. For these resources, supply the following information:

- Author's name (if known)
- The title of the posting (in quotation marks)
- The kind of communication (Online posting)
- The date of publication
- The name of the forum (Discussion group, News group)
- The access date
- Electronic address (URL), enclosed in angle brackets

Electronic mail (e-mail)

Finney, Jack. "Re: Time travel fiction." E-mail to Kelley

Griffith. 11 Oct. 1993.

For e-mail messages, give the following information:

- Author's name
- The subject line from the posting (in quotation marks)
- The recipient of the posting
- The date of publication (the day the message was sent)

For *all* electronic resources, you may find some of the information missing or difficult to come by. Don't be frustrated. Give as much of the information as you can, and omit what you cannot find.

Sample Entries for Other Nonprint Sources

An interview

Rogers, Fred. Interview with Noah Adams. All Things Con-

sidered. National Public Radio. WFDD, Winston-Salem. 19

Feb. 1993.

Trillin, Calvin. Personal interview. 16 Mar. 1993.

The basic information for interviews is (1) the interviewee's name, (2) the title or nature of the interview and the interviewer (if known), and

(3) the place and date of the interview. The first entry above indicates that Fred Rogers was interviewed on the radio program *All Things Considered* by Noah Adams. If you personally interviewed someone, your citation would look like the second entry.

A lecture

Gay, Geneva. "Ethnic Identity in a Diverse Society: The Chal-

lenge for Education." Temple University. Philadelphia. 30

Mar. 1993.

May, Marilyn. Class lecture. English 368: English Romantic

Poetry. University of North Carolina at Greensboro. 10

Apr. 1991.

For lectures, give the lecturer's name, then the title or nature of the lecture, and finally the place and date.

A television or radio program

Soundings. NPR. WFDD, Winston-Salem. 7 Mar. 1993.

Sixty Minutes. CBS. WFMY, Greensboro. 24 Jan. 1993.

"Mistaken Identity." Millennium: Tribal Wisdom and the Modern

World. Nar. Adrian Malone. WUNC, Chapel Hill. 12 Feb. 1992.

Radio and television programs should contain the following basic information: the title of the episode (in quotation marks), the title of the program (underlined), the network (CBS, NPR), the title of the series (no underscore), the call letters of the local station where you heard or saw the program, and the date of broadcast. The first entry above is a radio program, the second a television program. The third entry illustrates an episode in a program narrated by an individual.

A sound recording

Holbrook, Hal. "Journalism on Horseback." Mark Twain Tonight.

LP. Columbia, n.d.

McKennitt, Loreena. "The Lady of Shalott." The Visit. Music

by Loreena McKennitt. Lyrics by Alfred, Lord Tennyson.

Warner Brothers, 1991.

Thomas, Dylan. "Fern Hill." <u>Dylan Thomas Reading A Child's</u>

<u>Christmas in Wales and Five Poems</u>. LP. Caedmon, 1952.

For commercially available recordings, put the person cited first. Depending on your emphasis, this person may be the author, composer, performer, or director. Then list the title or titles, the artist or artists, the medium, the manufacturer, and the year of issue. If you do not know the year of issue, put *n.d.* ("no date"). If the medium is not compact disc, indicate the medium: audiocassette, audiotape, or LP (long-playing record).

A film or videotape recording

<u>Crete and Mycenae</u>. Prod. and dir. Hans-Joachim Horsfeld.

Videocassette. Kartes Video Communications, 1986.

<u>Star Wars</u>. Dir. George Lucas. Prod. Gary Kurtz. Screen-

play by George Lucas. Music by John Williams. Perf. Mark

Hamill, Harrison Ford, Carrie Fisher, Peter Cushing, and

Alec Guiness. Twentieth Century-Fox, 1977.

When citing films, begin with the title (underlined), then give information such as director, writer, performers, and conclude with distributor and date. For videotapes (and filmstrips and slide programs, as well), include the medium right before the name of the distributor, as in the first entry.

Frequently Used Abbreviations

Abbreviations save space. You will run into them when you read essays and books about literature, and you may want to use them yourself. Here, then, is a brief list. For a much longer list, see *The MLA Handbook*.

adapt.	adapter, adaptation, adapted by
app.	appendix
c., ca.	*circa*, "about" (usually used with dates when the exact date is not certain—for example, ca. 1594)
cf.	*confer*, "compare" (not the equivalent of "see")

ch., chs.	chapter, chapters
comp.	compiler
d.	died
ed., eds.	edited by, editor, editors
esp.	especially
e.g.	*exempli gratia,* "for example"
et al.	*et alii,* "and others"
etc.	*et cetera,* "and so forth"
i.e.	*id est,* "that is"
l., ll.	line, lines
ms., mss.	manuscript, manuscripts
NB	*nota bene,* "note well"
p., pp.	page, pages
par.	paragraph
pt.	part
rev.	revised by, revision; review or reviewed by (for reviews, use *review* where *rev.* might be confused with *revision* or *revised by*)
trans.	translated by
U, UP	university, university press (in documentation)
vol., vols.	volume, volumes

Sample Research Paper

The following sample student research paper illustrates the use of the MLA documentary style as well as the principles of the argumentative research essay. As in this paper, the first page of your paper should have your name and course information in the upper-left corner, the title centered just below this information, and the text just below the title. The *MLA Handbook* says that you do not need a title page, but you might ask your instructor for his or her preference. Usually, you do not need a title page. If you have endnotes, place them on a new page immediately following your text. Put your "Works Cited" list after the endnotes, beginning on a new page. For more detailed instructions on the format of your paper, see Chapter 10.

Harold Wright

Professor Helen May

English 105-06

12 April 2000

The Monster's Education in Mary Shelley's

Frankenstein

Education is a prominent endeavor in Mary

Shelley's Frankenstein. Nearly all the major

characters--Walton, Victor, Elizabeth, Henry, Safie,

and the monster--are at school or searching for

knowledge. Victor's education leads to the best

known event of the novel, his creation of a human

being. But the similarity of the monster to Mary

Shelley herself suggests that she uses the monster,

and especially his education, to express ideas that

were close to her heart.

The monster's education begins immediately

after his creation. His creator, Victor Franken-

stein, while at school in Germany, learns how to

bring dead tissue back to life. He assembles a

creature from body parts, but when he awakens it, he

shrinks from it in horror and runs away. Two years

later, the monster, now "grown up," meets Victor in

the Alps and tells him his story.

Although the monster's education is improbably

rapid, Shelley makes clear that it follows the pattern

of any person's growth from infancy to adolescence.

To establish the normality of the monster's growth and
education, she drew upon two works she read while
writing Frankenstein: John Locke's Essay Concerning
Human Understanding (1690) and Rousseau's Discourse on
the Origins of Human Inequality (1755). The monster's
childhood fits the pattern of Rousseau's noble savage,
who must learn how to survive in the wilderness by
trial and error. And he acquires knowledge according
to Locke's theory that everything people learn origi-
nates from sensations (Woodbridge pars. 15-17). At
the beginning of the monster's life, he is like any
newborn baby, completely innocent, empty of knowledge,
registering only sensations. Gradually he moves
into a kind of early childhood by learning to feel
hot and cold, to experience fear and pleasure, to
walk, eat, sleep, and clothe himself. His initial
encounters with human beings are not happy. The
first person who sees him runs shrieking away. When
he ventures into a village, the townspeople pelt him
with rocks and chase him out. After wandering cold
and hungry around the countryside, the monster comes
upon a cottage with a lean-to shed attached to it.
He crawls into the shed and makes it his home for
the next year (Shelley 98-101).

       The cottage is occupied by the De Laceys, a
family of political exiles from France. The family
consists of an old, blind father, a son, a daughter, and, somewhat later, the son's fiancée, the

daughter of a Turkish businessman. Through a chink
in a window, the monster observes and listens to
them. He is deeply impressed by this family, because, although they are poor, they love and care
for one another. Fearing that his appearance might
frighten them, he keeps himself out of sight. But
in imitation of them, he does acts of kindness. At
night, he piles firewood outside their door and
shovels snow from their pathways. The more he observes them, the more he yearns to join their warm
family circle (101-09).

His opportunity comes, he thinks, when the fiancée arrives. Since the fiancée cannot speak their
language and knows nothing about Europe, the family
begins to teach her, and as they do, the monster becomes her co-student. The monster is astonishingly
adept. He learns French more quickly than Safie,
the fiancée. He studies European history, eco-
nomics, and politics. He reads Goethe's The Sorrows
of Young Werther, Plutarch's Lives, and Milton's
Paradise Lost (109-123). As a result, he begins to
think about who he is: "My person was hideous and my
stature gigantic. What did this mean? Who was I?
What was I? Whence did I come? What was my desti-
nation?" (123).

He decides, finally, to reveal himself to the
family and beg them to accept him as one of their
own. One day, with fear and trepidation, while the

rest of the family is away, he visits the blind father. At first all goes well. The monster explains,
"I have good dispositions; my life has been hitherto
harmless and in some degree beneficial; but a fatal
prejudice clouds their [people's] eyes, and where
they ought to see a feeling and kind friend, they behold only a detestable monster" (128). The father
responds eagerly and recognizes in the monster a kin-
dred spirit: "I also am unfortunate; I and my family
have been condemned, although innocent; judge, therefore, if I do not feel for your misfortunes" (128).
The monster weeps in gratitude. But when the others
return, they view the monster with horror. The
daughter faints, Safie runs out of the cottage, and
the son beats the monster with a stick. Two days
later, the monster returns, finds the De Laceys
gone, and burns the cottage to the ground. Shortly
thereafter, when the monster rescues a little girl,
he completes his education. Instead of expressing
gratitude, the girl's companion shoots and wounds
him. The monster then vows revenge on all humankind. From this point onward, he becomes what he
is most famous for being. He becomes a killer
(123-135).

Mary Shelley's childhood and education parallel
the monster's in striking ways. She was born 30 August 1797 to two of the most notorious political
radicals of their day. Her father, William Godwin,

Wright 5

was a social critic, philosopher, political re-
former, and novelist. Her mother, Mary Wollstonecraft, was the first feminist author.
Together, they condemned tyrannical governments and
enthusiastically supported the French Revolution.
They shared a passionate and deeply satisfying relationship. Neither believed in marriage, but when
Wollstonecraft became pregnant, they married to protect the child. Ten days after Mary's birth, Wollstonecraft died from natal complications (Spark
3-11).

Mary grew up in a large and busy family, consisting of Godwin's new wife, Jane Clairmont, a
stepsister, stepbrother, half-sister, and half
brother. Although her brothers went to the best
schools, she had no formal education. Instead, she
was taught at home by her father, her stepmother,
and tutors. She read from her father's large library. She listened to the conversation of famous
visitors, like William Wordsworth, Charles Lamb, and
William Hazlitt. Once she hid behind the sofa to
hear Samuel Taylor Coleridge recite "The Rime of the
Ancient Mariner" (Spark 13).

By the time Mary was a teenager, relations with
her family had become strained. She didn't get
along with her stepmother, and her father distanced
himself from her. To escape tensions at home, she
made several extended visits to friends in Scotland.

It was after one of these that she met the poet
Percy Shelley, who had become a frequent visitor in
her father's house. He was five years older than
Mary, already married, and father of one child with
a second on the way. He and Mary fell in love and
began a passionate affair. After stormy opposition
from her family, they ran away together to Europe in
July 1814. Percy was twenty-one years old. She was
sixteen and had just discovered that she was pregnant (Spark 28-29).

Until Percy's death in 1822 from a boating accident, the couple lived a difficult, often tumul-
tuous life together. After they "eloped," her father
immediately condemned her and refused to see or write
to her for three and a half years. She and Percy
were almost always in financial difficulty, often, at
first, having no place to stay so that they slept
outdoors or in barns (Spark 28-29). Giving birth and
caring for babies dominated her relationship with
Percy. She was pregnant five times until Percy's
death. She had two miscarriages, the second of which
almost killed her. Two of her children died as in-
fants, and only one survived to adulthood. Amidst
these difficulties, Mary wrote <u>Frankenstein</u>. To create the novel, she drew upon the huge amount of reading she kept up during this period, the conversations
she had with Percy and their friends, her mother and
father's writings, and her own experiences. She began

the novel in July 1816 and finished it by May 1817.
It was published in January 1818 (Spark 56-60).

The difficulties of Mary's own education and
coming of age gave rise to the ideas she embedded in
the story of the monster's education. The first of
these ideas is that children who are abandoned or
neglected by their parents can become "monsters."
Ellen Moers argues that Mary's experience of continual pregnancy, childbirth, childcare, and child
death led her to write about a careless and inept
scientist who gives birth, so to speak, to a mis-
formed child. Moers calls <u>Frankenstein</u> a "birth
myth" (140). The novel is "interesting, most powerful, and most feminine" in its "motif of revulsion
against newborn life, and the drama of guilt, dread,
and flight surrounding birth and its consequences,"
especially in its dealing "with the retribution visited upon monster and creator for deficient infant
care" (142). Mary thus writes a "fantasy of the
newborn as at once monstrous agent of destruction
and piteous victim of parental abandonment" (148).

As a daring and anxious creator of life, Mary
is similar to Victor. But her childhood experiences,
gifts, and education link her also to the monster.
Like the monster she felt "abandoned" by her parents,
first, at childbirth by her mother, then by her father when he remarried and when she ran away with
Shelley (Sunstein 34, 114). "Obviously," Emily

Sunstein says, "the monster created from corpses reflects the primitive Mary Shelley: her guilt at being
her mother's killer-reincarnation, her rage that her
father abandoned her, and her resentment of her half
brother, William" (131). Like the monster Mary grew
up rapidly and was extremely young when she took on
the responsibilities of adulthood. Like the monster
she had to pick up an education by "looking on." Like
the monster she was very precocious, a rapid learner.
Like the monster she was something of an outlaw,
stepping across the border of conventional female
morality. Like the monster, she was scorned and ex-
iled.

Mary transfers her feelings of parental victim-
ization to the monster. Upon his first meeting with
Victor, he holds Victor accountable for mistreating
him: "Remember that I am thy creature; I ought to be
thy Adam, but I am rather the fallen angel, whom
thou drivest from joy for no misdeed" (95). Victor
reluctantly agrees: "For the first time, also, I felt
what the duties of a creator towards his creature
were, and that I ought to render him happy before I
complained of his wickedness" (97). The monster
compares the happy De Lacey family to his own lack
of family: "But where were my friends and relations?
No father had watched my infant days, no mother had
blessed me with smiles and caresses" (115). At the
end of his story, the monster once again accuses

Wright 9

Victor of failing as a parent: "You endowed me with perceptions and passions and cast me abroad an object for the scorn and horror of mankind" (133).

The second idea in Frankenstein suggested by Mary's life is that, like bad parents, an unjust society can create monsters. Her main source for this idea probably originated with her parents' ideas about the French Revolution. In her An Historical and Moral View of the Origin and Progress of the French Revolution (1794), Wollstonecraft responds to conservative critics of the French Revolution, like Edmund Burke, who labeled the revolutionaries as "monsters" (Sterrenburg 153). Wollstonecraft, Lee Sterrenburg says, "admits that rebels are monsters. But she resolutely insists that these monsters are social products. They are not the living dead, nor are they specters arisen from the tomb of the murdered monarchy. Rather, they are the products of oppression, misrule, and despotism under the ancien régime. The lower orders are driven to rebellion" (162).

The monster embodies Wollstonecraft's belief that social rebels are formed by society. At birth the monster is innocent. As he begins his education, he wants to do good deeds and to have loving relationships. But the failure of society (Victor, the De Laceys, other people) to accept him, love him, and treat him fairly causes him to become a

monster. He tells Victor, "I was benevolent and
good; misery made me a fiend" (95-96). After the
De Laceys drive him out of the cottage and the little girl's companion shoots him, he feels "the oppressive sense of injustice and ingratitude" of the
people who have hurt him and vows "eternal hatred
and vengeance to all mankind" (135). "I am mali-
cious," he says, "because I am miserable" (138).
As Sterrenburg says, "The Monster proves a very
philosophical rebel. He explains his actions in
traditional republican terms. He claims he has
been driven to rebellion by the failures of the
ruling orders. His superiors and protectors have
shirked their responsibilities toward him, im-
pelling him to insurrection" (161).

　　Although the monster is just one person, and an
unusual one, at that, Mary extends her social criticism to include others. She does so by means of his
education. Through his and Safie's reading of Volney's Ruins of Empires,[1] he hears about the tragic
history of human societies: "For a long time I could
not conceive how one man could go forth to murder
his fellow, or even why there were laws and governments; but when I heard details of vice and blood-
shed, my wonder ceased and I turned away with
disgust and loathing" (114). The De Laceys reveal
that society is unfair to all but a few citizens: "I
heard of the division of property, of immense wealth

and squalid poverty, of rank, descent, and noble
blood. [. . .] I learned that the possessions most
esteemed by your fellow creatures were high and un-
sullied descent united with riches" (115).

The De Laceys, Safie, Justine Moritz, the monster are all victims of an unjust society. So, too,
Mary no doubt believed, were the oppressed workers
of her own day. While she was writing Frankenstein,
England suffered from an economic depression that
caused widespread unemployment and hunger among
workers. These conditions led workers to hold
protest rallies that sometimes ended in violence.
The worst of these occasions was the "Peterloo" riot
of 1819, when 80,000 people demonstrated in St.
Peter's Fields in Manchester for political reform
and were fired upon by soldiers. Eleven people were
killed and 400 injured. The government's response
to such protests was unsympathetic, harsh, and repressive (Lerner 786). In Mary's mind, the monster
could have been any of these workers, driven to rebellion by poverty, hunger, and the meanness of powerful people.[2]

The third idea suggested by Mary's life is that
women, too, are made monstrous by society. Sandra
Gilbert and Susan Gubar hold that Mary saw herself as
a monster because women are taught to feel like monsters: "As we argued earlier, women have seen themselves (because they have been seen) as monstrous,

vile, degraded creatures, second-comers, and emblems
of filthy materiality, even though they have also
been traditionally defined as superior beings, angels, better halves" (240). Mary got a taste of
this attitude when she learned about her mother's
life and ideas. A year after Wollstonecraft's
death, Godwin published his <u>Memoirs of the Author of</u>
<u>A Vindication of the Rights of Woman</u> (1798), in
which, Emily Sunstein says, "he revealed the details
of her intimate life, which comparatively few had
known about: her love for Fuseli, her liaison with
Imlay, her premarital affair with him--'stripping his
dead wife naked,' said Robert Southey" (19). As a
result, the conservative press ruthlessly attacked
Godwin and her, calling her a "lascivious whore"
(Sunstein 20). Mary read Godwin's <u>Memoirs</u> when she
was fourteen, along with <u>A Vindication of the Rights</u>
<u>of Woman</u> (1794), Wollstonecraft's best-known book,
and her other works. Fully aware of the press's
charges against her mother, Mary became a fierce
partisan of Wollstonecraft's feminist beliefs. She
"worshiped" her mother, according to Sunstein, "both
as rational intellectual and romantic heroine" (53).
Through her mother's writings and actions, Mary saw
that women who advocate and practice liberation are
labeled "monsters."

     The monster's embodiment of women is most visi-
ble in his education. In <u>A Vindication of the</u>

Rights of Woman, Wollstonecraft declared the equal-
ity of the sexes and demanded equal rights for
women. She argued that the key to women's sharing
of power with men is education. Yet Mary, although
extremely able as a student, did not go to school.
Her brothers and husband went, but not she. And
there was probably no college or university at the
time that would have accepted females as students.
Instead, like the monster, Mary did much of her
learning on her own. As if to call attention to her
identity with the monster, she had him read the same
things that she had been reading under Percy's tute-
lage. The similarity of their reading program leads
Gilbert and Gubar to claim that Mary and the monster
are "parented, if at all, by books" (239).

The similarity of Mary's life to the monster's,
then, suggests that, through neglect and mistreat-
ment, three groups can be turned into "monsters":
children, citizens, and women. If the monster's experience is anything to go by, education, though ex-
citing, only adds to their monstrousness. It makes
them more aware of their alienation and unjust treatment. "Increase of knowledge," the monster tells
Victor, "only discovered to me more clearly what a
wretched outcast I was" (125). Furthermore, education drives them toward vengeance rather than acceptance: "My sufferings were augmented also by the
oppressive sense of the injustice and ingratitude of

Wright 14

their infliction. My daily vows rose for revenge--a
deep and deadly revenge, such as would alone compen-
sate for the outrages and anguish I endured" (135).
But the monster's education is also our education.
Just as he learned by looking over Safie's shoulder,
we learn by looking over his. Mary Shelley perhaps
hoped that if we shared the monster's education, we
might help prevent the creation of monsters--by caring for our children, by treating people fairly, and
by establishing just societies.

Notes

[1]One of Shelley's sources for the scene wherein the monster learns about the history of human vice is <u>Pygmalion et Galatée</u> (1803), a play by Stéphanie-Felicité Ducrest de Saint-Aubin, Comtesse de Genlis. In this play, a pure and innocent character, Galatea, is, like the monster, "awakened" to life fully grown. When an old servant fills her in on human history, she is shocked by revelations of human meanness and misery (slavery, tyranny, extreme distance between rich and poor, treachery). This play, Burton Pollin maintains, "helped to suggest the device of awakening and the actual injustices of society with which both naive intellects become acquainted" (101).

[2]Elizabeth Bohls claims that Mary extends her social criticism to "colonized" peoples: "Shelley weaves into her creature's indeterminate identity middle-class Britons' collective anxieties about otherness of more than one kind" (25). Safie, as a Turk and Christian, and the monster, as the alienated outlaw, represent colonized peoples (32). After reading Volney's book, they both lament the "genocide of the American Indians" (29). The monster's exclusion from happy middle class families like the Frankensteins and the De Laceys, "is inseparable from, in fact depends on, the violence their

civilization does to those whom its structure of

value needs to exclude and condemn" (29). In the

monster's expressions of alienation, we "hear the

anguish of a colonized self who has internalized

the values that judge him forever deficient" (32).

Wright 17

Works Cited

Bohls, Elizabeth A. "Standards of Taste, Discourses
    of 'Race,' and the Aesthetic Education of a
    Monster: Critique of Empire in Frankenstein."
    Eighteenth-Century Life (Nov. 1994): 23-36.

Gilbert, Sandra M., and Susan Gubar. The Madwoman
    in the Attic: The Woman Writer and the
    Nineteenth-Century Literary Imagination. New
    Haven, CT: Yale UP, 1979.

Lerner, Robert E., Standish Meacham, and Edward Mc-
    Nall Burns. Western Civilizations: Their His-
    tory and Their Culture. 11th ed. New York:
    Norton, 1988.

Moers, Ellen. Literary Women: The Great Writers.
    Garden City, NY: Anchor Books, 1977.

Pollin, Burton R. "Philosophical and Literary
    Sources of Frankenstein." Comparative Litera-
    ture 17 (Spring 1965): 97-108.

Shelley, Mary. Frankenstein: Or, The Modern
    Prometheus. New York: Signet Classic (New
    American Library), 1965.

Spark, Muriel. Mary Shelley. New York: Dutton, 1987.

Sunstein, Emily W. Mary Shelley: Romance and
    Reality. Boston: Little, Brown, 1989.

Woodbridge, Kim. "Mary Shelley and the Desire to
    Acquire Knowledge: Demonstrated in the Novel
    Frankenstein." Mary Shelley and Frankenstein.
    28 Aug. 2000 <http://desert-fairy.com/knowl-
    edge.shtml>.

Comments on the Research Paper

In the first paragraph—the introduction—the author states his purpose: to use Mary Shelley's life as a means of identifying important ideas in *Frankenstein*. He indicates that he will focus on one part of the novel, the section about the monster's education. Although he does not state his purpose in the form of a question, we can infer the question that lies behind his purpose: How might the monster's education apply to the real world? Put another way, what ideas might Shelley have wanted to convey in her story of the monster's education?

The body of the paper is structured by three answers to this question. First, neglectful parents can turn children into monsters. Second, unjust societies can turn citizens into monsters. Third, prejudiced societies can turn women into monsters. Each of these claims constitutes a major unit of the paper. Within each unit the author draws upon details from the novel, information about Mary Shelley's life, and opinions of critics to explain and support his claims.

In the final paragraph, the author's conclusion, he restates his three major claims. This summary, the first sentence of the paragraph, is his thesis. He then uses the thesis to make a conjecture about what his line of thought adds up to, how the monster's education might apply to people today. Throughout the paper, he follows MLA procedure for introducing facts and testimony in his text. He includes two explanatory notes, which he places at the end of the paper. His parenthetical references refer clearly to the sources in the "Works Cited" list.

Notice that for all the author's inclusion of secondary sources, the paper is nonetheless his argument, his creative investigation of the meaning of the novel. He never presents facts and other people's opinions as ends in themselves, but rather as support for his own ideas. As such, his paper is a fine model of a research essay about literature.

Taking Essay Tests

So far, this book has dealt with essays written outside the classroom. Tests and examinations, however, are work you do in class, usually within a given time frame. When your instructor tests you, he or she wants to know two things: how familiar you are with the course material (the literature, the instructor's lectures, the secondary material you may be required to read) and how creatively you can think about this material. Tests fall into two categories—objective and essay. Sometimes, the instructor may include questions or assignments from both categories on the same test.

Objective tests ask you to account for, explain, and identify details about the course material. Essay tests ask you to state your ideas about literary works and to support those ideas with facts and reasoning. Some essay tests call for short, one-paragraph essays; some call for long essays. The same methods for writing out-of-class essays apply to test essays, short or long. Your test essays are arguments: They should have a thesis and should try to convince an audience of the validity of that thesis. They should use sound logic and apt illustrations. Most of all, because of time limits, they need good organization. Perhaps the most important general consideration to keep in mind is that your grade will depend on how well you *perform* on a particular assignment, not simply on how much you know. You may know the material very well, but if you do not perform well, your grade will not reflect the abundance or quality of your knowledge. The following guidelines should help you perform well on essay tests.

Guidelines for Taking Essay Tests

1. **Prepare thoroughly.**
   a. First, learn the facts of the work or works on which you are being tested. Know who the characters are, what they do, and what happens to them, as well as the specifics of setting, and so forth. When you are taking the test, you should know the details so well that they emerge from your memory almost automatically. This subliminal knowledge saves your creative energy for dealing with the interpretive problems the instructor gives you. If you have to dredge up facts from your memory slowly, you waste valuable test time.
   b. Systematically review the key problems or subjects relevant to the works, literary periods, or genres covered by the test. A wise first step is to review the aspects of the works the instructor has emphasized in class. Then ask questions about the works, as you would for finding essay topics. Here, however, cover a range of important questions. Focus on the elements of literature. How does the author handle setting, characterization, theme, point of view, and so forth. If the test covers a number of works, consider ways in which the works are linked together. Assume that your instructor will ask you to compare works, noting similarities and differences among them.
   c. When you review class notes, do so *along with* a review of the literary works. Reviewing your notes on the instructor's class comments will help you to pinpoint important aspects of the works and should help you anticipate test questions. Remember, however, that memorizing class notes is no substitute for reviewing the works themselves. The two should be done together.

2. **Understand the assignment.** When you get the test, read all of the assignments carefully before you begin writing. If you do not understand any of them, ask the instructor to explain more fully. Sometimes instructors unintentionally write ambiguous assignments. You have a right to know exactly what you are supposed to do.

3. **Plan your answer.**
   a. *Think through* your answer by making a short, topical outline. Making an outline frees you from worrying about relevance and completeness while you write. Instead, once you have planned your answer and jotted down an outline of your plan, you can devote your writing time to a creative development of each main

point. If you have fifty minutes to write an essay, ten minutes making an outline is time well spent. Your outline might look something like this:

Thesis (state it in a phrase)
Claim # 1 (state it in a phrase)
    Supporting facts (list several)
Claim # 2
    Supporting facts
Claim # 3
    Supporting facts

b. Cross through items on your outline that do not fit the topic.
c. Arrange the remaining items in a logical order. Descending order of importance is probably best. That way, if you run out of time, you will have covered the most important items.
d. Once you have edited your outline, you are ready to write. If you think of additional items to cover, add them in the appropriate place to your outline.

4. **Respond directly to the assignment.** One or two sentences at the beginning of the essay and at strategic places throughout should do the job. This way the instructor will know that you have kept the assignment in mind and that you have tried to deal with it. Your direct response to the assignment is the thesis of your essay and therefore should usually come near the beginning or end of your essay. Note the following example:

Assignment: Huck tricks Jim into believing that he dreamed they were separated in the fog. But Jim finally sees the trick for what it is. What does Huck learn from Jim's reaction?

Direct Response: Huck learns that Jim has feelings and dignity just as white people do.

The complete answer, of course, would explain and illustrate this point, but the direct response connects the whole answer to the assignment. Without a direct response, your answer may seem irrelevant.

5. **Write on one side of the page.** Writing on both sides of the page is messy and hard to read (ink bleeds through). Also, the instructor might overlook what's on the back side, especially if it is just a few

sentences. To avoid these problems, write on one side of the page. Do this even if you use blue books.

6. **Add inserts when necessary.** It is acceptable, after you have read your answer through, to add new material. This is another reason to write on only one side of the page. If the new material is short, write it in the margin, with an arrow to indicate where it fits. If the new material is long, write the words "insert (see the back of this page)" in the margin, accompanied with the arrow, and write the new material on the back of the page.

7. **Write clear, simple, and correct prose.** The limited time and the pressure of the occasion make some mechanical slips likely, but strive to avoid them. Be wary of serious errors such as sentence fragments, ambiguous pronoun references, and subject–verb disagreements. If your handwriting is normally difficult to read, take care to make it legible.

8. **Develop your answer thoroughly.**
   a. State claims that respond directly to the assignment. Often, these claims will serve as topic sentences for paragraphs.
   b. Offer specific details from the works that support and illustrate your claims.
   c. Represent the work or works adequately. The more thoroughly and appropriately you relate the work to your claims (and thus to the assignment), the better your answer will be.
   d. Your answer is an argument. Back up claims with evidence. Show your readers, do not just tell them.

9. **Be creative.** Some instructors want you to reproduce what they have said in class. Studying for their tests is straightforward. Just memorize what the instructor has said and paraphrase it on the test. The more perfect your reproduction, the better your grade. Other instructors, however, want more—and they design their tests to get more. They want *your* thinking, not just their own. They want your creativity. But how can you be creative on tests? The answer is— think for yourself! Here are some ways to do so.
   a. Use the instructor's points, but provide your own facts from the works. This shows that you are doing more than just memorizing lectures. It shows that you have thought through and applied the instructor's ideas on your own.
   b. Make your own claims. Although instructors try to cover the most important aspects of a work, limited class time makes it impossible for them to cover every aspect, even all the important

ones. There are usually plenty of other claims to be made. Study the work yourself, and come up with your own claims. Read what others have said about the work and discover claims that way. Do not neglect claims made by the instructor, but make other claims as well.

c. Describe and take a stand on controversies—disagreements about meaning—in works of literature. Instructors often enjoy presenting controversies for class discussion. You can dip into them yourself by reading criticism of the works you are studying. Understanding literary controversies can sharpen your perception of the work. Showing your awareness of them and taking a stand on them will demonstrate your creative involvement with the work.

d. Be detailed in your support and illustration of points. The more details you provide, the clearer your creative involvement becomes, especially if you include details you have noticed on your own.

Sample Test Essays

All of the following essays respond to the assignment below. The writers had about twenty minutes to write their essays.

> Assignment: Explain the possible symbolic meanings of the rocking horse in D. H. Lawrence's "The Rocking-Horse Winner."

Essay 1

```
Paul seems desperately to want his mother to love him.

He senses that somehow she disapproves of him, that he

stands in her way of achieving happiness.  He seeks so-

lace in the rocking horse.  She has told him that "luck"

means having money, so he rides the horse to get money.

He hopes that by giving his mother money, he can buy his

way into her heart.  But, unfortunately, when he gives

her an enormous sum of money, she is even more unhappy

than before.  Paul returns to the rocking horse to get
```

```
more money for her.  He frantically rides the horse one
last time.  But although he wins the jackpot, he dies
from overexcitement and exhaustion.
```

Comments on Essay 1

Although this essay has good qualities, it is nonetheless mediocre because it does not directly address the assignment. It describes the action of the story accurately. It is clearly written. Its organization is easy to follow. It seems to have the assignment vaguely in mind, but nowhere does it say what the rocking horse symbolizes. The instructor may guess what the writer has in mind, but he or she cannot know for sure. The essay also omits important details. The writer does not say, for example, how Paul uses the horse to win money. The instructor may wonder whether the writer has read the story carefully.

Essay 2

```
Paul's mother claims that she is "unlucky," and she ex-
plains to Paul that being unlucky means having no money.
But the details of the story suggest that Paul's family
does have money, because they live very well.  The family
has the trappings of wealth--a nurse, a large house, com-
fortable furnishings, and a gardener.  The mother, then,
isn't really poor but is obsessed with money.  Her chil-
dren sense this obsession.  Most sensitive of all is Paul,
who hears voices saying, "There must be more money." As a
result, Paul sets out to win his mother's love by being
"lucky." His means of achieving luck and thus his mother's
love is the rocking horse.  He finds that by riding the
horse hard enough, he can predict winners of horse races.
The rocking horse, then, symbolizes the love his mother
has withheld from him.  He even experiences something like
```

the ecstasy of love when riding the horse to a winner. But his plan fails when his gift of 5,000 pounds only makes his mother's greed greater. He then becomes so desperate for love that he rides the rocking horse to his death.

Comments on Essay 2

This is a good essay. It not only recounts details from the story accurately, it also directly responds to the assignment, and it relates all the details cited from the story to that response. In other words, the details become "evidence." Because it deals directly with the assignment, it treats the story more specifically and thoroughly than does essay 1.

Essay 3

The rocking horse symbolizes many things in "The Rocking-Horse Winner." Paul's mother complains that she has no money, and she tells Paul that to be "lucky" is to have money. Paul is very impressed by what she says and decides to prove to her that he is lucky. He wants also to stop the voices in the house that incessantly demand more money. He feels that the rocking horse can take him where luck is. Sure enough, when he rides the rocking horse and it takes him "there," he can predict the winners of horse races and make a great deal of money. So one thing the rocking horse symbolizes is luck, which, in turn, means money.

But the rocking horse also seems to represent a second idea. Paul's uncle says after Paul dies that he is better off being dead than living in a world where he had to ride a rocking horse to find a winner. The implication is that Paul was using the rocking horse to get what his

mother never gave him: her love. So the rocking horse
also symbolizes Paul's need for love and his parents'
failure to give him love.

Finally, the rocking horse symbolizes success. When
Paul rides the rocking horse far enough, it brings him
financial success. But this success is only ironic, for
it never brings him the "success" he desperately wants--
his mother's love--and in the end it brings him death.
Lawrence seems to suggest that some kinds of success
are better than others; it is better to be loved than to
be rich.

Comments on Essay 3

This is an excellent answer. Like essay 2, the essay responds to the assignment directly, and it plausibly and logically connects details of the story to its points. But it is more detailed and creative than essay 2. The writer makes a strong case for the complexity of the rocking horse as symbol and, by so doing, points to the multiple meanings and richness of the story.

Sample Essays

This chapter contains four sample essays: one on a poem, one on a short story, one on a play, and one on a novel. All essays about literature are different. Interpretive questions vary enormously from essay to essay; authors employ different methods of answering them. These essays, then, are not models to be slavishly imitated. They do, however, embody the main points of this book: that essays about literature are interpretations, that they address explicit or implicit questions, that their theses answer those questions, and that, as arguments, they employ sound logic and well-supported claims.

Essay on a Poem

RICHARD CORY

BY EDWIN ARLINGTON ROBINSON

[FIRST PUBLISHED IN 1897]

Whenever Richard Cory went down town,
We people on the pavement looked at him:
He was a gentleman from sole to crown,
Clean favored, and imperially slim.

And he was always quietly arrayed,
And he was always human when he talked;
But still he fluttered pulses when he said,
"Good-morning," and he glittered when he walked.

And he was rich—yes, richer than a king—
And admirably schooled in every grace:
In fine, we thought that he was everything
To make us wish that we were in his place.

So on we worked, and waited for the light,
And went without the meat, and cursed the bread;
And Richard Cory, one calm summer night,
Went home and put a bullet through his head.

Cannon 1

George Cannon

Professor Landsdown

English 251-10

12 February 1999

Point of View in Edwin Arlington Robinson's

"Richard Cory"

Yvor Winters, an American critic, condemns Edwin
Arlington Robinson's poem "Richard Cory" for containing "a superficially neat portrait of the elegant man
of mystery" and for having a "very cheap surprise
ending" (52). It is true that because Richard Cory
fits the stereotype of "the man who has everything,"
his suicide at the end is surprising, even shocking.
But the poet's handling of point of view makes the
portrait of Richard Cory only apparently superficial
and the ending only apparently "cheap."

In the second line of the poem, we learn that
the speaker is not Robinson himself (the omniscient
narrator), but someone with a limited view of
things. He is one of the "people" of the town (38).

Cannon 2

It is as if he has cornered a visitor on a sidewalk
somewhere and is telling him about a fellow townsman
whose suicide has puzzled and troubled him. He cannot understand it, so he talks about it. Throughout
this speaker's narration, we learn a lot about him
and his peers and how they regarded Richard Cory.

Clearly they saw him as something special. The
imagery of kings and nobility ("crown," "imperially
slim" and "richer than a king") permeates their conception of Richard Cory. To them he had the bearing
and trappings of royalty. He was a "gentleman," a
word that suggests courtliness as well as nobility.
He had good taste ("he was always quietly arrayed").
He was wealthy. He had good breeding (he was "admirably schooled in every grace"). He "glittered
when he walked," suggesting, perhaps, that he wore
jewelry and walked with confidence. Because of this
attitude, the speaker and his peers placed themselves in an almost feudal relationship to Cory.
They saw themselves as "people on the pavement," as
if they walked on the ground and Richard Cory somehow walked above them. Even if he did not literally
walk above them, they saw him as "above" them socially. They seemed to think it unusual that he was
"human when he talked." The word <u>human</u> suggests several things. One is that the people saw Cory as
somehow exempt from the problems and restrictions of
being a human being (thus "human") but that when he

talked, he stepped out of character. Another is
that he, who was so much above them, could be kind,
warm, and thoughtful (another meaning of "human").
They were so astonished by this latter quality that
when he did such a simple and obvious thing as say
"Good-morning," he "fluttered pulses."

In the final stanza, the speaker brings out the
most important differences between the people and
Richard Cory. Most obvious is that he was rich and
they were poor; they "went without the meat, and
cursed the bread." But another difference is suggested by the word light: "So on we worked, and
waited for the light." Light in this context most
apparently means a time when things will be better,
as in the expression "the light at the end of the
tunnel." But another meaning of "light" is revelation. Light has traditionally symbolized knowledge
and truth, and it may be that this is the meaning
the speaker--or at least Robinson--has in mind. If
so, another difference that the people saw between
Richard Cory and themselves was that Cory had knowledge and understanding and they did not. After all,
they had no time to pursue knowledge; they needed
all their time just to survive. But Richard Cory
did have the time. He was a man of leisure who had
been "schooled." If anyone would have had the
"light"--a right understanding of things--then
Richard Cory would have been that person.

Although Robinson does not tell us why Richard
Cory killed himself, he leaves several hints. One of
these is the assumptions about Richard Cory held by
the narrator and the "people." Cory may have been a
victim of their attitude. The poem gives no evidence
that he sought to be treated like a king or that he
had pretensions to nobility. He seems, in fact, to
have been democratic enough. Although rich, well-
mannered, and tastefully dressed, he nonetheless came
to town, spoke with kindness to the people, and
greeted them as if they deserved his respect. Could
he even have wanted their friendship? But the people's attitude may have isolated Richard Cory. Every
time he came to town, they stared at him as if he
were a freak in a sideshow (lines 1-2). In their
imagination, furthermore, they created an ideal of
him that was probably false and, if taken seriously
by Richard Cory, would have been very difficult to
live up to. Cory did not, at least, have the "light"
that the people thought he had. His suicide attests
to that. He was, in short, as "human" as they; but,
unlike them, he lacked the consolation of fellowship.
Ironically, then, the people's very admiration of
Richard Cory, which set him apart as more than human
and isolated him from human companionship, may have
been the cause of his death.

Had Robinson told Cory's story as an omniscient
narrator, Winters's complaint about the poem would

Cannon 5

be justified. The poem would seem to be an attempt to shock us with a melodramatic and too-obvious irony. But Robinson has deepened the poem's meaning by having one of Cory's fellow townspeople tell his story. This presentation of Cory's character, his relationship to the townspeople, and his motives for suicide open up the poem to interpretation in a way that Winters does not acknowledge or explore.

Works Cited

Robinson, Edwin Arlington. <u>Tilbury Town: Selected</u>
     <u>Poems of Edwin Arlington Robinson</u>. New York:
     Macmillan, 1951.

Winters, Yvor. <u>Edwin Arlington Robinson</u>. Norfolk:
     New Directions, 1946.

Note: Normally, the "Works Cited" list would appear on a separate page, but we print it here, right after the essay, to save space.

Essay on a Short Story

THE CASK OF AMONTILLADO

BY EDGAR ALLAN POE

[FIRST PUBLISHED IN 1846]

The thousand injuries of Fortunato I had borne as I best could, but when he ventured upon insult I vowed revenge. You, who so well know the nature of my soul, will not suppose, however, that I gave utterance to a threat. At *length* I would be avenged; this was a point definitely set-tled—but the very definitiveness with which it was resolved precluded the idea of risk. I must not only punish but punish with impunity. A wrong is unredressed when retribution overtakes its redresser. It is equally unredressed when the avenger fails to make himself felt as such to him who has done the wrong.

It must be understood that neither by word nor deed had I given Fortunato cause to doubt my good will. I continued, as was my wont, to smile in his face, and he did not perceive that my smile *now* was at the thought of his immolation.

He had a weak point—this Fortunato—although in other regards he was a man to be respected and even feared. He prided himself on his connoisseurship in wine. Few Italians have the true virtuoso spirit. For the most part their enthusiasm is adopted to suit the time and opportunity, to practice imposture upon the British and Austrian *millionaires*. In painting and gemmary, Fortunato, like his countrymen, was a quack, but in the matter of old wines he was sincere. In this respect I did not differ from him materially;—I was skilful in the Italian vintages myself, and bought largely whenever I could.

It was about dusk, one evening during the supreme madness of the carnival season, that I encountered my friend. He accosted me with excessive warmth, for he had been drinking much. The man wore motley. He had on a tight-fitting parti-striped dress, and his head was surmounted by the conical cap and bells. I was so pleased to see him that I thought I should never have done wringing his hand.

I said to him—"My dear Fortunato, you are luckily met. How remarkably well you are looking to-day. But I have received a pipe of what passes for Amontillado, and I have my doubts."

"How?" said he. "Amontillado? A pipe? Impossible! And in the middle of the carnival!"

"I have my doubts," I replied; "and I was silly enough to pay the full Amontillado price without consulting you in the matter. You were not to be found, and I was fearful of losing a bargain."

"Amontillado!"

"I have my doubts."

"Amontillado!"

"And I must satisfy them."

"Amontillado!"

"As you are engaged, I am on my way to Luchresi. If any one has a critical turn it is he. He will tell me—"

"Luchresi cannot tell Amontillado from Sherry."

"And yet some fools will have it that his taste is a match for your own."

"Come, let us go."

"Whither?"

"To your vaults."

"My friend, no; I will not impose upon your good nature. I perceive you have an engagement. Luchresi—"

"I have no engagement;—come."

"My friend, no. It is not the engagement, but the severe cold with
which I perceive you are afflicted. The vaults are insufferably damp.
They are encrusted with nitre."

"Let us go, nevertheless. The cold is merely nothing. Amontillado!
You have been imposed upon. And as for Luchresi, he cannot distinguish Sherry from Amontillado."

Thus speaking, Fortunato possessed himself of my arm; and
putting on a mask of black silk and drawing a *roquelaire** closely
about my person, I suffered him to hurry me to my palazzo.

There were no attendants at home; they had absconded to make
merry in honor of the time. I had told them that I should not return until
the morning, and had given them explicit orders not to stir from the
house. These orders were sufficient, I well knew, to insure their immediate disappearance, one and all, as soon as my back was turned.

I took from their sconces two flambeaux, and giving one to Fortunato, bowed him through several suites of rooms to the archway that
led into the vaults. I passed down a long and winding staircase, re-
questing him to be cautious as he followed. We came at length to the
foot of the descent, and stood together upon the damp ground of the
catacombs of the Montresors.

The gait of my friend was unsteady, and the bells upon his cap
jingled as he strode.

"The pipe," he said.

"It is farther on," said I; "but observe the white web-work which
gleams from these cavern walls."

He turned towards me, and looked into my eyes with two filmy
orbs that distilled the rheum of intoxication.

"Nitre?" he asked, at length.

"Nitre," I replied. "How long have you had that cough?"

"Ugh! ugh! ugh!—ugh! ugh! ugh!—ugh! ugh! ugh!—ugh! ugh!
ugh!—ugh! ugh! ugh!"

My poor friend found it impossible to reply for many minutes.

"It is nothing," he said, at last.

"Come," I said, with decision, "we will go back; your health is
precious. You are rich, respected, admired, beloved; you are happy,
as I once was. You are a man to be missed. For me it is no matter. We

*A long cloak

will go back; you will be ill, and I cannot be responsible. Besides, there is Luchresi—"

"Enough," he said; "the cough is a mere nothing; it will not kill me. I shall not die of a cough."

"True—true," I replied; "and, indeed, I had no intention of alarming you unnecessarily—but you should use all proper caution. A draught of this Medoc will defend us from the damps."

Here I knocked off the neck of a bottle which I drew from a long row of its fellows that lay upon the mould.

"Drink," I said, presenting him the wine.

He raised it to his lips with a leer. He paused and nodded to me familiarly, while his bells jingled.

"I drink," he said, "to the buried that repose around us."

"And I to your long life."

He again took my arm, and we proceeded.

"These vaults," he said, "are extensive."

"The Montresors," I replied, "were a great and numerous family."

"I forget your arms."

"A huge human foot d'or, in a field azure; the foot crushes a serpent rampant whose fangs are imbedded in the heel."

"And the motto?"

"*Nemo me impune lacessit.*"*

"Good!" he said.

The wine sparkled in his eyes and the bells jingled. My own fancy grew warm with the Medoc. We had passed through long walls of piled skeletons, with casks and puncheons intermingling, into the inmost recesses of the catacombs. I paused again, and this time I made bold to seize Fortunato by an arm above the elbow.

"The nitre!" I said; "see, it increases. It hangs like moss upon the vaults. We are below the river's bed. The drops of moisture trickle among the bones. Come, we will go back ere it is too late. Your cough—"

"It is nothing," he said; "let us go on. But first, another draught of the Medoc."

I broke and reached him a flagon of De Grâve. He emptied it at a breath. His eyes flashed with a fierce light. He laughed and threw the bottle upwards with a gesticulation I did not understand.

I looked at him in surprise. He repeated the movement—a grotesque one.

"You do not comprehend?" he said.

*No one attacks me with impunity.

"Not I," I replied.

"Then you are not of the brotherhood."

"How?"

"You are not of the masons."

"Yes, yes," I said; "yes, yes."

"You? Impossible! A mason?"

"A mason," I replied.

"A sign," he said, "a sign."

"It is this," I answered, producing from beneath the folds of my *roquelaire* a trowel.

"You jest," he exclaimed, recoiling a few paces. "But let us proceed to the Amontillado."

"Be it so," I said, replacing the tool beneath the cloak and again offering him my arm. He leaned upon it heavily. We continued our route in search of the Amontillado. We passed through a range of low arches, descended, passed on, and descending again, arrived at a deep crypt, in which the foulness of the air caused our flambeaux rather to glow than flame.

At the most remote end of the crypt there appeared another less spacious. Its walls had been lined with human remains, piled to the vault overhead, in the fashion of the great catacombs of Paris. Three sides of this interior crypt were still ornamented in this manner. From the fourth side the bones had been thrown down, and lay promiscuously upon the earth, forming at one point a mound of some size. Within the wall thus exposed by the displacing of the bones, we perceived a still interior crypt or recess, in depth about four feet, in width three, in height six or seven. It seemed to have been constructed for no especial use within itself, but formed merely the interval between two of the colossal supports of the roof of the catacombs, and was backed by one of their circumscribing walls of solid granite.

It was in vain that Fortunato, uplifting his dull torch, endeavored to pry into the depth of the recess. Its termination the feeble light did not enable us to see.

"Proceed," I said; "herein is the Amontillado. As for Luchresi—"

"He is an ignoramus," interrupted my friend, as he stepped unsteadily forward, while I followed immediately at his heels. In an instant he had reached the extremity of the niche, and finding his progess arrested by the rock, stood stupidly bewildered. A moment more and I had fettered him to the granite. In its surface were two iron staples, distant from each other about two feet, horizontally. From one of these depended a short chain, from the other a padlock. Throwing the links about his waist, it was but the work of a few seconds to secure it. He was to much astounded to resist. Withdrawing the key I stepped back from the recess.

"Pass your hand," I said, "over the wall; you cannot help feeling the nitre. Indeed, it is *very* damp. Once more let me *implore* you to return. No? Then I must positively leave you. But I must first render you all the little attentions in my power."

"The Amontillado!" ejaculated my friend, not yet recovered from his astonishment.

"True," I replied; "the Amontillado."

As I said these words I busied myself among the pile of bones of which I have before spoken. Throwing them aside, I soon uncovered a quantity of building stone and mortar. With these materials and with the aid of my trowel, I began vigorously to wall up the entrance of the niche.

I had scarcely laid the first tier of the masonry when I discovered that the intoxication of Fortunato had in a great measure worn off. The earliest indication I had of this was a low moaning cry from the depth of the recess. It was *not* the cry of a drunken man. There was then a long and obstinate silence. I laid the second tier, and the third, and the fourth; and then I heard the furious vibrations of the chain. The noise lasted for several minutes, during which, that I might hearken to it with the more satisfaction, I ceased my labours and sat down upon the bones. When at last the clanking subsided, I resumed the trowel, and finished without interruption the fifth, the sixth, and the seventh tier. The wall was now nearly upon a level with my breast. I again paused, and holding the flambeaux over the mason-work, threw a few feeble rays upon the figure within.

A succession of loud and shrill screams, bursting suddenly from the throat of the chained form, seemed to thrust me violently back. For a brief moment I hesitated, I trembled. Unsheathing my rapier, I began to grope with it about the recess; but the thought of an instant reassured me. I placed my hand upon the solid fabric of the catacombs, and felt satisfied. I reapproached the wall; I replied to the yells of him who clamoured. I re-echoed, I aided, I surpassed them in volume and in strength. I did this, and the clamorer grew still.

It was now midnight, and my task was drawing to a close. I had completed the eighth, the ninth and the tenth tier. I had finished a portion of the last and the eleventh; there remained but a single stone to be fitted and plastered in. I struggled with its weight; I placed it partially in its destined position. But now there came from out the niche a low laugh that erected the hairs upon my head. It was succeeded by a sad voice, which I had difficulty in recognizing as that of the noble Fortunato. The voice said—

"Ha! ha! ha!—he! he! he!—a very good joke, indeed—an excellent jest. We will have many a rich laugh about it at the palazzo—he! he! he!—over our wine—he! he! he!"

"The Amontillado!" I said.

"He! he! he!—he! he! he!—yes, the Amontillado. But is it not getting late? Will not they be awaiting us at the palazzo, the Lady Fortunato and the rest? Let us be gone."

"Yes," I said, "let us be gone."

"*For the love of God, Montresor!*"

"Yes," I said, "for the love of God!"

But to these words I hearkened in vain for a reply. I grew impatient. I called aloud—

"Fortunato!"

No answer. I called again—

"Fortunato!"

No answer still. I thrust a torch through the remaining aperture and let it fall within. There came forth in return only a jingling of the bells. My heart grew sick; it was the dampness of the catacombs that made it so. I hastened to make an end of my labour. I forced the last stone into its position; I plastered it up. Against the new masonry I re-erected the old rampart of bones. For the half of a century no mortal has disturbed them. *In pace requiescat!**

Long 1

Blake Long

Prof. Johnson

English 212-04

3 April 2000

Montresor's Fate in Edgar Allan Poe's

"The Cask of Amontillado"

Montresor, the narrator of Edgar Allan Poe's

story "The Cask of Amontillado," tells the story not

---

*May he rest in peace.

Long 2

to us but to someone else. We see this in the first
two sentences: "The thousand injuries of Fortunato I
had borne as I best could, but when he ventured upon
insult I vowed revenge. You, who so well know the
nature of my soul, will not suppose, however, that I
gave utterance to a threat" (167). In the story,
Montresor reveals that fifty years ago he murdered
Fortunato and no one found out. He committed the
perfect crime. Why would he be telling anyone about
it now?

Details in the story suggest that Montresor's
listener is a priest and that the story is a confes-
sion. If this is correct, Montresor's motive for
telling the story would be to gain absolution for
his sin. Montresor is the right age to worry about
the fate of his soul. At the time of the crime, he
had to be old enough to live through Fortunato's
"thousand injuries" and worldly wise enough to plan
his complicated revenge. Let's say he was about
thirty. Fifty years have passed, so Montresor is
now around eighty. Death is staring him in the
face. His categorization of the listener as someone
who "so well" knows "the nature of my soul" points
to someone whose calling is to care for souls--a
priest. The final line of the story--<u>In pace requi-
escat</u>!--echoes the words a priest would say at the
end of a service for the dead: "May he rest in
peace." A priest would know these words as a pious

expression. Montresor perhaps thinks that the
priest will take them as an expression of remorse,
as if, after much reflection, Montresor is sorry for
what he did and now wishes "peace" for Fortunato in
the afterlife. In his own mind, Montresor might
also be applying the phrase to himself: "Since I am
about to die, may I rest in peace. And I will if
this priest will only absolve me."

If the listener is indeed a priest, will he do
this, grant Montresor absolution? Since the story
ends before the listener speaks, Poe leaves it to us
to imagine the ensuing scene. What will the priest
decide? In order to answer this question, we need to
judge two things: the magnitude of Montresor's crime
and his attitude toward it. First, did Fortunato deserve to die? A priest might be willing to grant absolution if Montresor had been an instrument of
justice. Maybe Fortunato had done terrible deeds but
escaped the law. In that case, Montresor's crime
would have visited just retribution upon Fortunato.
From what we see of Fortunato, he is not especially
likable. He is so egotistical that he goes on a wild
goose chase just to prove his superiority to
Luchresi, his rival in wine connoisseurship. He pooh
poohs his ill-health with macho bravado, as if he is
above mortal limitations. His pretense of not knowing Montresor's family crest (171) reveals his dis-
dain for people. His drunkenness and costume--that

of a fool--underscore his boorishness and stupidity.
All of these qualities support Montresor's claim that
Fortunato is guilty of committing "injuries" and "insults." But does someone deserve to die for being
boorish and stupid? Montresor doesn't say what the
injuries are, but they don't seem to have harmed him
greatly. He is still alive, still the owner of a
palazzo, still a person of high station. His unwill-
ingness to specify what Fortunato did makes us suspicious that Fortunato wounded Montresor's pride rather
than caused him serious harm. The punishment Montresor dishes out seems to far outweigh the "injuries"
and "insults" of which Fortunato stands accused.

Well, OK, Montresor went too far. Perhaps he
realizes that now. Does he show contrition for
killing Fortunato? If so, the priest might grant
him absolution. No, Montresor does not. The tone
of his narrative reflects pride in his cleverness,
not sorrow for his deed. Presenting his plan for
revenge as a kind of game, he states the "rules" at
the beginning: "A wrong is unredressed when retribution overtakes its redresser. It is equally unredressed when the avenger fails to make himself felt
as such to him who has done the wrong" (167). He
proceeds to gloat about how clever he was in getting
Fortunato to go down into the catacombs. Montresor
is an astute psychologist. He knows that if he
plucks the strings of Fortunato's vanity, Fortunato

will keep on walking. All he has to do is mention
Luchresi and Fortunato's cold, and Fortunato will
keep going. Montresor revels in telling how he
sadistically needled Fortunato about his cold by
calling attention to the nitre and dampness. Montresor also enjoys his little jokes. When Fortunato says he "shall not die of a cough," Montresor
replies "True--true" (170). When Fortunato asks him
if he is a Mason, Montresor assures him he is and
pulls out a trowel (172). After Montresor enchains
Fortunato, he says, "Once more let me implore you
to return" (173). Montresor does exhibit some behavior that might suggest feelings other than self-
congratulation. Fortunato's screams give Montresor
pause: "For a brief moment I hesitated, I trembled"
(174). But he trembles from fear of discovery, not
contrition. When Fortunato appeals to Montresor's
sense of divine mercy ("For the love of God, Montresor!"), Montresor blows him off: "'Yes,' I said,
'for the love of God!'" (175). The only hint of
remorse comes when, after hearing the bells on Fortunato's costume, Montresor says, "My heart grew
sick" (175). In his heart of hearts, Montresor may
be revolted by his crime. But this recognition
never reaches the surface of his consciousness.
Instead, he attributes his feeling to "the dampness
of the catacombs" (175). His concluding statement--
"For the half of a century no mortal has disturbed

Long 6

[Fortunato's bones]"--seems like pride of accomplishment rather than anything close to remorse.

On two counts, then, Montresor fails the test for absolution: His crime was not justified and he expresses no remorse for committing it. We might join the priest here in saying, "May you fry in hell!" But a final twist in the story is that Montresor has already, for fifty years, been in hell, a mental hell. He knows the details of this story so well that we can see it as a kind of movie that he has replayed in his mind over and over for years and years. Now he wants a different story, one of ascent: ascent to heaven. The story he will get, however, is one of descent: deeper and deeper into the earth, past the remains of the dead, through cold and damp, ending at the final crypt. He may not have realized it at first, but surely he has become aware that his story was not just about a descent to Fortunato's death, but to his own as well. And it looks like he will soon make one more step down--to the eternal punishments of hell.

Work Cited

Poe, Edgar Allan. "The Cask of Amontillado." Complete Works of Edgar Allan Poe. Ed. James A. Harrison. Vol. 5. New York: Fred De Fau, 1902.

Note: Normally the "Works Cited" list would appear on a separate page, but we print it here, right after the essay, to save space.

Essay on a Play

TRIFLES

BY SUSAN GLASPELL

The first performance of the one-act play *Trifles* took place at the Wharf Theater, Provincetown, Massachusetts, on 8 August 1916. Susan Glaspell played the part of Mrs. Hale.

■ Characters

George Henderson (County Attorney)   Mrs. Peters

Henry Peters (Sheriff)   Mrs. Hale

Lewis Hale (a neighboring farmer)

SCENE: *The kitchen is the now abandoned farmhouse of* JOHN WRIGHT, *a gloomy kitchen, and left without having been put in order—unwashed pans under the sink, a loaf of bread outside the bread-box, a dish-towel on the table—other signs of incompleted work. At the rear the outer door opens and the* SHERIFF *comes in followed by the* COUNTY ATTORNEY *and* HALE. *The* SHERIFF *and* HALE *are men in middle life, the* COUNTY ATTORNEY *is a young man; all are much bundled up and go at once to the stove. They are followed by the two women—the* SHERIFF's *wife first; she is a slight wiry woman, a thin nervous face.* MRS. HALE *is larger and would ordinarily be called more comfortable looking, but she is disturbed now and looks fearfully about as she enters. The women have come in slowly, and stand close together near the door.*

COUNTY ATTORNEY: (*rubbing his hands*) This feels good. Come up to the fire, ladies.

MRS. PETERS: (*after taking a step forward*) I'm not—cold.

SHERIFF: (*unbuttoning his overcoat and stepping away from the stove as if to mark the beginning of official business*) Now, Mr. Hale, before we move things about, you explain to Mr. Henderson just what you saw when you came here yesterday morning.

COUNTY ATTORNEY: By the way, has anything been moved? Are things just as you left them yesterday?

SHERIFF: (*looking about*) It's just the same. When it dropped below zero last night I thought I'd better send Frank out this morning to make a fire for us—no use getting pneumonia with a big case on, but I told him not to touch anything except the stove—and you know Frank.

COUNTY ATTORNEY: Somebody should have been left here yesterday.

SHERIFF: Oh—yesterday. When I had to send Frank to Morris Center for that man who went crazy—I want you to know I had my hands full yesterday. I knew you could get back from Omaha by today as long as I went over everything here myself—

COUNTY ATTORNEY: Well, Mr. Hale, tell just what happened when you came here yesterday morning.

HALE: Harry and I had started to town with a load of potatoes. We came along the road from my place and as I got here I said, "I'm going to see if I can't get John Wright to go in with me on a party telephone." I spoke to Wright about it once before and he put me off, saying folks talked too much anyway, and all he asked was peace and quiet—I guess you know about how much he talked himself; but I thought maybe if I went to the house and talked about it before his wife, though I said to Harry that I didn't know as what his wife wanted made much difference to John—

COUNTY ATTORNEY: Let's talk about that later, Mr. Hale. I do want to talk about that, but tell now just what happened when you got to the house.

HALE: I didn't hear or see anything; I knocked at the door, and still it was quiet inside. I knew they must be up, it was past eight o'clock. So I knocked again, and I thought I heard somebody say, "Come in." I wasn't sure. I'm not sure yet, but I opened the door—this door (*indicating the door by which the two women are still standing*) and there in that rocker—(*pointing to it*) sat Mrs. Wright.

(*They all look at the rocker.*)

COUNTY ATTORNEY: What—was she doing?

HALE: She was rockin' back and forth. She had her apron in her hand and was kind of—pleating it.

COUNTY ATTORNEY: And how did she—look?

HALE: Well, she looked queer.

COUNTY ATTORNEY: How do you mean—queer?

HALE: Well, as if she didn't know what she was going to do next. And kind of done up.

COUNTY ATTORNEY: How did she seem to feel about your coming?

HALE: Why, I don't think she minded—one way or other. She didn't pay much attention. I said "How do, Mrs. Wright it's cold, ain't it?" And she said, "Is it?"—and went on kind of pleating at her apron. Well, I was surprised; she didn't ask me to come up to the stove, or to set down, but just sat there, not even looking at me, so I said, "I want to see John." And then she—laughed. I guess you would call it a laugh. I thought of Harry and the team outside, so I said a little sharp: "Can't I see John?" "No," she says, kind o' dull like. "Ain't he home?" says I. "Yes," says she, "he's home." "Then why can't I see him?" I asked her, out of patience. "'Cause

he's dead," says she. *"Dead?"* says I. She just nodded her head, not getting a bit excited, but rockin' back and forth. "Why—where is he?" says
I, not knowing what to say. She just pointed upstairs—like that (*himself
pointing to the room above*) I got up, with the idea of going up there. I
walked from there to here—then I says, "Why, what did he die of?" "He
died of a rope round his neck," says she, and just went on pleatin' at her
apron. Well, I went out and called Harry. I thought I might—need help.
We went upstairs and there he was lyin'—
COUNTY ATTORNEY: I think I'd rather have you go into that upstairs,
where you can point it all out. Just go on now with the rest of the story.
HALE: Well, my first thought was to get that rope off. It looked . . . (*stops, his
face twitches*) . . . but Harry, he went up to him, and he said, "No, he's
dead all right, and we'd better not touch anything." So we went back
down stairs. She was still sitting that same way. "Has anybody been no-
tified?" I asked. "No," says she unconcerned. "Who did this, Mrs.
Wright?" said Harry. He said it business-like—and she stopped pleatin'
of her apron. "I don't know," she says. "You don't *know?*" says Harry.
"No," says she. "Weren't you sleepin' in the bed with him?" says Harry.
"Yes," says she, "but I was on the inside." "Somebody slipped a rope
round his neck and strangled him and you didn't wake up?" says Harry.
"I didn't wake up," she said after him. We must 'a looked as if we didn't
see how that could be, for after a minute she said, "I sleep sound." Harry
was going to ask her more questions but I said maybe we ought to let her
tell her story first to the coroner, or the sheriff, so Harry went fast as he
could to Rivers' place, where there's a telephone.
COUNTY ATTORNEY: And what did Mrs. Wright do when she knew that
you had gone for the coroner?
HALE: She moved from that chair to this one over here (*pointing to a small
chair in the corner*) and just sat there with her hands held together and
looking down. I got a feeling that I ought to make some conversation, so
I said I had come in to see if John wanted to put in a telephone, and at
that she started to laugh, and then she stopped and looked at me—
scared. (*the* COUNTY ATTORNEY, *who has had his notebook out,
makes a note*) I dunno, maybe it wasn't scared. I wouldn't like to say it
was. Soon Harry got back, and then Dr. Lloyd came, and you, Mr. Peters, and so I guess that's all I know that you don't.
COUNTY ATTORNEY: (*looking around*) I guess we'll go upstairs first—and
then out to the barn and around there. (*to the* SHERIFF) You're convinced
that there was nothing important here—nothing that would point to any
motive.
SHERIFF: Nothing here but kitchen things.

(*The* COUNTY ATTORNEY, *after again looking around the kitchen, opens the door of a cupboard closet. He gets up on a chair and looks on a shelf. Pulls his hand away, sticky.*)

COUNTY ATTORNEY: Here's a nice mess.

(*The women draw nearer.*)

MRS. PETERS: (*to the other woman*) Oh, her fruit; it did freeze. (*to the* LAWYER) She worried about that when it turned so cold. She said the fire'd go out and her jars would break.

SHERIFF: Well, can you beat the women! Held for murder and worryin' about her preserves.

COUNTY ATTORNEY: I guess before we're through she may have something more serious than preserves to worry about.

HALE: Well, women are used to worrying over trifles.

(*The two women move a little closer together.*)

COUNTY ATTORNEY: (*with the gallantry of a young politician*) And yet, for all their worries, what would we do without the ladies? (*the women do not unbend. He goes to the sink, takes a dipperful of water from the pail and pouring it into a basin, washes his hands. Starts to wipe them on the roller-towel, turns it for a cleaner place*) Dirty towels! (*kicks his foot against the pans under the sink*) Not much of a housekeeper, would you say ladies?

MRS. HALE: (*stiffly*) There's a great deal of work to be done on a farm.

COUNTY ATTORNEY: To be sure. And yet (*with a little bow to her*) I know there are some Dickson county farmhouses which do not have such roller towels.

(*He gives it a pull to expose its length again.*)

MRS. HALE: Those towels get dirty awful quick. Men's hands aren't always as clean as they might be.

COUNTY ATTORNEY: Ah, loyal to your sex, I see. But you and Mrs. Wright were neighbors. I suppose you were friends, too.

MRS. HALE: (*shaking her head*) I've not seen much of her of late years. I've not been in this house—it's more than a year.

COUNTY ATTORNEY: And why was that? You didn't like her?

MRS. HALE: I liked her all well enough. Farmers' wives have their hands full, Mr. Henderson. And then—

COUNTY ATTORNEY: Yes—?

MRS. HALE: (*looking about*) It never seemed a very cheerful place.

COUNTY ATTORNEY: No—it's not cheerful. I shouldn't say she had the homemaking instinct.

MRS. HALE: Well, I don't know as Wright had, either.

COUNTY ATTORNEY: You mean that they didn't get on very well?

MRS. HALE: No, I don't mean anything. But I don't think a place'd be any cheerfuller for John Wright's being in it.

COUNTY ATTORNEY: I'd like to talk more of that a little later. I want to get the lay of things upstairs now.

(*He goes to the left, where three steps lead to a stair door.*)

SHERIFF: I suppose anything Mrs. Peters does'll be all right. She was to take in some clothes for her, you know, and a few little things. We left in such a hurry yesterday.

COUNTY ATTORNEY: Yes, but I would like to see what you take, Mrs. Peters, and keep an eye out for anything that might be of use to us.

MRS. PETERS: Yes, Mr. Henderson.

(*The women listen to the men's steps on the stairs, then look about the kitchen.*)

MRS. HALE: I'd hate to have men coming into my kitchen, snooping around and criticising.

(*She arranges the pans under sink which the* LAWYER *had shoved out of place.*)

MRS. PETERS: Of course it's no more than their duty.

MRS. HALE: Duty's all right, but I guess that deputy sheriff that came out to make the fire might have got a little of this on. (*gives the roller towel a pull*) Wish I'd thought of that sooner. Seems mean to talk about her for not having things slicked up when she had to come away in such a hurry.

MRS. PETERS: (*who has gone to a small table in the left rear corner of the room, and lifted one end of a towel that covers a pan*) She had bread set. (*Stands still.*)

MRS. HALE: (*eyes fixed on a loaf of bread beside the bread-box, which is on a low shelf at the other side of the room. Moves slowly toward it*) She was going to put this in there. (*picks up loaf, then abruptly drops it. In a manner of returning to familiar things*) It's a shame about her fruit. I wonder if it's all gone. (*gets up on the chair and looks*) I think there's some here that's all right, Mrs. Peters. Yes—here; (*holding it toward the window*) this is cherries, too. (*looking again*) I declare I believe that's the only one. (*gets down, bottle in her hand. Goes to the sink and wipes it off on the outside*) She'll feel awful bad after all her hard work in the hot weather. I remember the afternoon I put up my cherries last summer.

(*She puts the bottle on the big kitchen table, center of the room. With a sigh, is about to sit down in the rocking-chair. Before she is seated realizes what chair it is; with a slow look at it, steps back. The chair which she has touched rocks back and forth.*)

MRS. PETERS: Well, I must get those things from the front room closet. (*she goes to the door at the right, but after looking into the other room, steps back*) You coming with me, Mrs. Hale? You could help me carry them.

(*They go in the other room; reappear,* MRS. PETERS *carrying a dress and skirt,* MRS. HALE *following with a pair of shoes.*)

MRS. PETERS: My, it's cold in there.

(*She puts the clothes on the big table, and hurries to the stove.*)

MRS. HALE: (*examining the skirt*) Wright was close. I think maybe that's why she kept so much to herself. She didn't even belong to the Ladies Aid. I suppose she felt she couldn't do her part, and then you don't enjoy things when you feel shabby. She used to wear pretty clothes and be lively, when she was Minnie Foster, one of the town girls singing in the choir. But that—oh, that was thirty years ago. This is all you was to take in?

MRS. PETERS: She said she wanted an apron. Funny thing to want, for there isn't much to get you dirty in jail, goodness knows. But I suppose just to make her feel more natural. She said they was in the top drawer in this cupboard. Yes, here. And then her little shawl that always hung behind the door (*opens stair door and looks*) Yes, here it is

(*Quickly shuts door leading upstairs.*)

MRS. HALE: (*abruptly moving toward her*) Mrs. Peters?

MRS. PETERS: Yes, Mrs. Hale?

MRS. HALE: Do you think she did it?

MRS. PETERS: (*in a frightened voice*) Oh, I don't know.

MRS. HALE: Well, I don't think she did. Asking for an apron and her little shawl. Worrying about her fruit.

MRS. PETERS: (*starts to speak, glances up, where footsteps are heard in the room above. In a low voice*) Mr. Peters says it looks bad for her. Mr. Henderson is awful sarcastic in a speech and he'll make fun of her sayin' she didn't wake up.

MRS. HALE: Well, I guess John Wright didn't wake when they was slipping that rope under his neck.

MRS. PETERS: No, it's strange. It must have been done awful crafty and still. They say it was such a—funny way to kill a man, rigging it all up like that.

MRS. HALE: That's just what Mr. Hale said. There was a gun in the house. He says that's what he can't understand.

MRS. PETERS: Mr. Henderson said coming out that what was needed for the case was a motive; something to show anger, or—sudden feeling.

MRS. HALE: (*who is standing by the table*) Well, I don't see any signs of anger around here. (*she puts her hand on the dish towel which lies on the table, stands looking down at table, one half of which is clean, the other half messy*) It's wiped to here. (*makes a move as if to finish work, then turns and looks at loaf of bread outside the breadbox. Drops towel. In that voice of coming back to familiar things.*) Wonder how they are finding things upstairs. I hope she had it a little more red-up up there. You

know, it seems kind of *sneaking.* Locking her up in town and then coming
out here and trying to get her own house to turn against her!

MRS. PETERS: But Mrs. Hale, the law is the law.

MRS. HALE: I s'pose 'tis. (*unbuttoning her coat*) Better loosen up your
things, Mrs. Peters. You won't feel them when you go out.

> (MRS. PETERS *takes off her fur tippet, goes to hang it on hook at back
> of room, stands looking at the under part of the small corner table.*)

MRS. PETERS: She was piecing a quilt.

> (*She brings the large sewing basket and they look at the bright
> pieces.*)

MRS. HALE: It's log cabin pattern. Pretty, isn't it? I wonder if she was goin'
to quilt it or just knot it?

> (*Footsteps have been heard coming down the stairs. The* SHERIFF
> *enters followed by* HALE *and the* COUNTY ATTORNEY.)

SHERIFF: They wonder if she was going to quilt it or just knot it!

> (*The men laugh, the women look abashed.*)

COUNTY ATTORNEY: (*rubbing his hands over the stove*) Frank's fire didn't
do much up there did it? Well, let's go out to the barn and get that
cleared up.

> (*The men go outside*)

MRS. HALE: (*resentfully*) I don't know as there's anything so strange, our
takin' up our time with little things while we're waiting for them to get the
evidence. (*she sits down at the big table smoothing out a block with decision*) I don't see as it's anything to laugh about.

MRS. PETERS: (*apologetically*) Of course they've got awful important things
on their minds.

> (*Pulls up a chair and joins* MRS. HALE *at the table.*)

MRS. HALE: (*examining another block*) Mrs. Peters, look at this one. Here,
this is the one she was working on, and look at the sewing! All the rest of
it has been so nice and even. And look at this! It's all over the place!
Why, it looks as if she didn't know what she was about!

> (*After she has said this they look at each other, then start to glance
> back at the door. After an instant* MRS. HALE *has pulled at a knot
> and ripped the sewing.*)

MRS. PETERS: Oh, what are you doing, Mrs. Hale?

MRS. HALE: (*mildly*) Just pulling out a stitch or two that's not sewed very
good. (*threading a needle*) Bad sewing always made me fidgety.

MRS. PETERS: (*nervously*) I don't think we ought to touch things.

MRS. HALE: I'll just finish up this end. (*suddenly stopping and leaning forward*) Mrs. Peters?

MRS. PETERS: Yes, Mrs. Hale?

MRS. HALE: What do you suppose she was so nervous about?

MRS. PETERS: Oh—I don't know. I don't know as she was nervous. I sometimes sew awful queer when I'm just tired. (MRS. HALE *starts to say something, looks at* MRS. PETERS, *then goes on sewing*) Well I must get these things wrapped up. They may be through sooner than we think. (*putting apron and other things together*) I wonder where I can find a piece of paper, and string.

MRS. HALE: In that cupboard, maybe.

MRS. PETERS: (*looking in cupboard*) Why, here's a bird-cage. (*holds it up*) Did she have a bird, Mrs. Hale?

MRS. HALE: Why, I don't know whether she did or not—I've not been here for so long. There was a man around last year selling canaries cheap, but I don't know as she took one; maybe she did. She used to sing real pretty herself.

MRS. PETERS: (*glancing around*) Seems funny to think of a bird here. But she must have had one, or why would she have a cage? I wonder what happened to it.

MRS. HALE: I s'pose maybe the cat got it.

MRS. PETERS: No, she didn't have a cat. She's got that feeling some people have about cats—being afraid of them. My cat got in her room and she was real upset and asked me to take it out.

MRS. HALE: My sister Bessie was like that. Queer, ain't it?

MRS. PETERS: (*examining the cage*) Why, look at this door. It's broke. One hinge is pulled apart.

MRS. HALE: (*looking too*) Looks as if someone must have been rough with it.

MRS. PETERS: Why, yes.

(*She brings the cage forward and puts it on the table.*)

MRS. HALE: I wish if they're going to find any evidence they'd be about it. I don't like this place.

MRS. PETERS: But I'm awful glad you came with me, Mrs. Hale. It would be lonesome for me sitting here alone.

MRS. HALE: It would, wouldn't it? (*dropping her sewing*) But I tell you what I do wish, Mrs. Peters. I wish I had come over sometimes when *she* was here. I—(*looking around the room*)—wish I had.

MRS. PETERS: But of course you were awful busy, Mrs. Hale—your house and your children.

MRS. HALE: I could've come. I stayed away because it weren't cheerful—and that's why I ought to have come. I—I've never liked this place. Maybe because it's down in a hollow and you don't see the road. I dunno what it is, but it's a lonesome place and always was. I wish I had come over to see Minnie Foster sometimes. I can see now—(*shakes her head*)

MRS. PETERS: Well, you mustn't reproach yourself, Mrs. Hale. Somehow we just don't see how it is with other folks until—something comes up.

MRS. HALE: Not having children makes less work—but it makes a quiet house, and Wright out to work all day, and no company when he did come in. Did you know John Wright, Mrs. Peters?

MRS. PETERS: Not to know him; I've seen him in town. They say he was a good man.

MRS. HALE: Yes—good; he didn't drink, and kept his word as well as most, I guess, and paid his debts. But he was a hard man, Mrs. Peters. Just to pass the time of day with him—(*shivers*) Like a raw wind that gets to the bone (*pauses, her eye falling on the cage*) I should think she would 'a wanted a bird. But what do you suppose went with it?

MRS. PETERS: I don't know, unless it got sick and died.
(*She reaches over and swings the broken door, swings it again, both women watch it.*)

MRS. HALE: You weren't raised round here, were you? (MRS. PETERS *shakes her head*) You didn't know—her?

MRS. PETERS: Not till they brought her yesterday.

MRS. HALE: She—come to think of it, she was kind of like a bird herself—real sweet and pretty, but kind of timid and—fluttery. How—she—did—change. (*silence; then as if struck by a happy thought and relieved to get back to everyday things*) Tell you what, Mrs. Peters, why don't you take the quilt in with you? It might take up her mind.

MRS. PETERS: Why, I think that's a real nice idea, Mrs. Hale. There couldn't possibly be any objection to it, could there? Now, just what would I take? I wonder if her patches are in here—and her things.
(*They look in the sewing basket.*)

MRS. HALE: Here's some red. I expect this has got sewing things in it. (*brings out a fancy box*) What a pretty box. Looks like something somebody would give you. Maybe her scissors are in here. (*Opens box. Suddenly puts her hand to her nose*) Why—(MRS. PETERS *bends nearer, then turns her face away*) There's something wrapped up in this piece of silk.

MRS. PETERS: Why, this isn't her scissors.

MRS. HALE: (*lifting the silk*) Oh, Mrs. Peters—it's—
(MRS. PETERS *bends closer.*)

MRS. PETERS: It's the bird.

MRS. HALE: (*jumping up*) But, Mrs. Peters—look at it! It's neck! Look at it's neck! It's all—other side *to*.

MRS. PETERS: Somebody—wrung—its—neck.
(*Their eyes meet. A look of growing comprehension, of horror. Steps are heard outside. MRS. HALE slips box under quilt pieces, and sinks into her chair. Enter SHERIFF and COUNTY ATTORNEY. MRS. PETERS rises.*)

COUNTY ATTORNEY: (*as one turning from serious things to little pleasantries*) Well ladies, have you decided whether she was going to quilt it or knot it?

MRS. PETERS: We think she was going to—knot it.

COUNTY ATTORNEY: Well, that's interesting. I'm sure. (*seeing the bird-cage*) Has the bird flown?

MRS. HALE: (*putting more quilt pieces over the box*) We think the—cat got it.

COUNTY ATTORNEY: (*preoccupied*) Is there a cat?

(MRS. HALE *glances in a quick covert way at* MRS. PETERS.)

MRS. PETERS: Well, not now. They're superstitious, you know. They leave.

COUNTY ATTORNEY: (*to* SHERIFF PETERS, *continuing an interrupted conversation*) No sign at all of anyone having come from the outside. Their own rope. Now let's go up again and go over it piece by piece (*they start upstairs*) It would have to have been someone who knew just the—

(MRS. PETERS *sits down. The two women sit there not looking at one another, but as if peering into something and at the same time holding back. When they talk now it is in the manner of feeling their way over strange ground, as if afraid of what they are saying, but as if they can not help saying it.*)

MRS. HALE: She liked the bird. She was going to bury it in that pretty box.

MRS. PETERS: (*in a whisper*) When I was a girl—my kitten—there was a boy took a hatchet, and before my eyes—and before I could get there—(*covers her face an instant*) If they hadn't held me back I would have (*catches herself, looks upstairs where steps are heard, falters weakly*)—hurt him.

MRS. HALE: (*with a slow look around her*) I wonder how it would seem never to have had any children around. (*pause*) No, Wright wouldn't like the bird—a thing that sang. She used to sing. He killed that, too.

MRS. PETERS: (*moving uneasily*) We don't know who killed the bird.

MRS. HALE: I knew John Wright.

MRS. PETERS: It was an awful thing was done in this house that night, Mrs. Hale. Killing a man while he slept, slipping a rope around his neck that choked the life out of him.

MRS. HALE: His neck. Choked the life out of him.

(*Her hand goes out and rests on the bird-cage.*)

MRS. PETERS: (*with rising voice*) We don't know who killed him. We don't know.

MRS. HALE: (*her own feeling not interrupted*) If there'd been years and years of nothing, then a bird to sing to you, it would be awful—still, after the bird was still.

MRS. PETERS: (*something within her speaking*) I know what stillness is. When we homesteaded in Dakota, and my first baby died—after he was two years old, and me with no other then—

MRS. HALE: (*moving*) How soon do you suppose they'll be through, looking for the evidence?

MRS. PETERS: I know what stillness is. (*pulling herself back*). The law has got to punish crime, Mrs. Hale.

MRS. HALE: (*not as if answering that*) I wish you'd seen Minnie Foster when she wore a white dress with blue ribbons and stood up there in the choir and sang. (*a look around the room*) Oh, I wish I'd come over here once in a while! That was a crime! That was a crime! Who's going to punish that?

MRS. PETERS: (*looking upstairs*) We mustn't—take on.

MRS. HALE: I might have known she needed help! I know how things can be—for women. I tell you, it's queer, Mrs. Peters. We live close together and we live far apart. We all go through the same things—it's all just a different kind of the same thing. (*brushes her eyes, noticing the bottle of fruit, reaches out for it*) If I was you, I wouldn't tell her her fruit was gone. Tell her it *ain't*. Tell her it's all right. Take this in to prove it to her. She—may never know whether it was broke or not.

MRS. PETERS: (*takes the bottle, looks about for something to wrap it in; takes petticoat from the clothes brought from the other room, very nervously begins winding this around the bottle. In a false voice*) My, it's a good thing the men couldn't hear us. Wouldn't they just laugh! Getting all stirred up over a little thing like a—dead canary. As if that could have anything to do with—with—wouldn't they *laugh!*

(*The men are heard coming down stairs.*)

MRS. HALE: (*under her breath*) Maybe they would—maybe they wouldn't.

COUNTY ATTORNEY: No, Peters, it's all perfectly clear except a reason for doing it. But you know juries when it comes to women. If there was some definite thing. Something to show—something to make a story about—a thing that would connect up with this strange way of doing it—

(*The women's eyes meet for an instant. Enter* HALE *from outer door.*)

HALE: Well, I've got the team around. Pretty cold out there.

COUNTY ATTORNEY: I'm going to stay here a while by myself. (*to the* SHERIFF) You can send Frank out for me, can't you? I want to go over everything. I'm not satisfied that we can't do better.

SHERIFF: Do you want to see what Mrs. Peters is going to take in?

(*The* LAWYER *goes to the table, picks up the apron, laughs.*)

COUNTY ATTORNEY: Oh, I guess they're not very dangerous things the ladies have picked out. (*Moves a few things about, disturbing the quilt pieces which cover the box. Steps back*) No, Mrs. Peters doesn't need supervising. For that matter, a sheriff's wife is married to the law. Ever think of it that way, Mrs. Peters?

MRS. PETERS: Not—just that way.

SHERIFF: (*chuckling*) Married to the law. (*moves toward the other room*) I just want you to come in here a minute, George. We ought to take a look at these windows.

COUNTY ATTORNEY: (*scoffingly*) Oh, windows!

SHERIFF: We'll be right out, Mr. Hale.

(HALE *goes outside. The* SHERIFF *follows the* COUNTY ATTORNEY *into the other room. Then* MRS. HALE *rises, hands tight together, looking intensely at* MRS. PETERS, *whose eyes make a slow turn, finally meeting* MRS. HALE's. *A moment* MRS. HALE *holds her, then her own eyes point the way to where the box is concealed. Suddenly* MRS. PETERS *throws back quilt pieces and tries to put the box in the bag she is wearing. It is too big. She opens box, starts to take bird out, cannot touch it, goes to pieces, stands there helpless. Sound of a knob turning in the other room.* MRS. HALE *snatches the box and puts it in the pocket of her big coat. Enter* COUNTY ATTORNEY *and* SHERIFF.)

COUNTY ATTORNEY: (*facetiously*) Well, Henry, at least we found out that she was not going to quilt it. She was going to—what is it you call it, ladies?

MRS. HALE: (*her hand against her pocket*) We call it—knot it, Mr. Henderson.

(CURTAIN)

```
                                          Briner  1

     Carolyn Briner

     Prof.  Hesterman

     English 104-12

     12 September 1998

               The Meaning of Physical Objects

                 in Susan Glaspell's Trifles

          In most performances of plays, the audience

     sees physical objects on stage--the sets and props

     that locate the action in time and space.  The title

     of Susan Glaspell's play Trifles calls attention to
```

the importance of such objects. Most of them are
the "trifles" that mark the extreme difference between the way the male and female characters value
women's work. They are also the evidence in the im-
promptu trial enclosed by the play: Mrs. Wright is
charged with murdering her husband; the county attorney is the prosecutor; Mr. Hale and the sheriff
(Mr. Peters) are the witnesses; and the women, Mrs.
Hale and Mrs. Peters, are the jury. We, the audience, join the women as jurors. Like them, we piece
together Mrs. Wright's character and her past by
discovering what the physical objects mean.

The action of the play takes place in Mrs.
Wright's kitchen. The characters have arrived the
day after Mr. Hale discovered Mr. Wright's body.
The men have come to find evidence to prove that
Mrs. Wright strangled her husband with a rope. They
have brought the women along, not to help them find
evidence but to gather items to take to Mrs. Wright
in jail. The key exchange, which names the play and
sets the trial in motion, occurs near the beginning:

> COUNTY ATTORNEY: [to the SHERIFF] You're con-
>   vinced that there was nothing important here-
>   -nothing that would point to any motive.
> SHERIFF: Nothing here but kitchen things.
> COUNTY ATTORNEY: [after noticing spilled pre-
>   serves in the cupboard.] Here's a nice mess.

Briner 3

MRS. PETERS: [to Mrs. Hale] Oh, her fruit; it did

freeze. [to the County Attorney] She worried

about that when it turned so cold. She said

the fire'd go out and her jars would break.

SHERIFF: Well, can you beat the women! Held

for murder and worryin' about her preserves.

COUNTY ATTORNEY: I guess before we're through

she may have something more serious than

preserves to worry about.

HALE: Well, women are used to worrying over

trifles.

COUNTY ATTORNEY: And yet, for all their worries,

what would we do without the ladies? [no-

tices the dirty hand towel.] Dirty towels!

[kicks the pans under the sink.] Not much of

a housekeeper, would you say, ladies?

MRS. HALE: [stiffly] There's a great deal of

work to be done on a farm. (38)

 In this exchange, the men dismiss the very evi-

dence that is crucial to the case, evidence that es-

tablishes Mrs. Wright's guilt and her motive. This

evidence--objects the men label as "trifles"--shows

three things about Mrs. Wright. First, it shows

that Mrs. Wright was a hard worker and fine crafts-

man. The men don't understand this, since, as the

passage above indicates, they undervalue women's

work and conclude that Mrs. Wright was "a bad house-

keeper." But the objects in the kitchen, as the

women know, tell a different story. The broken jars
of preserves represent Mrs. Wright's hard work and
skill. "She'll feel awful bad," Mrs. Hale says,
"after all her hard work in the hot weather. I remember the afternoon I put up my cherries last summer" (39). An expert herself, Mrs. Hale holds the
one good jar to the window and sees that it's all
right. Equally telling are the loaf of bread, covered with a cloth, waiting to be placed in the
breadbox, and the quilting pieces the women find in
her sewing basket. "It's log cabin pattern," Mrs.
Hale says. "Pretty, isn't it?" The sewing is "nice
and even" (41). The kitchen has been Mrs. Wright's
domain. As playgoers, we view its objects--stove,
table, breadbox, loaf of bread, jar of cherries,
cupboard, sewing basket, quilting pieces--and see
them as the tools of her craft and the products of
her hard work.

The second thing that physical objects show
about Mrs. Wright is that she led a difficult life
with her husband. Even Mr. Hale knows that Mr.
Wright was indifferent to his wife: "I didn't know
as what his wife wanted made much difference to
John" (36). Mrs. Hale admits that Mr. Wright was
"good" in that he abstained from drinking, kept his
word, and paid his debts. But "he was a hard man,
Mrs. Peters. Just to pass the time of day with him--
[shivers] Like a raw wind that gets to the bone"

(42). Coldness is the dominant atmosphere of the
play and represents the Wrights' life together. At
the beginning, we are told that the night before the
temperature was below zero (36). Ironically, the
object that signifies coldness is the stove. Although the stove is constantly referred to, it never
seems adequate to heat the house, to make it warm
and cosy. When Mrs. Peters returns from the front
room, she says, "My, it's cold in there" (40). When
the men come from upstairs, the County Attorney says,
"Frank's fire didn't do much up there, did it?" (41).
Mr. Wright was stingy and did not talk much. The
house is "down in a hollow" where "you don't see the
road" (42). There was no telephone in the house.
The severity of Nebraska winters, the isolation of
the house, its location in a low place, the stingy
and obdurate nature of Mr. Wright all make the house
emotionally as well as physically "cold."

The third thing that physical objects show
about Mrs. Wright is her motivation for killing her
husband. The most important objects here are the canary and the birdcage. Glaspell openly associates
Mrs. Wright with the canary. Mrs. Hale says,
"She--come to think of it, she was kind of like a
bird herself--real sweet and pretty, but kind of
timid and--fluttery" (43). Before she married Mr.
Wright, she was Minnie Foster, who used to sing (42)
and wear pretty clothes (40). But after marrying

him, she didn't socialize: "I suppose she felt she
couldn't do her part, and then you don't enjoy things
when you feel shabby" (40). The canary also represents the children she never had, which Mr. Wright
may have denied her. "I wonder," Mrs. Hale says,
"how it would seem never to have had any children
around. [. . .] No, Wright wouldn't like the bird--a
thing that sang. She used to sing. He killed that,
too" (44). The canary's death, Mrs. Peter's specu-
lates, must have caused an alienating "stillness":
"When we homesteaded in Dakota, and my first baby
died--after he was two years old, and me with no
other then--. [. . .] I know what stillness is" (44).

We can guess that to Mrs. Wright the canary
represented the sum total of what she was as Minnie
Foster: young, pretty, sweet, lively, a person who
took pleasure in singing, in wearing attractive
clothes, in other people's company, in hopes for the
future. She must have equated Mr. Wright's strangling of the canary to his destroying the Minnie
Foster that was her former self. The birdcage, too,
represents this violation. Mrs. Hale, upon seeing
it, says, "Looks as if someone must have been rough
with it." She then immediately connects it to the
house: "I don't like this place" (42). The broken
birdcage is equivalent to Minnie Foster's violated
self. It is the shell of her privacy, the container
of her true self. Mr. Wright breaks into it to find

and destroy her. The bird and birdcage, in other
words, make clear to the women and to us that Mrs.
Wright did in fact kill her husband and that she had
a strong motive.

The men, dense as ever, never see any of this.
From what they say, Mrs. Wright is likely to be ac-
quitted or to get off with a light sentence. They
can't find a motive for the crime, and juries, the
county attorney says, are easy on women (44). But
the women know the truth. They "vote" for acquittal
by suppressing the evidence--the dead canary--and by
withholding an interpretation of the "trifles" that
would make the case against Mrs. Wright. Their last
act is to gather objects to take to Mrs. Wright. In
choosing them, they seem almost to communicate with
Mrs. Wright, to express their solidarity with her,
as if the objects belong to a language that only
women know: her apron (for hard work), her jar of
cherries (for achievement), her quilting pieces (for
work still to do), and her shawl (for warmth).

Work Cited

Glaspell, Susan. <u>Trifles. Plays by Susan Glaspell</u>.
Ed. C. W. E. Bigsby. Cambridge: Cambridge
UP, 1987.

Note: Normally, the "Works Cited" list would appear on a separate page, but we print it here, right after the essay, to save space.

Essay on a Novel

Mary Ann Evans, the author of *Adam Bede,* wrote under the pen name George Eliot. The novel was first published in 1859. The action takes place in 1799 in an English farm village. The events of the novel featured in the essay below are as follows: Hetty Sorrel, a working-class teenager, and Arthur Donnithorne, an aristocrat, fall in love. Not knowing that she is pregnant, he breaks off the relationship. When she can no longer hide her pregnancy, she undertakes an arduous journey in search of him. She fails to find him, gives birth, and, in a confused state of mind, abandons the baby in the woods. After being tried for infanticide and condemned to hang, she gains a reprieve and is transported to Australia. Dinah Morris, a devout Methodist preacher, ministers to her in prison.

Forrest 1

Shalita Forrest

Professor Griffith

English 110-02

2 November 1999

First Love, Lost Love in George Eliot's <u>Adam Bede</u>

In George Eliot's <u>Adam Bede</u>, I was drawn to Hetty Sorrel. Hetty's first experience of love somewhat resembles my own. Hetty is misunderstood by many of the other characters, but I understood her from the beginning of the book. Hetty is young, in love for the first time, and blinded by love. I know this feeling, because I have been there and experienced a love similar to Hetty's. There are similarities between Hetty's first love and my first love, but we handled our situations in totally different ways.

The first similarity between Hetty and me is the
type of men we fell in love with. Hetty and I both
loved men who could never be completely ours. Hetty
is in love with Arthur Donnithorne, who is on a different social level from her. Arthur belongs to the
aristocracy, and Hetty comes from the working class.
This class difference creates a tremendous barrier
between them. Hetty can never have Arthur. She
knows, however, that Arthur is interested in her:
"Hetty had become aware that Mr. Arthur Donnithorne
would take a good deal of trouble for the chance of
seeing her" (99). Despite their class difference,
she welcomes his attentions anyway. I was also in
love with a man who I knew could never be true to
one woman. The man I loved wanted his cake plus his
ice cream, too. He had many other women and was not
willing to give them up to be with me. Yet I pur-
sued him anyway, knowing that it was nothing but
trouble, just as Hetty does.

When you pursue something you know can never
be, you subject yourself to a lot of heartache.
Hetty receives a letter from Arthur, the man of her
dreams, telling her that their relationship has to
end, and this crushes her heart. The same thing
happened to me. I was in love and I got a letter
saying that we could not be together because he was
not ready for a serious relationship. Since this
was my first love and I had never been rejected like

Forrest 3

this before, I hurt more than anything in the world.
It was as if the person I loved took a knife and
stabbed me in the heart.

Another way in which Hetty and I are alike is
that we both lost the will to live. In Hetty's case,
she travels to find the man who broke her heart. The
journey is not easy for her. Times get harder, the
nights get colder, and her money begins to disappear.
Hetty is so unhappy she wants to kill herself: "It
was because I was so very miserable," She tells
Dinah, the Methodist minister. "I didn't know where
to go . . . and I tried to kill myself before, and I
couldn't. O, I tried so to drown myself in the pool,
and I couldn't. [. . .] I went to find him, as he
might take care of me; and he was gone, and then I
didn't know what to do" (451-52). Hetty has given
up on life: "I wished I'd never been born into this
world" (452). In my case I was young and didn't
know any better. My first love broke my heart, and
I did not think that my life could go on without
him. I did not believe there was anything to move
on to. There were times when I hoped that I would
not wake up the next day.

The last similarity between Hetty and me is
that we both got pregnant at a very young age.
Hetty and I were very young and very naive. We were
just in love; at least, that is what we thought.
Not at one time did we ever stop to think about the

consequences of sharing ourselves and our hearts
with the men we believed we loved. When Hetty gets
pregnant she hides it from everybody for months, because she knows it would not be accepted. In her
society, getting pregnant out of wedlock is totally
unacceptable. Not only can Hetty not tell anyone,
she also worries what people will think about her
relationship with Arthur: "I daredn't go back home
again--I couldn't bear it. I couldn't have bore to
look at anybody, for they'd have scorned me" (452).
When I got pregnant, I hid it also, because I knew
that I would let my family down. I knew that they
would be disappointed. I was a very good student
with a lot of potential, and I thought that they
would only look down on me.

Even though Hetty and I experienced the same
first love but lost love, we handled our situations
differently. Hetty runs after Arthur when she gets
pregnant. She leaves her family behind, the family
she believes will not help her. Hetty leaves home
to find Arthur, thinking that they can be together:
"But it must be done--she must get to Arthur: oh,
how she yearned to be again with somebody who would
care for her!" (371). Hetty never gives up trying
to find Arthur; she never stops to think about what
she is doing. She continues to let herself hurt.

At one point I did leave home, and I did turn my
back on my family, but I had to stop and think about

what I was doing. I was tired of being unhappy. The
relationship was too intense. It caused me to be
miserable and never content. I made a very big decision, and that was to give up and go back home. I
realized that love was not supposed to hurt. Every
day with him I felt the agonizing pain that he was
putting me through and that I allowed myself to go
through. I realized that I deserved better. I knew
when to get out, when enough was enough. Hetty did
not have the sense to know when enough was enough.

I turned to my family and friends for support.
They helped me make it through a very rough time in
my life. I was only sixteen years old when I gave
birth. Daily, I asked myself, "How am I supposed to
raise a child, when I am just a child myself?" I realized then that I could no longer consider myself a
child. At that point in my life, I felt I had to
take on the responsibilities of a woman, so that I
could be a good mother to my child, and care for
her, support her, and love her as a mother should.
My family and friends made me realize that life goes
on and that I had too much going for myself to give
up on life. My family and friends gave me strength
to live and to go on with my life.

Hetty, on the other hand, leaves her child in
the woods, thinking that someone will find it so that
she can return home and continue as if nothing has
happened. Things turn out badly for Hetty. After

Hetty leaves the child, it dies: "I did do it,
Dinah . . . I buried it in the wood . . . the little
baby . . . and it cried . . . I heard it cry . . . ever
such a way off . . . all night . . . and I went back because it cried. [. . .] I didn't kill it--I didn't
kill it myself. I put it down there and covered it
up, and when I came back it was gone" (451). Hetty
does not think that this act will cause her to spend
the rest of her days in prison or to be hanged: "I
thought I should get rid of all my misery, and go back
home, and never let 'em know why I ran away" (452).

I understand the confusion and the sorrow Hetty
feels from lost love. It is a love so deep and con-
suming that Hetty cannot make a rational decision
about the child she is carrying. Hetty should realize
that the conception of this child will have to be a
symbol of her lost love and to do her best to raise
and love this child as every child deserves. Hetty is
overcome with grief for a man who does not love her.
She does not know how to handle this heartbreak. I,
on the other hand, am raising and loving my child, because she is a part of the man I loved and a part of
me, and just simply because she is my first love!

Work Cited

Eliot, George. <u>Adam Bede</u>. Oxford World's Classics.
New York: Oxford UP, 1998.

Note: Normally, the "Works Cited" list would appear on a separate page, but we print it here, right after the essay, to save space.

Index of Concepts and Terms

Index of Critics, Authors, and Works